NATIONALISM AND ~~ISM~~
CONFLICT IN IRELAND, 1885–1921

Nationalism and Unionism
Conflict in Ireland, 1885–1921

PETER COLLINS

Editor

The Institute of Irish Studies
The Queen's University of Belfast

First published 1994

Reprinted 1994
Reprinted with corrections 1996
The Institute of Irish Studies
The Queen's University of Belfast

© Editor and Authors

British Library Cataloguing-in-Publication Data. A catalogue record for this book is available from the British Library.

ISBN 0 85389 495 7

Printed by W. & G. Baird Ltd., Antrim
Cover design by Rodney Miller, Associates.

CONTENTS

ILLUSTRATIONS

NOTES ON CONTRIBUTORS

George Boyce is Professor of Political Theory and Government at University College Swansea. An Ulsterman, he has written many books on the Irish Question including *Nationalism in Ireland*, *Nineteenth-Century Ireland : The Search for Stability*, *The Irish Question and British Politics* and *(ed.) The Revolution in Ireland 1879–1923*.

Patrick Buckland is Professor and Director of the Institute of Irish Studies at Liverpool University. His many works on Ireland include *Irish Unionism I: The Anglo-Irish and the New Ireland, 1885–1922*, *Irish Unionism II, Ulster Unionism and the Origins of Northern Ireland, 1886–1922*, *James Craig, Lord Craigavon*, *The Factory of Grievances: Devolved Government in Northern Ireland 1921–39*, and *A History of Northern Ireland*.

Peter Collins has taught in Belfast for twenty years. He was development officer for the Young Historian Scheme based at the Institute of Irish Studies at Queen's University Belfast. His doctoral thesis was on the Belfast Labour movement at the turn of the century. He has contributed to several books on Irish history and is a founder and curriculum editor of the magazine *History Ireland*.

Tim Pat Coogan is a well known journalist and broadcaster. He has written a history of the IRA. More recently he has produced important biographies of Michael Collins and Eamon de Valera.

Tom Fraser is Professor and head of the History Department at the University of Ulster. He works mainly in the area of comparative and international history. Most relevant to this volume among his works is *Partitioning Ireland, India and Palestine* .

Alvin Jackson is a lecturer in the School of Modern History at Queen's University Belfast. His major work *The Ulster Party: Irish Unionists in the House of Commons 1884–1911* looks at the Irish Question in relation to the high politics of the time.

Keith Jeffery is a reader in the History Department at the University of Ulster. He is a specialist in military history and among his works are *The British Army and the Crisis of Empire 1918–22*. He has edited *The Military Correspondence of Field Marshal Sir Henry Wilson 1918–22*, on whose biography he is currently working.

Gearóid. Ó Tuathaigh is Associate Professor of History and Vice-President at University College Galway. His publications, mainly in Irish and British history of the 19th and 20th centuries, include, *Ireland Before the Famine 1798–1848* and *Thomas Drummond and the Government of Ireland 1835–41*.

Eamonn Phoenix teaches in St. Malachy's College Belfast where he is archivist and Head of Cultural Heritage. His doctoral thesis was on Northern Nationalists. He was the editor of the 1991 centenary supplement of *The Irish News* which will soon be published in book form. His *Nationalist Politics, Partition and the Catholic Minority in Northern Ireland 1890–1940* is due for publication in early 1994.

Catherine Shannon is Professor of History at Westfield State College in Massachusetts. She studied at U.C.D. and recently was a senior fellow at the Institute of Irish Studies at Queen's University Belfast. She is active in the American Commitee for Irish Studies and other Irish-American academic and cultural bodies. She is the author of *Arthur J. Balfour and Ireland 1874–1922*.

Brian Walker is Director of the Institute of Irish Studies at Queen's University Belfast. Among his works are *Ulster Politics : The Formative Years 1868–86* and *Parliamentary Election Results in Ireland 1801–1922* and *Parliamentary Election Results in Ireland, 1918–92*

INTRODUCTION

Peter Collins

This volume is to a great extent the epilogue of the Young Historian Scheme (YHS), of which I was development officer during its existence from Sepember 1989 to August 1992. One of the most important aspects of YHS was the annual series of sixth form conferences at which academics from all over the British Isles gave lectures to A level students from Northern Ireland schools. The lectures covered all aspects of the A level history syllabus, but because the Irish history special paper is the most popular choice, most were on the period covered in this volume. Almost all the chapters here originated as YHS lectures and I am grateful to our contributors for putting the extra work into retooling their papers.

The original aim of this volume was to cater for students in their final year at school and this has been achieved. However, the various contributors are acknowledged authorities in their fields and the volume is a major contribution to the understanding of Irish history, in the late 19th and early 20th centuries, both for scholars at all levels and the lay reader. It is not my intention here to provide a detailed introduction or overview of the period as I believe that this has been more than adequately accomplished within the various contributions.

We open with Ireland in the late 1880's when Home Rule comes onto the political agenda. Brian Walker shows that the elections of 1885 and 1886 saw the convergence of somewhat disparate political forces into the two main opposing blocs, Nationalist and Unionist, which were to mould the basic character of politics during this whole period. Catherine Shannon, in addition to a synopsis of her earlier major biography of Balfour, provides as well an analysis of Conservative policy and attitudes to Ireland both in and out of government. We go on into the 20th century with Alvin Jackson's study of the transformation of the Irish Unionism of 1905 into the Ulster Unionism of 1920. Gearóid Ó Tuathaigh looks at the changes that went on within Nationalism as a whole, leading to the supplanting of the Parliamentary Party by Sinn Féin and indeed the ongoing tensions between constitutionalists and militarists within Republicanism up to the Civil War. Patrick Buckland looks at the leaders of Unionism, Carson and Craig, and brings out the essential differences between them in personality and in political aims, most notably in relation to partition.George Boyce concentrates on the enormous impact of the Irish Question on British politics and how this in turn affected British policy in Ireland.

Eamon Phoenix analyses the attitudes of northern Nationalists through their leader Joe Devlin in particular to the questions of Home Rule and Partition and their relationship with their Unionist neighbours. Peter Collins addresses the question of why the Irish Labour movement, though strong in its industrial side, with brilliant political leaders like Larkin, Connolly and Walker, failed to make the transition from the periphery to the political centre stage. Tim Pat Coogan, the biographer of Michael Collins, paints a personal picture of this enigmatic figure, the lost leader whose massive impact in a few short years pointed to a potential that was tragically never to be realised. Keith Jeffery, in a study of British security policy, looks at the often contradictory politico-military considerations in a conflict, perhaps unique at the time, which has too often been repeated throughout the world since. Finally Tom Fraser considers the question of partition in Ireland, Palestine and India. He looks at Ireland as a precedent and considers in the light of the experience of all three, whether or not partition was a formula British response to communal disintegration.

Peter Collins, January 1994.

Acknowledgements are due to many people who have assisted either with the Young Historian Scheme or the publication of this book. Members of the Young Historian Scheme steering committee gave valuable assistance during the life of the project – Professor RH Buchanan, Professor DW Harkness, Dr Richard McMinn, Dr Frank Thompson, Dr Brian Lambkin, Mr Dan McCall, Ms Wendy Gunning and Mr Dave Brittan of the Department of Education, Northern Ireland (Community Relations Branch). We are grateful to the Department for a grant to assist the publication of the book. At the publishers, Mr Patrick McWilliams, Ms Brenda Graham, Ms Kate Newmann and Dr Brian Walker were all very helpful. I am grateful to the Deputy Keeper of the PRONI for permission to use the Allison photograph.

Finally I would like to thank all the contributors who in spite of busy schedules, have delivered their papers so willingly both at the lectures and in these subsequent chapters.

Riots in Belfast, 1886, after the defeat of the first Home Rule Bill *Illustrated London News*, 19 June 1886

CHAPTER ONE

The 1885 and 1886 General Elections –
A Milestone in Irish History
by
B.M.Walker

In the recent history of Ireland, both north and south, certain events are seen in retrospect to have been crucial in establishing the basis of our parties and political divisions. Modern politics in the Republic are viewed as rooted in the 1916 rising in Dublin and in the civil war of the early 1920s, while politics in Northern Ireland are regarded as based on the outcome of the events of 1912–14 and the Government of Ireland Act of 1920. Undoubtedly, these episodes were very important but it should be realised that they influenced a political situation that had already emerged in its essential form at the general elections of 1885 and 1886.[1] These elections saw the birth of modern political parties based on a new mass electorate that embraced nearly every household in the country. Even more significantly, these years witnessed the emergence, for the first time throughout Ireland, of distinct Nationalist/Unionist politics linked to a clear Protestant/Catholic division. Later events of 1912–16 and 1918–23 would determine the final shape of the territorial and constitutional structures for the two new political units of modern Ireland, but the outcome of these elections established the basic character of late nineteenth and twentieth century politics in both parts.

To appreciate more fully the significance of developments in these crucial years 1885–6, it is valuable to look at the state of politics in Ireland prior to this time. Conflict over Nationalism was not new to elections in 1885–6, but in the past there had usually been a wide range of political opinion and swings in popular support often occurred. Daniel O'Connell's Repeal Party and the Young Irelanders had laid the grounds for a nationalist movement. In the 1850s and 1860s, however, the political scene in Ireland had been dominated by the Liberal and Conservative parties which accepted the United Kingdom framework. It was not until the general election of 1874 with the appearance of the Home Rule movement, linked to the issues of land and educational reform, that constitutional Nationalism became again an important

1

political force. Still, the general election of 1880 returned not just 62
Home Rule MPs, but also 15 Liberals and 26 Conservatives. There were
important regional variations. On the eve of the 1885 general election, 3
Home Rulers only, plus 9 Liberals and 17 Conservatives were returned
for Ulster compared with 62 Home Rulers, 7 Liberals and 9 Conservatives for the rest of Ireland.[2]

Rivalry between denominations was also not new to Irish politics in
1885, but at previous elections the influence of religious division in
relation to political matters was rarely clear cut. Protestants tended to
vote Conservative and Catholics tended to vote Liberal, but there were
times of marked exception such as the general election of 1859 when
many Catholics voted Conservative, and the general elections of 1868–
80 when many Protestants, in particular northern Presbyterians, voted
Liberal. The Home Rule party won largely Catholic support, although
in 1874 and 1880 there were considerable numbers of Protestant Home
Rule MPs. Elections prior to 1885 reflected reasonably well changes in
political attitudes, but the franchise was restricted to limited categories
of property owners and occupiers. There were some well run local
political associations in Ireland before 1885, especially in Ulster, but
generally speaking parties were organised on an ad hoc basis in the
constituencies.

From 1885–6 onwards, however, conflict over the nationalist issue,
based very largely on a Protestant/Catholic divide, remained at the
centre of Irish elections right up to 1921, and significantly affected the
nature of politics that emerged post 1921 in Northern Ireland and the
Irish Free State. These political divisions were strongly felt throughout
the whole community, thanks to the new household vote and effective
political organisations, both local and central. The first part of this study
will be concerned with an account of the run up to the elections followed by an analysis of the polling. The second part of the study will
look at the background to these events. How important were social,
economic and religious factors? Finally, the impact of political developments in these two years must be assessed. The particular forms of
nationalism and unionism to emerge at this time will be analysed. We
need to explain why the outcome of these two general elections has
proved to have had such a lasting significance for politics in Ireland,
both north and south.

I

Changes in electoral law provided important new conditions for these
two general elections. Thanks to the 1883 Corrupt Practices Act, the

amount of money that candidates could spend on their election campaigns was restricted, and so new, voluntary party organisations were now required. Throughout the country, constituencies of roughly equal size were established due to the 1885 Redistribution Act, which expanded the number of constituencies from 64 to 101. The Franchise Act of 1884 extended the vote to adult male householders and thus increased the number of Irish voters by over 200 per cent between 1884 and 1885. Important sections of the population, in particular the labourers and small farmers, were enfranchised for the first time.[3] A parliamentary return of 1884–5 showed Catholic majorities in all constituencies except for half of the Ulster divisions.These changes presented the existing parties with considerable problems and opportunities.

Other challenges also faced the parties on the eve of the 1885 general election. Throughout the community there was a heightened sense of political consciousness, aroused originally over the land question. Agrarian protest had resulted not only in the 1881 Land Act, which gave farmers new rights, but it undermined the landlords who had traditionally played a key role in Irish politics. After the 1881 Tyrone by election, one observer commented: 'The fact is the Protestants as well as the Roman Catholics do not want an Orangeman or even a Fenian if he is a gentleman or a landlord.'[4] By 1885 landlord-tenant relations were no longer the major issue, which meant that other divisions such as those between farmers and labourers, urban and rural interests, and Protestant and Catholic, asssumed new importance for the parties, as did interest groups and internal conflicts.

The various parties responded in different ways to these new challenges. After the 1880 general election C.S. Parnell had taken over the leadership of the Home Rule party, the largest party in Ireland with 63 seats, but until 1885 it remained a loosely organised body with little discipline among the members in parliament and ad hoc organisational structures in the constituencies. In early 1885 it was reckoned that Parnell could count on the wholehearted support of only some 20–30 MPs of his Home Rule group and he had to deal with both agrarian activists and radical Nationalist elements.[5] Parnell, however, was also head of the National League which had been set up to harness agrarian and Nationalist protest after the suppression of the Land League. During 1885 the Home Rule movement underwent marked reorganisation and growth under the direction of Parnell and his followers in the National League.

In common parlance the term 'Homeruler' gave way to 'Nationalist'. The National League provided for the Nationalist party an effective organisation through its local branches which expanded rapidly in 1885. County conventions selected parliamentary candidates, under the supervision of representatives from the organising committee of the League, which was controlled by Parnell. A pledge was introduced to bind the MPs together into a tightly disciplined party. Thus, as Dr Conor Cruise O'Brien has remarked, the National League turned the Home Rule movement from a loose grouping of independent elements into a 'well-knit political party of a modern type . . . effectively monopolising the political expresssion of national sentiment'.[6] This reorganisation allowed the Nationalist party to face the general election very effectively. The National League embraced small farmers and labourers as well as larger farmers and so helped to mitigate chances of social division. Efforts by Michael Davitt and others to radicalise the movement, in particular to organise the labourers, were thwarted and the influence of Nationalist radicals was largely destroyed.

Vital for this socially cohesive, countrywide organisation was the forging of a 'very effective, if informal, clerical-Nationalist alliance' as Professor Emmet Larkin has called it.[7] Acceptance of Catholic claims on education won the party the approval of the hierarchy in mid-1885. The intervention of Archbishop Walsh of Dublin ensured that all Catholic clergy should have the right to attend Nationalist conventions to select parliamentary candidates.[8] Catholic clergy now played an important role at these conventions as well as in many cases, such as in Co. Westmeath,[9] providing local leadership for National League branches. In the months immediately preceeding the election, candidates were selected for every consituency, except those Ulster divisions with a Protestant majority. So successful was the party in capturing the Nationalist electorate, that only in one Irish constituency did an independent Nationalist stand. In early October Parnell declared that the party platform would consist of a single plank 'the plank of legislative independence'.[10]

In response to this Nationalist reorganisation the Irish Loyal and Patriotic Union was formed in Dublin in May 1885 by a number of southern businessmen, landowners, and academics. It sought to organise opposition in the three southern provinces to the Nationalists, and to unite Liberals and Conservatives on a common platform of maintenance of the Union. The Irish Loyal and Patriotic Union also published pamphlets and leaflets which were widely circulated. In its aim of bringing together Liberals and Conservatives the ILPU was successful, and in some cases candidates came forward in the election simply as 'loyalists'. A total of 54 of the southern seats were contested by anti-Home Rule candidates.[11]

In Ulster, however, appeals for unity between supporters of the Union went unheeded and the Liberal and Conservative parties continued to operate separately. The election of 1885 in Ulster involved not only Nationalists against pro-union supporters but rivalry between Liberal and Conservative. Before the general election, the Ulster Liberals, whose support lay chiefly with the tenant farmers and included both Catholics and Presbyterians, held 9 seats. With an impressive headquarters at the recently built Reform Club in Belfast, they sought to develop new local divisional associations. In spite of a good central office, however, and contrary to later claims of a strong Liberal effort, the evidence of Liberal activity at the registration courts and in the constituencies during the campaign reflected lack of vitality and effective local organisation.[12] Attempts were made to embrace labourers in their new divisional associations, but with little success, partly due to the identification of the Liberals with the farmers' cause. On the eve of the 1885 general election, the Liberals still retained considerable support among Presbyterian farmers, even if it was clear that the Nationalist movement was proving very attractive to Catholic farmers in Ulster who had formerly voted Liberal. Liberal candidates declared their support for the Union between Great Britain and Ireland and also called for further land reform.

Before the 1885 general election the Conservatives held 17 seats in Ulster. Seen as the former landlord party, their electoral prospects must have appeared poor. Conservative party organisation had developed to some extent in the province over the previous ten years with the growth of a number of county and borough Conservative associations, but these bodies had a limited popular involvement. Historians have sometimes painted a bleak picture of Conservative organisation during 1885, but this picture relies on the evidence of party apathy and disunity in Counties Armagh and Fermanagh.[13] Elsewhere, however, matters were very different, especially in the north east of Ulster. Under the energetic leadership of E.S. Finnigan, a full-time party organiser based in Belfast, the Conservatives extensively reorganised in 1885. Finnigan helped to set up, with strong local involvement, many divisional associations, especially in the key areas of Belfast and Counties Antrim and Down.[14]

A vital aspect of these new branches was the involvement of the Orange Order. Local lodges were given special positions in many of the new organisations. Speaking, for example, in Ballynahinch, Co. Down, on 7 May 1885, E.S. Finnigan, described proposals to set up a broadly based local committee: 'The Orange Association would have a well defined position. The district master and district officers . . . would be appointed . . . upon each committee.'[15] At this stage the Order was a minority movement among Protestants, but it embraced many of the newly enfranchised labourers, and therefore it was an important means of integrating the labourers into the Conservative party. Such arrangements went smoothly in Counties Antrim and Down but ran into trouble in Belfast, and Counties Armagh and Londonderry where Orange labourers felt that they were being given no influence in the new Conservative party machine. In Armagh and Londonderry they rebelled against the local Conservative organisers and forced them to accept candidates agreeable to them, while in the case of two Belfast seats, they ran independent candidates. In a number of cases, Conservative party organisers co-operated secretly with Nationalist party organisers to undermine the Liberals and the middle ground. Conservative candidates emphasised their support for the Union.

In Ulster the Nationalist party had started the election campaign in a weak position. Only 3 of the former Ulster MPs were Home Rulers, thanks to a weak Home Rule organisation in the past and to the success of the Ulster Liberals in attracting the anti-Conservative vote. During 1885, however, the National League expanded considerably in many parts of Ulster. A government report on National League activity (1 January – 30 June 1885) commented, 'the most noteworthy feature is the progress that the League is making in Ulster, especially in Armagh, Down, Fermanagh, Tyrone and Monaghan; three new branches have even been started in Co Antrim.'[16] League organisers from Dublin, such as Timothy Harrington, played an important role in the spread of the movement and in its preparations for the elections. Conventions, under the chairmanship of a representative of the party leadership, were held to select candidates for those constituencies with a Catholic majority. Mid Armagh, with a Protestant majority, was an exceptional case. In both the conventions and the National League branches, Catholic clergy played an important part in most constituencies. Only in Co. Londonderry was there an effort, among both clergy and leaders, to avoid a clerical image.[17]

Early in the campaign, strong efforts were made to promote Nationalist unity. National League branches in Belfast, favourable to Michael Davitt, were closed down in late 1884, early 1885, and other steps were taken to weaken his influence, including the removal of the editor of the *Morning News*, C.J. Dempsey, who later commented to John Pinkerton 'I am too great a disciple of Davitt's . . . the MPs want me effaced from Ulster politics.'[18] In some areas Nationalist organisers co-operated secretly with Conservative organisers to keep all Catholics together in the Nationalist movement and also to undermine the Liberals. For example, to thwart Dempsey standing for South Armagh, the local convention under the chairmanship of T.M. Healy had picked a compromise candidate, Alex Blane, a tailor by trade. Since in Healy's words, 'nobody knew him and snobbery was rampant', this aroused the threat of an independent Nationalist splitting the Catholic vote, a danger only averted by Healy secretly arranging for a Conservative to come forward in South Armagh, which obliged the independent to step down. In return for this Conservative favour, Healy agreed to put forward a Nationalist candidate in Mid Armagh to damage the Liberal candidate's chances.[19] In other areas where there was no Nationalist candidate, the Catholic vote was given to the Conservatives to help destroy the Liberals and any potential cross community electoral support.[20]

The outcome of the election was a resounding victory for the Nationalist party which won 85 seats throughout Ireland, plus a seat in Liverpool. It held 17 out of 33 Ulster constituencies. Apart from two Dublin University seats held by the Conservatives, pro-union candidates were successful only in Ulster where the Conservative party took 16 seats while the Liberal party failed to win a single division. These Conservative figures include 2 successful independent candidates in Belfast who were subsequently adopted by the official Conservative associations. Out of 85 Nationalists 80 were Catholic: all Ulster Nationalist MPs were Catholic. All the 19 Conservatives were members of the Church of Ireland except 3 Presbyterians and 1 Methodist: most of the unsuccessful Liberals had been Presbyterian. Parnell now returned to parliament with a strong, disciplined Nationalist party. For their part the Ulster Conservatives had emerged as the clear leaders of pro-union support in Ireland.

An analysis of the voting for the two sides shows a high degree of religious polarisation in the constituencies. It is clear that nearly all Catholics, who voted, backed the Nationalists, except in some northern constituencies where there were no Nationalist candidates and Catholics voted Conservative for tactical reasons. In perhaps as many as 6 divisions, last minute Catholic support for the Conservative against the Liberal proved significant.[21] In a few southern constituencies small numbers of Catholics may have voted for pro-union candidates. It is also evident that nearly all Protestants, who voted, supported pro-union candidates. Although Protestants were nearly 10 per cent of the population outside Ulster they were too widely dispersed to win any seats. In Co. Londonderry there is evidence of some Protestants voting for a Nationalist, (due both to the candidate's reputation on the land question and efforts in the county to present a non-sectarian image). Generally it is clear, however, that the electorate had polarised sharply along denominational lines throughout the country. Protestant Nationalists such as C. S. Parnell, or Jeremiah Jordan from Co. Fermanagh, and Catholic Unionists such as Daniel O'Connell, grandson of The Liberator, and W.T. McGrath from Belfast were rare exceptions.

Within nine months there occurred another general election, which would copperfasten the outcome of the 1885 general election. Early in

1886 Gladstone announced his support for Home Rule and in April the first Home Rule Bill was introduced but defeated. Gladstone's action now caused a split among the Liberals. In Ulster, the vast majority of Liberals became Liberal Unionists and in the general election of mid 1886 joined with the Conservatives in a common pro-union front. Various social and denominational differences between the former Liberals and Conservatives were ignored in the new Unionist movement. A small group of pro-Gladstone supporters fought the election as Gladstonian Liberals. There also appeared a new organisation called the Irish Protestant Home Rule Association with the aim to promote the principle of Home Rule among Protestants.[22]

At the 1886 general election only 33 constituencies in Ireland were contested compared with 79 in 1885, outside Ulster a mere 7 divisions out of 68 saw a poll. Out of 70 Nationalist candidates, 62 were returned unopposed in the southern provinces, the 8 who were opposed were returned with large majorities. Most Ulster divisions were contested.[23] In these contests, Conservatives faced Nationalists (including some Protestant Nationalist candidates) in 17, Liberal Unionists fought Nationalists in 5 and in another 5 Gladstonian Liberals opposed Conservatives. The bulk of former Liberals in the main Unionist constituencies in the north east played little active part in the election, leaving the Unionist political organisations to be effectively controlled by the Conservative victors of 1885. The outcome in Ulster was the election of 15 Conservatives, 2 Liberal Unionists and 16 Nationalists. Overall the Nationalists won 84 seats, plus a seat in Liverpool. The Conservatives won 17 (including 2 Dublin University seats) and the Liberal Unionists 2, a result which reflected accurately the comparative strength of the two groups in the new Unionist movement.

Viewed broadly it is evident that again most Catholic voters supported Nationalist candidates and most Protestant voters backed Unionist candidates. Some Protestants did vote for Nationalists, although it is difficult to put a precise figure on their numbers. Probably it is fair to say that only around 3,000 Protestants (mainly former Liberals) voted for Gladstonian Liberals or Nationalist candidates. Under the Unionist flag were now both former Conservatives and Liberals, with the former fully in control. The latter would survive as a minor grouping within the Unionist family until the full incorporation of the Ulster Liberal Unionist Society into the Unionist party in 1911. The Nationalist party would split over the Parnell divorce but eventually would successfully realign itself along the lines established in 1885. This period, therefore, saw the emergence of Nationalism and Unionism in Ireland and the polarisation of politics along religious grounds. In spite of later attempts at accommodation, the divisions that emerged at this time with Catholic and Nationalist on one side and Protestant and Unionist on the other, remained central to Irish politics up to 1921 and formed a basic background to the politics that emerged thereafter.

II

To understand the outcome of these elections it is essential that such political events should not be viewed in isolation. Social and economic factors formed an important background to the rise of Nationalism and Unionism in Ireland. In 1841 the population of Ireland was three times that of Scotland and more than half that of England and Wales.[24] Fifty years later, however, after the Famine and continuous emigration in Ireland, and massive industrialisation in Great Britain, the picture was very different. By 1891, Ireland's population had fallen to slightly less than that of Scotland and one eighth of the population of England and Wales.[25] Such developments helped to encourage Nationalism. To many Nationalists this economic decline was seen as linked to the union. In November 1885 Thomas Sexton declared: 'We look back to the year of the Union, along that level plain of years to see the shameful, the miserable results of English rule in Ireland . . . The population of Ireland was greater than now, the comfort of the people was greater . . .'[26]

In Ulster the nineteenth century social and economic experience was rather different. Although parts of Ulster witnessed population decline similar to that elsewhere in Ireland, other parts, especially in the north-east experienced considerable prosperity, thanks to industrialisation. In 1841 Ulster's population was 29 per cent of that of the whole of Ireland, but by 1891 this figure stood at 34 per cent. In 1841 Belfast's population was 70,447, or one third of Dublin's population of 232,726, but by 1891 Belfast's figure was 276,114 compared to Dublin's 269,716.[27] Belfast grew faster than any other urban centre in the British Isles in the second half of the nineteenth century. The Grand Trades Arch in Donegall Place in Belfast for the royal visit of 1885 captured well the spirit of Victorian Belfast with slogans such as 'Trade is the golden girdle of the globe' and 'Employment is nature's physician'.[28] For Unionists in Ulster the period of the Union was seen as a time of rising prosperity.

The land question was another source of division between Ireland and Great Britain and between Ulster and the rest of Ireland. The Great Famine, with its enormous human toll, affected Ulster far less than elsewhere in Ireland, thanks to northern industrialisation and the availability of other crops. After the Great Famine, rising agricultural prices brought a growth in prosperity throughout the Irish country-side,[29] but the question of tenure continued as a major source of discontent until the reforms of the 1880s, which followed the land war of 1879-81. In Ulster, however, farmers benefited from the Ulster custom which gave certain rights to farmers. While this custom had weaknesses which were to help cause tenant unrest at various points in the nineteenth century, it gave greater security to Ulster farmers than elsewhere and so the question of land reform, whether in the early 1850s or the 1870s, seems to have caused less bitterness in the north than elsewhere.

Such major social and economic divisions, which influenced the rise of Irish Nationalism, could have helped to create a straightforward split between a totally Unionist Ulster and the rest of Ireland which was entirely Nationalist. To understand why this did not happen it is essential to look at the religious factor. In 1881 Catholics were around 76 per cent of the Irish population, while in Great Britain the population was predominantly Protestant. Within Ireland, Protestants were 24 per cent of the total population, with only 9 per cent outside Ulster, but they were in a small majority in all Ulster and a substantial majority in the north east. Three quarters of Irish Protestants were to be found in Ulster, but Catholics in Ulster were only 21 per cent of their whole community in Ireland.[30] For Catholics and Protestants in nineteenth century Ireland, both religious conflict and the strength of denominational bonds had an important impact on their political positions. Religious division was important not only between Ireland and Britain but within Irish society.

Religious issues such as Catholic emancipation had been the cause of considerable political unrest in the first half of the nineteenth century. Although most specifically religious issues were settled by the 1870s, this whole area still coloured people's views on broader political matters, including the question of the link with Great Britain and community relations within Ireland. Religious controversies, particularly that over education, continued to cause Catholic disillusionment with Westminster, a feeling not experienced by Protestants. The strengthening of denominational ties and identities in Ireland, influenced greatly by the revivalism which occurred among all the main denominations in the second half of the nineteenth century, meant that for most people in Ireland, the links with their respective religious groups were very important.[31] Until the mid 1880s, nonetheless, the correlation between religious and political divisions was far from complete. There were sharp divisions in voting behaviour between Presbyterians and members of the Church of Ireland in Ulster and there were differences between Catholics in Ulster and elsewhere in how they voted.

During 1885–6, however, denominational ties and identities emerged as the main determining factor in political behaviour, regardless of regional or class differences. In these years nearly all Ulster Catholics, of every social rank, identified with the political aspirations of their co-religionists elsewhere in Ireland and voted Nationalist. In March 1886, Dr Patrick MacAllister, the new Catholic bishop of Down and Connor, expressed his satisfaction at 'seeing the Catholics of Belfast working in harmony with the rest of Ireland in the cause of nationality.'[32] Most Protestants, Presbyterians as well as members of the Church of Ireland, in Ulster and in the rest of Ireland, came together in support of the Union, although only in Ulster were they able to elect Unionist MPs. Social and economic differences between Ulster and the rest of Ireland go part of the way to help explain the rise of Nationalism and Unionism, but in the new political alignments that finally emerged in 1885–6, the division between Protestant and Catholic proved of great importance.

Economic and social tensions between Protestant and Catholic probably played some part in the rise of the opposing camps of Unionist and Nationalist, but their importance should not be exaggerated, chiefly because the other main divisions and conflicts in society did not correlate to a simple Protestant Catholic divide. Members of the Church of Ireland owned most of the land and dominated official positions, at the expense not just of Catholics but also of Presbyterians. In Ulster, Catholics were over-represented among unskilled labourers and small farmers while Presbyterians dominated the skilled jobs and larger farm sector, but most ordinary members of the Church of Ireland had little or no special advantage in these latter areas.[33] Social divisions in Ireland often crossed religious divisions. At the end of the day, however, religion served not only to provide a key source of grievance, namely education, but it united people on a denominational community basis. The new political arrangements of 1885–6 established firmly the link between parties and religious division.

III

The political developments of 1885–6 had a vital effect on how Nationalism and unionism emerged finally in their particular forms. These two years were the climax to a period of great political change and mobilisation in the whole country. The extension of the franchise and changes in electoral law, as well as the high degree of popular excitement over the issues that now held the public attention, meant that entirely new demands were placed on party organisations and leaders. Their response to this situation not only affected immediate party fortunes, but also influenced greatly the whole nature of politics to emerge at this time. The structure and spirit of the new party organisations had a very important bearing on the type of politics and society to develop. These parties reflected certain divisions in society and particular elements had key roles in the new organisational structures. The religious divisions in Irish society had often had some bearing on party divisions, but in 1885–6 the two victorious parties based firmly their respective movements on denominational differences. The decisions by both the Nationalist and Conservative party leadership to adapt their organisations in the way they did (important, no doubt, to meet the challenges of 1885–6 and to win the elections) had a far-reaching influence on the new political and social confrontations to materialise at these elections.

Many special features of Nationalism and Unionism were the result of these years. The new Nationalist movement that emerged had support from throughout the island of Ireland, but in practice it represented only the Catholic community.[34] The events of this period meant that Irish Nationalism emerged as a Catholic movement with strong clerical support. There had been connections in the past between Irish Nationalism and Catholicism but events of the mid 1880s established the link in a formal and thorough way. Ironically, it was a Protestant leader of the Nationalist party, C.S.Parnell, who was responsible for the alliance of 1884–5 between Nationalism and the Catholic church in Ireland which played a vital part in the electoral success of his party in 1885. Undoubtedly, as Professor Emmet Larkin has argued, this link had democratic benefits in that it prevented the emergence of an all powerful central party,[35] but it did help to give Irish Nationalism a strong denominational character. Parnell was very successful at creating a strong, united Nationalist movement, in Ireland and at Westminster, but it was at the expense of excluding most of the Protestant population in Ireland.

The new Unionist movement was concerned with defending the Union, but because of the events of 1885–6 it represented just Protestants and won seats only in Ulster. The failure of the Ulster Liberals to hold Catholic support meant that the new combination of former Liberals and Conservatives represented just one part of the Ulster population. This new Unionist movement, furthermore, was dominated by the Conservative, Orange-backed element in Ulster society, with the gentry still prominent, at the expense of the more radical, Liberal section. Ironically, the tactical support given by Nationalists to Conservative candidates in 1885 played a vital role in moving power in the pro-union community to Conservative elements. The link between the Orange lodges and the new Unionist associations did introduce a populist, democratic element into Unionist politics but it also served to reinforce the denominational nature of Unionism. The individual responsible for this Orange/Unionist link was E.S. Finnigan and not as often alleged, Lord Randolph Churchill whose 'Orange card' remarks were made only in 1886 and related primarily to English power politics. Outside of Ulster, Unionists formed an important minority but their only parliamentary representation came from the two Dublin University seats.

The 1885–86 general elections marked the birth of modern politics in both parts of Ireland.[36] In the succeeding three and a half decades up to 1923 there would be significant developments which would affect the new territorial and constitutional arrangements to emerge in the early 1920s, but which would not alter the essentials of the conflict that materialised in 1885–6. Unionism would move from a concern to maintain all Ireland for the Union, to a defence of Ulster and then to support for only six of the Ulster counties. Nationalism would witness the collapse of the parliamentary Nationalist party and the triumph of Sinn Féin. Support from the main parties in Britain affected the fortunes of both Nationalists and Unionists. The threat or use of violence played an important role. The two new states would be marked by the turmoil of their establishment, 1921–3. All these developments, however, took place within the basic framework established in 1885–6 and served to modify but not to replace the fundamental confrontations and alliances to emerge at this time.

Conflict over Nationalism remained the key factor, whether between Nationalist and Unionist pre-1921, between pro-treaty and anti-treaty Nationalists in the Irish civil war or between Unionists and Nationalists in Northern Ireland post 1921. The new party systems to emerge in both the Irish Free State and Northern Ireland were greatly influenced by this conflict, which effectively diminished the importance of other social and regional divisions. The connection between politics and religious division remained very strong. Both sides could sometimes win supporters across the denominational barriers such as the Catholic unionist MP Denis Henry, or the Protestant Sinn Féin MP, Ernest Blythe. At the end of the day, however, Unionism and Nationalism were rooted firmly in their respective religious camps. Post 1921, in the south most Protestants were politically marginalised outside the main parties, while in the north political and religious divisions remained strongly linked. The creation of two new political units in Ireland in 1921 and the political systems 'without social bases', that emerged in both parts thereafter, are directly linked to the 1885–6 general elections and the emergence of a Nationalist/Unionist conflict with its associated religious division.

Why were these elections of 1885–6 so important? Other elections in the nineteenth century had witnessed significant events but none had such obvious lasting relevance. Part of the answer to this question lies in the nature of some of the broader changes that occurred. Key social and economic developments, in particular the main resolution of the land question, the enormous growth of Belfast and the strengthening of religious identities, all of which set the scene for modern Ireland, occurred in the preceding period. This was the era when for the first time the vast majority of the people could read and write. The other part of the answer lies in the very significant extension of the franchise and the rise of modern political parties, that took place in these years of mass political mobilisation and electoral change. Although there was not yet universal suffrage, most households had a vote. There was now an extensive network of local political associations with popular involvement, and, especially in the Nationalist case, a strong central party organisation.

The importance of such developments has been noted elsewhere by political scientists.[37] In many parts of Europe the particular divisions that emerged as important at the end of the nineteenth and the beginning of the twentieth centuries have remained significant. Party systems have continued remarkably true to the traditions and shape of the politics established at this point, where broad based modern parties with a wide franchise came into being for the first time. People have then voted simply for the same parties as their parents. Even when particular parties have collapsed and new ones have arisen, they have often remained within the basic framework of the party system established at this earlier stage. Nationalism and Unionism along with religious divisions, emerged at this key formative period to dominate modern politics in Ireland.

Neither the polarisation of politics along denominational lines nor the emergence of nationalism were unique to Ireland but have strong parallels in contemporary Europe. Although it was no longer a major factor in politics in Great Britain by this stage, religious conflict remained important in other parts of Western Europe. In Germany, Switzerland and Holland there were significant divisions between Protestant and Catholic parties.[38] Various European countries, such as Norway and Italy, also experienced the rise of Nationalist politics with important consequences for party cleavages.[39] The situation in Ireland, however, differed from the situation in these countries in that, besides religious differences, there was also a split over the national question and, because of the changes we have witnessed, each division powerfully reinforced the other.

These elections of 1885–6, then, saw the emergence of two distinct political movements, based firmly on particular religious groups, with strongly opposed views on the nature of the nation, the state and the central issue of sovereignty.[40] Both sides would claim ancient historical roots for their position but in fact the conflict that emerged was greatly influenced by contemporary political and social developments. At this key period, party leaders, organisers and supporters, influenced and aided by the social, economic and religious developments of their age, created a new order of politics where the religious and national divisions were firmly related in a form that would prove long lasting. The 1885–6 general elections are an important milestone in the modern political development of both parts of Ireland.

Arthur Balfour at demonstration in Belfast, 1893
Illustrated London News, 15 April 1893

CHAPTER TWO

The Legacy of Arthur Balfour to Twentieth-century Ireland
by
Catherine B.Shannon

While most readers are well aware of the crucial role of Charles Stewart Parnell in nurturing modern Irish Nationalism in the 1880s, Arthur J. Balfour's role in shaping the contours of twentieth century Ireland is less well known. Both men entered politics in the 1870s when the Irish Question moved onto centre stage at Westminster, Balfour as Tory MP for Hertford, Parnell representing Meath for the Buttite Home Rule Party. Both came from landed families and attended Cambridge University. Of course, the wealth and political influence enjoyed by Balfour as the nephew of Robert Cecil, the 3rd Marquis of Salisbury entirely dwarfed that available to Parnell. Whereas Balfour had a respectable university experience which established his life long interest in science and philosophy, Parnell's academic career was a disaster which perhaps foreshadowed his adult indifference to intellectual matters and reading. The controversies of the Land Question and Home Rule would draw Parnell and Balfour into a bitter symbiotic relationship in the House of Commons debates, where Balfour's innate respect for parliamentary tradition clashed sharply with Parnell's clever exploitation of parliamentary rules so as to publicise Ireland's multiple grievances. While Balfour was happiest among his parliamentary colleagues, Parnell was never seduced by the aura of Westminster. If Parnell was the champion of modern Irish Nationalism, Balfour was one of its most determined and outspoken critics. Yet this should not blind us to the importance of Arthur J. Balfour in modern Irish history. In this essay, I hope to provide a sense of Balfour's persona and political ideology and of his crucial importance in the shaping of twentieth century Ireland.

A study of Balfour's involvement with Ireland over his long political career, starting first as Chief Secretary from 1887–1891 and continuing as Tory Leader of the House of Commons, Prime Minister and senior party leader down to 1921 provides useful insights on how and why the ideas, interests and prejudices of the British establishment hindered a

peaceful solution to the Irish Question and why Ulster continued to
haunt Anglo-Irish relations long after 1921.

When preparing his memoirs with his niece, Blanche Dugdale, in
1928, Arthur Balfour proclaimed with pride that the political and economic stability which the fledgling Irish Free State enjoyed after 1923
was a result of 'the Ireland we made'. Balfour asserted that twenty years
of progressive Unionist policy between 1887 and 1905 provided the
foundations for the success which the Free State achieved compared
with other new nations in the post World War I era. Balfour might well
have added 'Ireland Made Me', for it was as Irish Chief Secretary from
1887 to 1891 that he earned his political stripes as a witty and effective
debater and as a fearless administrator in Dublin Castle. Balfour's
vigorous enforcement of his Criminal Amendment Act of 1887 brought
him instant fame in England and earned him the sobriquet 'Bloody
Balfour' in Irish folk history. His use of coercion against William
O'Brien's rural agitation known as the 'Plan of Campaign' has been
well documented by Perry Curtis, Lawrence Geary, and more recently
by Margaret O'Callaghan, so I propose to focus mainly on the conciliatory aspects of Balfour's policy and his views on Ulster.

This will demonstrate that while the Balfourian legacy regarding
land, local government and educational reform and the Congested
Districts Board was a source of legitimate pride, the results of Tory
policy on Ulster are more problematic. This analysis will take us beyond
Balfour's exit from the Irish office in 1891, for the policies of Gerald
Balfour and George Wyndham, his successors in the Irish Office drew a
great deal from Arthur's earlier example. Furthermore, Arthur was a
key figure in the formulation of party policy when the Tories were in
opposition from 1910 to 1914 and Home Rule and the Ulster issue
dominated political debate. His influence was present again when the
Government of Ireland Act of 1920 which established the present border was being formulated.

Three aspects of Balfour's personality and general outlook ought to
be stressed initially. First, similar to his uncle and political mentor, Lord
Salisbury, Balfour had a strong distrust for democracy. He viewed the
newly enfranchised masses as 'uninstructed children whom he and
others had to keep out of mischief'. He believed the Tory party had a
special obligation to protect, through careful management of the democracy, the institutions, privileges and power of the landed aristocracy. Secondly, Balfour was convinced of the superiority of Anglo-Saxon
culture and institutions, and believed that the adoption of these by
other peoples, like the Irish, was a prerequisite to their enjoying the
progress and prosperity experienced by Britain. Though his anti-Irish
prejudice was not as extreme as some of his contemporaries, he was not

immune from the prevailing anti-Irish sentiment, nor from a tendency to display a condescending and patronising attitude toward the Irish. On more than one occasion, Balfour's imagery and analogies when speaking publicly echoed the unflattering portraits created by Punch cartoonists.

Thirdly, Balfour was a philosophic sceptic who disdained the display of emotion, enthusiasm or zeal, prompting one of his lady friends to comment, 'Arthur is the most fascinating of them all ... because he lives with his windows shut, and has a few false windows'. Another commentator observed: 'You feel he would give you the same smile in sending you to the scaffold as he would in passing the salt.' Throughout his adult life Balfour maintained this personal aloofness, an almost Olympian detachment, from all but his most intimate friends and relatives. This detachment was not just aristocratic snobbery, but a product of a philosophic temperament that found relaxation and renewal in music, literature, art, tennis and golf rather than in racing, hunting and team sports- the typical diversions of the landed class. He once explained his aversion to fox hunting by saying, 'I did not see why I should break my neck because a dog chose to run after a nasty smell.'

His approach to politics was cold and calculating. He attacked political and administrative problems in a clinical way, never letting sentiment obstruct his fundamental resolve to preserve the interests of his class, the Tory Party and Britain. His letters and state papers reflect both his habit and ability to weigh all sides of an issue and admit, although never publicly, the merits of his opponents' case. It was his cool, witty and unflappable manner that the MPs found so exasperating when Balfour was Irish Secretary. A typical example was his response in an 1891 debate to Tim Healy's lengthy and impassioned pleas for a little justice for his country. Balfour drily replied, 'There isn't enough to go around.' In Lord Salisbury's eyes, this ability to deflect attacks and his indifference to what was said of him constituted Balfour's unique qualification for the Irish position.

Such was the young man who first entered Parliament in 1874 at the age of twenty-six. There is no evidence that he gave Ireland even a second thought during his first six years in Parliament, a reflection not only of a general Tory indifference toward Ireland during Disraeli's last administration, but perhaps also the disdain which his Cecilian relatives held toward Ireland and her peoples. While Salisbury's Hottentot remark is well-known Lady Salisbury once proclaimed :

> ... as to Ireland I have made a vow never to read any speeches on the subject on either side, there is nothing much to be said but lies on one side and contradictions on the other, and as I have never believed the

first, why should I trouble about the last . . .. The only cure for the evils of Ireland is the total extermination of the inhabitants.[1]

While such remarks may have been dinner-time repartee, they are revealing nonetheless. Balfour's 1881 description of the Irish multitudes as potentially more dangerous and easily led than the English public, whom he claimed at least demanded some external appearance of reason from their agitators, may reflect this family opinion as much as the impact of the on-going land war and the obstructionist tactics which the Irish Parliamentary Party employed to disrupt the Commons debate in 1877–79.

Balfour abandoned his parliamentary reticence on Ireland in response to Gladstone's attempts to quell the land war with the 1881 Land Act which gave the three f's; fixity of tenure, judicially fixed fair rents, and free sale of the tenant improvements upon the expiration of a lease. Balfour attacked this measure on both pragmatic and theoretical grounds. First, he thought it an unwise concession to the forces of crime and disorder which would only encourage further lawlessness from a tenantry he considered easy prey for socialist agitators. Second, although he appreciated the importance of the landlord system in nurturing Irish alienation, he did not believe this could be diminished by the legalized dual ownership principle inherent in the measure. To Balfour, the proposal was a foolish attempt to revive an archaic and irrational Gaelic communal land system, and he had no sympathy with the historicist argument popular in Gladstonian circles, that the incorporation of the Brehon system in contemporary land legislation was appropriate. More important, as a Conservative dedicated to the defence of property rights, he was anxious that the bill's principles threatened the principles of property for the landed as well as the industrial leaders throughout the United Kingdom. Considering his own extensive holdings in Scotland (over 180,000 acres), his attitude is perhaps understandable and accounts for his explaining the crofter no-rent campaigns in 1886 to the contagious example of the Irish, sentiments which were echoed by other Scots landlords like Lord Cranbrook and the Duke of Argyle.

In his 1881 analysis of the causes of Irish rural unrest, Balfour ignored altogether the serious effects of the agricultural depression and the poor harvests of 1879–81 on the solvency of Irish tenants. He shared the British aristocracy's tendency to consider all Irish claims of distress as exaggerated, although many British landowners were responsive to economic misery among their own countrymen. Indeed, in 1879, when his own Scottish tenants were adversely affected by agricultural failure, Balfour was not unsympathetic and granted a 25% reduction to his 'suffering tenants' on the following year's rents, and another 25%

reduction on his gross rentals in 1882 following a similar collapse of the harvest. Yet appeals of Land League figures and Irish MPs for voluntary reductions in Irish rents were dismissed as incitement of criminal confiscation.

During the mid-eighties, Balfour's views on the Irish land question matured and gradually took on a more positive aspect. By 1883 he recognized that the land agitation had radicalized the Irish farmer to the point that peasant ownership, not dual ownership, had become the ultimate aim of most tenant farmers. Having observed Parnell's successful co-option of the land issue into the program of the Irish Parliamentary party, Balfour concluded that only peasant proprietorship would eliminate both rural unrest and Irish disaffection for the Union. Although the kernels of Balfour's future ideas on the Irish land question were recognizable in his support of Lord George Hamilton's 1883 resolution in support of expanding the purchase provisions of the 1881 Land Act, it was not until responsibility for Irish affairs was firmly in the hands of the Tories after 1886 that he would fully work out the implications of his analysis of Irish discontent.

By the time of Salisbury's caretaker ministry of 1885 he believed a state-aided program of peasant purchase was the most effective means to liberate the allegedly gullible Irish tenant farmers from being the pawns of those he considered professional agitators and Fenian firebrands such William O'Brien, Michael Davitt and John Dillon. Moreover, by this time, Balfour appreciated the benefits of a state-aided purchase program for the landlords in providing them with an opportunity to sell their holdings before the combined effects of statutory rent reductions, diminishing land values and chronic rural agitation reduced their estates' value to nihil. The economic crisis facing many Irish landlords was reflected by the fate of Lord Lansdowne, Balfour's old school chum, whose rental income from his Irish properties fell from £13,000 to £500 between 1880 and and 1885 under the impact of the land war and the judicial rent reductions.

Although Balfour agreed with Salisbury's decision to disregard Lord Carnarvon's proposals for a conciliatory Irish policy on local government and education during the Caretaker Ministry of 1885, he endorsed heartily the ministry's experimental Ashbourne Act which provided £5 million to tenants for the full purchase price of their holdings, repayable at 4% over 49 years. However, when the Tories became aware of Gladstone's growing proclivities toward Home Rule in the fall of 1885, there was little incentive to sponsor further conciliatory measures, believing as they did that an alliance between Gladstone and Parnell would ultimately split the Liberal party beyond repair. Indeed, following his December social visit to Eaton Hall, it was Balfour who confirmed for Salisbury Gladstone's Home Rule leanings and predicted the subsequent Liberal split over the issue.

Back in office in July 1886 following the defeat of the First Home Rule Bill, the Tories had to move beyond mere resistance to Home Rule. With the revival of agrarian agitation in the form of the 'Plan of Campaign' in late 1886, Salisbury grew impatient with the conciliatory approach of his Chief Secretary Sir Michael Hicks Beach. In March 1887 the Prime Minister took the opportunity provided by Beach's illness to replace him with his nephew Arthur whom he knew would have no hesitation in applying the Cecilian formula of 'resolute government'. Within three months the infamous Jubilee Coercion Act was on the statute book and Balfour showed no hesitation in arresting even those leaders of the 'Plan' who held parliamentary seats, such as William O'Brien and Timothy Harrington. By late 1888, vigorous law enforcement and a co-ordinated plan of landlord resistance secretly inspired by Balfour succeeded in reducing agrarian crime substantially. Between 1887 and 1891, 1800 arrests were made. Moreover, Balfour conducted a highly effective propaganda campaign by insuring that the findings of the Parnell Commission would implicate National League members with agrarian crimes committed at the beginning of the decade, thus casting a pall of criminality over all Parnellite constitutional Nationalists.

Meanwhile, as part of the 1887 tenants' relief legislation, Balfour moved the state-aided land purchase policy beyond the experimental stage by securing an additional five million pounds to supplement the Ashbourne Act. His plans to introduce a more comprehensive purchase measure were delayed until 1891 when he succeeded in obtaining 45 million pounds which enabled 47,000 tenants to purchase their holdings. Balfour's conviction that the land purchase policy would effectively douse the fires of the Home Rule engine drove him to work diligently to overcome the reluctance, and on occasion, outright opposition of Lord Salisbury, Treasury officials as well as the English radicals to this imperially subsidised program.

When the Tories returned to office in 1895 following the three year Liberal interlude, the higher priority now accorded to Irish policy was reflected in Salisbury's appointment of a Cabinet subcommittee composed of both Balfours, Lords Cadogan, Ashbourne and Lansdowne. Arthur Balfour would wage many a battle against ultra-conservative Irish landlords such as Lord Ardiluan, who considered the Government purchase policy close to thievery. Even after leaving the Irish office, Balfour encouraged and supported his brother Gerald's proposal to increase purchase funding by 36 million pounds in his 1896 Land Act. Equally, George Wyndham found Balfour's support as Prime Minister absolutely crucial in overcoming Treasury opposition and some Cabinet reluctance to his 1903 Land Bill, the biggest one of all, which provided 83 million pounds to finance purchase. While Balfour acknowledged the extra-ordinary cost this placed on the Treasury, he insisted to the King and the Duke of Devonshire among others, that this was necessary in the interests of the Government's larger Irish policy. The political success of the 1903 legislation is perhaps best reflected in the virtual disappearance of land agitation by 1906 and the 85,000 purchase agreements concluded between tenants and their landlords by March 1906.

There were naturally other factors that account for Balfour's consistent advocacy of state-aided land purchase, some politically pragmatic and some theoretical. The Conservatives retained power after 1886 by virtue of their alliance with Joseph Chamberlain and his dissident followers who abandoned Gladstone over Home Rule in 1886. The terms of the Liberal Unionist-Tory alliance demanded that concession be made to the legislative priorities of these former Liberals, and land purchase had figured prominently in Chamberlain's early prescription for Ireland's ills, as well as in the priorities which the Ulster Liberal Unionists laid before the Tory administration in 1886. The need to retain the loyalty of Ulster Unionists was acutely appreciated in 1887, and again in 1895 and 1902 when T. W. Russell's agitation championing the interests of the Ulster tenant farmers seemed to endanger the Tory-Liberal Unionist alliance. Thus the dictates of party interests complemented the long range Tory plan for shoring up the foundations of the Union. Moreover, good Victorian that he was, Balfour held that property owning would effect a moral reformation in the average Irish countryman whom he viewed as gullible, immature, feckless, lazy, clannish and thoroughly deficient in initiative and ambition. Indeed, on one occasion after a serious potato failure in Connaught in 1890 he linked the disaster to deficiencies he perceived in Irish character:

> I wish to heaven we could induce the Irish to grow some food of a more trustworthy character than the potato . . .The readiness to accept new ideas to engage on new enterprises is precisely the characteristic most wanting in the population. If it were not so they would have refused to squat generation after generation on the bogs of the inclement West.[2]

Balfour believed that proprietorship and education were essential to inculcate those virtues of orderliness, initiative, self-help, responsibility and respect for the law that he and his contemporaries valued as the foundations of Victorian progress and prosperity. Seeing these values as particularly lacking among the population of the west of Ireland, he ordered close supervision of road-building and railroad building projects to insure that 'a day's work for a day's pay' prevailed so that the inhabitants would be lifted out of 'the demoralizing slough of insolvency through the hard work, discipline and punctuality learned on the job.'[3]

Contrary to widely held principles of laissez-faire, Balfour's establishment of the Congested Districts Board in 1891 indicates his willingness to advocate a considerable amount of state paternalism to address the difficult problems of terrain, isolation and unemployment that plagued the west of Ireland. The board did important work in promoting forestry, livestock and poultry breeding as well as native weaving and spinning crafts. Its activities constituted an important segment of Balfour's program of moral uplift and anglicization of language, education and cultural values in the Gaelic west. It is noteworthy that Parnell supported the Congested District Board (CDB) initiative in Balfour's bill. The work of the CDB earned praise from virtually all sides of the political spectrum, and it was under Nationalist pressure that the jurisdiction of the board was increased to include half of Ireland and 1/3 of its population. By the time of the board's dissolution in 1923, approximately 1,000 estates comprising 2 million acres had been purchased, and 60,000 holdings had been created or improved, work which the ex-Fenian and Land Leaguer Michael Davitt described as 'enlightened state socialism'

By 1920 the combined effects of the Tory land acts, and the additional financing provided by Birrell's 1909 measure, over 157 million pounds in Government funds had been loaned to finance peasant purchase of over 9 million acres of Irish land, enabling over 200,189 tenants to buy their holdings. Whereas only 3% of the Irish population were owners in 1870, by 1916 63.9 were owners of their occupations. This represented the virtual undoing of the conquests and confiscations of the 16th and 17th centuries. To say the least, this initiated the most profound, if quietist economic and social revolution in modern Irish history.

The defects in Balfour's analysis of the land and national question became obvious in time. He was, of course mistaken in not recognizing a genuine political Nationalism in much of the Home Rule enthusiasm, and also in not recognizing that the land hunger was not solely economic, but also a reflection of a deeply-rooted Nationalist desire to regain ancestral land considered to have been unjustly seized. Balfour underestimated the strong undercurrent of Fenian sympathy in the countryside, maintaining up to about 1910 that exposure to British values and institutions eventually would satisfy legitimate Irish grievances and make the average Irishman content with the Union. On the other hand, Balfour was correct in predicting that peasant proprietorship would end the Irish tenant farmer's flirtation with agrarian socialism. The social and political conservatism that has dominated rural Ireland down to the present day was nurtured in large measure by the nature of the land settlement. Yet his Anglo-Saxonism prevented him from seeing as Parnell clearly did that this was a conservatism that could potentially work against the Union he was trying to save. While the purchase programme saved the Ascendency from financial ruin, it contributed to terminating the relationships between the native Irish and the Anglo-Irish gentry. The democratisation of Irish county and local government under Gerald Balfour's Local Government Act of 1898 was another reform conceded under heavy Liberal Unionist pressure and the Government's pressing need to quench bi-partisan Irish anger regarding an 1896 royal commission finding that Ireland had been overtaxed which came hard on the heels of land purchase. The Local Government Act drove the majority of the gentry in the south and west of Ireland into political and social isolation, and indeed in some sections of the north. The results of the first county council elections in 1898 emphasize this clearly. Across the country 551 Nationalists were elected to the first county councils in 1899. Unionists won only 125 seats, 86 of them in Ulster. These developments made it much easier for the Gaelic and Irishing of Ireland forces such as the GAA and the Irish language movement to influence the southern and western countryside prior to World War I.

Moreover, the popularly controlled local government institutions provided useful forums for Irish farmers and labourers to forward programmes that improved their economic and social conditions. For instance, the first county councils, in conjunction with the newly established Department of Agriculture and Technical Instruction, established during Gerald Balfour's tenure, had 121 itinerant instructors teaching 551 farm extension courses to 39,000 students by 1904. Antrim, Armagh and Down were the only counties without some scheme of local government sponsored technical instruction. Although jobs may have been more plentiful in this area closest to Belfast, it is interesting to note that these were the counties with the least Nationalist councillors on their councils. County councils addressed the scandalous housing conditions of agricultural labourers, and the multiplication of labourers' cottages after 1900 through council support represented a significant improvement for this hitherto neglected segment of the community.

From early on, Balfour accepted the legitimacy of the Catholic grievance over university education. Since Trinity College Dublin was a Protestant institution and the Royal University only an examining body, there was little opportunity for Irish Roman Catholics to obtain a university education. Balfour's efforts to solve this problem, though pragmatically motivated by the hope this might encourage the hierarchy to support of Dublin Castle's law enforcement policy, can be attributed also to his belief that university education was essential to counter the irrational, authoritarian and obscurantist characteristic he perceived in Roman Catholicism. Similar to many Victorians, Balfour associated the progress and enlightenment of modern history with the triumph of Protestantism and its values. Manifestations of increased Catholic power, as evidenced by rising vocations, church construction and lay participation, which abounded in the last quarter of the century, undoubtedly nurtured his negative perceptions and account for his insistence that the role and power of the Irish hierarchy be kept at an absolute minimum in any Unionist scheme for a state supported Irish university system. He believed that exposure to the rationalist scientific tradition that he equated with English universities would nurture habits of independent thought, and correct a mythical and sentimental view of the past which he believed prompted the Home Rule enthusiasm of middle class Irish Catholics. Balfour's analysis failed to recognize that limitations on clerical influence in politics were supported not only by Parnell but subsequently by other Nationalists such as John Redmond, John Dillon and Michael Davitt. His recognition of anti-clericalism within the Fenian tradition was offset by his abhorrence of the separatist Republicanism within Fenian ideology. It should be said as well that Balfour permitted, even welcomed, political involvement by the Roman Catholic clergy if it facilitated the Government. This was exemplified by his back door efforts through the Duke of Norfolk at the Vatican in 1887 to secure a papal rescript against the 'Plan of Campaign'.

Although as early as 1889, Balfour began drawing up preliminary plans for a state-funded university scheme for Irish Roman Catholics, his efforts floundered on a combination of Cabinet reluctance and rank and file anti-Catholic prejudice within the Unionist coalition. The opposition of Trinity College Dublin to any scheme that might infringe upon its privileged position was yet another hurdle, as was the refusal of the Irish hierarchy to support any plan that excluded them from the governing body. Meanwhile, the considerable opposition from northern Protestants who resented any Government plans to endow a Catholic educational institution, caused Balfour to complain to his uncle in September 1891, 'I am everlasting being denounced as a Jesuit in disguise ...' Although no substantial moves were taken to redress the university grievance while he was Chief Secretary, in 1898 Balfour delegated Richard B. Haldane, who had written the London University charter, to draft plans for an Irish university after secret consultations with Archbishops Walsh and Logue as well as with Irish Parliamentary Party members. For a variety of financial and partisan reasons that would be too lengthy to develop here, the Haldane plan was pigeon-holed in 1899 and again in 1903. However, the Irish University Bill which Augustine Birrell piloted through the Commons in 1908 and which established the current National University of Ireland, was based primarily upon the Balfour-Haldane plan that emerged from the earlier Haldane-Balfour initiative of 1898.

In my view the problematic area of Balfour's legacy to twentieth century Ireland relates to his general views on Ulster and northern Protestants, and especially to his political actions during the 1910–1914 crisis. Whereas Parnell's eight visits to Ulster between 1883–1891 led to an appreciation of the complexities of Ulster's party political allegiances and religious demography, Balfour's sole visit there did little to encourage movement beyond the stereotype of a solid Unionist hegemony in the north-east. He never focused sharply enough on Ulster at this time to recognize that a solid anti-Home Rule sentiment existed in only three Ulster counties in 1885, and that the existence of over 287 Ulster branches of the National League gave evidence of a more complex situation. It is clear that Balfour did not like northern Protestants particularly. The sectarianism associated with Orangeism and the inclination of northern Unionists to political paranoia as demonstrated in the 1904 devolution crisis, offended his intellectual and political sensibilities. Indeed, he never returned to Belfast after he delivered a rousing anti-Home Rule speech in the Ulster Hall when the second bill was before Parliament. Yet Balfour was a firm and consistent champion of Protestant Ulster in the resistance to Home Rule from the 1880's right down to the drafting of the Government of Ireland Act of 1920. Pragmatic political strategy dictated a good deal of this through 1914. Balfour never forgot that it was the 'Orange Card' that rallied wide and decisive British opposition to the first Home Rule Bill, and laid the cornerstone of the Tory/Liberal Unionist alliance, an alliance in which Ulster Liberal Unionists were of no mean importance. As we have seen, the positive aspects of his legislative programme suggest his recognition of their political and electoral significance.

Although Parnell attempted to assuage Protestant anxieties regarding Catholic power and stressed the role of Ulster in preserving religious liberty throughout the island during an 1891 Belfast appearance, his appeal never registered with Balfour. Instead Balfour enthusiastically took up his role as the chief Unionist critic of the 1893 bill in the Commons, and rallied the forces of northern Unionism with his Ulster Hall speech in 1893. Before a packed audience, he condemned Home Rule for sacrificing the 'orderly', 'prosperous' and 'loyal' north to the 'inferior' and 'disorderly' south, and asserted that religious divisions within Ireland made the Home Rule policy folly and madness. The contrast between this address and Parnell's address is palpable. Not only did Balfour's characterisation ignore the sectarian rioting that plagued Belfast since the 1850's, but certainly it overlooked the deliberate defiance by Orange leaders of the Party Processions Act against Orange parades in the mid 1860's. Balfour came so close to playing the Orange card in his Belfast speech that demands were made for his arrest for inciting riot when Belfast Protestants attacked Catholics after his visit, (and a follow-up one by Lord Salisbury a few weeks later).

After the two 1910 elections and the Parliament Act made Home Rule a virtual certainty, Balfour not only failed to accept the democratic implications of the Parliament Act, but also increasingly used Ulster as the bludgeon to frustrate the will of the Commons. For example, in March 1912 he drafted a memorandum advocating that the King be pressured by the Unionists to dissolve Parliament and force Asquith into an election. This memo appears to have inspired subsequent appeals by Lord Lansdowne and Andrew Bonar Law (who had succeed Balfour as Tory leader in 1911) to George V to dismiss Asquith and appoint others who would hold a general election on Home Rule. The King greatly resented this pressure and refused these requests.

In late 1913–4 Balfour gave every encouragement in Parliament and in public to the Ulster Protestant resistance. Although he supported the June 1912 amendment of the Liberal MP Agar-Robartes calling for the exclusion of the four northeast Ulster counties, he did so chiefly as a wrecking device in hopes it would destroy both the Home Rule bill and the Asquith ministry. Despite mounting evidence of illegal arms importation and drilling by the UVF in 1913, he continued to portray the northern loyalists as loyal and patriotic citizens. By September of that year even Bonar Law began to worry about the potential for civil war that the Ulster campaign had unleashed while Balfour's anxiety that the UVF would find Nationalist imitators in the south ultimately proved prophetic. It was against this background in late September 1913 that Bonar Law agreed to the King's suggestion of secret negotiations with Prime Minister Asquith to find a compromise on the basis of a temporary Ulster exclusion. Although Balfour advised Law that he could hardly refuse to participate, Balfour showed little enthusiasm about these Cherkley meetings, and particularly so after the Tories won two by-elections after the second meeting. In the midst of these negotiations, while publicly demanding that all of Ulster be excluded from Home Rule, Balfour confided to Bonar Law his agreement with Joe Devlin's contention that an Ulsterless Ireland would be a disaster:

> I take Devlin's view, and were I an Irish Nationalist, I think I should refuse Home Rule on the terms proposed. With all the industrial

energy and all the money left out of the new community, and nothing left in it but the Irish genius for parliamentary debate and political organization, I do not see that they have much prospect of playing a satisfactory part in the world's history.[4]

Although privy to the imminent danger of a European war in early 1914, Balfour approved of the Tory plan to amend the Army Bill so as to prevent the use of the Crown Forces against the UVF, a plan that was ultimately abandoned as too extreme. Instead of admitting any Unionist responsibility for an atmosphere that encouraged General Gough and his officers to their breach of military discipline in March 1914, he attributed the Curragh affair to a plan of Winston Churchill '. . . in one of his Napoleonic moods' to strangle Ulster into submission. Similarly he defended the Larne gun-runners and subsequently condemned the Nationalists who ran guns into Howth in July 1914. Meanwhile, he supported Carson in his flat dismissal of Asquith's offer of a six year Ulster exclusion in March, 1914.

Analysing the motivations governing Balfour's role in these events between 1914–19 is no easy task. Certainly his portrayal of the Liberal Home Rule Bill as the product of a corrupt bargain between Irish and the Liberals with the former getting the parliamentary veto and Home Rule in return for support of Lloyd George's budget provided a convenient issue to camouflage the deep divisions in the Unionist ranks over fiscal policy. At the same time this ensured that Ulster Unionists, still harbouring the memories of the devolution affair, would not cause further division in the Tory ranks and jeopardize the Unionist seats regained since 1906. This helps account for his refusal in the midst of the constitutional crisis in 1910 to seriously consider the proposal of some younger party men associated with the imperial federation movement, that federalism could provide an alternative to Home Rule that might meet the requirements of both Nationalists and Unionists. (Indeed at this stage he rejected outright an offer from Lloyd George suggesting that a coalition Government might be able to solve the Irish question as well as address the pressing concerns of defense, social reform and industrial regeneration. In explaining his rejection he said he couldn't do what Peel had done. There is a good deal of archival evidence that Ireland was still being used as a political football as late as November 1913. The American Ambassador Walter Hines Page was not far off the mark when he observed in May 1914:

The Conservatives have used Ulster and its army as a club to drive the Liberals out of power; and they have gone to the very brink of civil war.They don't really care about Ulster. I doubt whether they care much about Home Rule. They'd slip Ireland out to sea without much worry except their own financial loss. Its the Lloyd George programme that infuriates them, and Ulster and anti-Home rule are mere weapons to stop the general Liberal revolution.[5]

Office hunger and an unconscious need to avenge the loss of his almost hereditary position as Tory party leader merged with the usual historic and strategic objections to Home Rule to make up the rationale of Balfour's actions in this period. Yet it is clear that the seeds of a two-nations theory were implanted in Balfour's thinking on the north even before 1913–14. Organised Orangeism and the collapse of the Liberals as a force in Ulster politics in the mid-1880s blinded Balfour to any symptoms of Irish identity that a considerable number of Irish Presbyterians had displayed in the past. His disdain for the Gaelic elements in Irish culture, his Anglo-Saxon pride and the memories of his 1893 Belfast visit predisposed him to a two-nations view, and led to his conclusion that it was an accident of geography that Protestant Ulster lay adjacent to the Roman Catholic and Gaelic south. The Easter Rising, the anti-conscription campaign and the Anglo-Irish war reinforced these attitudes as evidenced by his description of the 1918 Sinn Fein electoral victory as '. . . the blessed refusal of the Sinn Feiners to take the oath of allegiance.' Meanwhile, the fact that 23 of the 26 Unionist seats won in the 1918 election lay in the six counties was never far from his mind when the Lloyd George Coalition took up the Irish Question again in late 1919. From this point until the signing of the Treaty in 1921, Balfour consistently advocated letting the south go, and retaining the link with the Protestant north east.

Although busy at Versailles in 1919, Balfour kept in close contact with Walter Long's Cabinet committee which was responsible for drafting legislation to provide separate self-governing structures in Dublin and Belfast. In November 1919, Balfour learned that Long's committee was recommending a nine-county division (which would have included Catholic Donegal, Monaghan and Cavan) as the best means of promoting eventual Irish unity. He fired back an immediate protest to London. Emphasizing that there was no historic or geographical basis for an all Ireland political unit, he proclaimed it was a violation of self-determination to force the Protestant north into the same political mould as the disloyal and Catholic South through the proposed Council of Ireland. He was present at the 19th of December Cabinet at which his memorandum was considered and which resulted in the six-county division, subsequently announced by Lloyd George in the Commons on 22nd December. When the combined objections of the Irish Hierarchy, southern Unionists and the remaining Nationalist members caused Lloyd

George in February 1920 to revert back to the nine-county division and to concede further powers to the Council of Ireland, once again it was Balfour's objections in an additional memorandum that appear to have been crucial in the Treaty committee's return to the six-county division that ultimately became the boundary in the Government of Ireland Act. Balfour's timely interventions countered Long's and Chamberlain's early hopes that the bill could be constructed so as not to preclude eventual Irish unity. This gave considerable leverage to James Craig and his Ulster followers who wanted to insure a permanent partition by having a smaller Ulster. Indeed, it was leverage which enabled them to extract a secret agreement from Long that despite the provision for the Council of Ireland, the partition provided for in the Government of Ireland Bill of 1920 was to be permanent. This promise was kept, as we know, despite the incentive of the Boundary Commission that Lloyd George held out to the Irish delegates during the 1921 Treaty negotiations. (In fact, on the eve of the meeting of the Boundary Commission, Balfour published in the Times a letter which F. E. Smith had sent him in 1921 indicating that the Treaty provisions would not endanger the line drawn by the 1920 Act.)

Two days after the signing of the Treaty, Lloyd George wrote to Balfour thanking him for his advice on Irish affairs, and he indicated that 'the happy consummation of our five years of work would not have been possible without your support.'[6] Meanwhile, Balfour wrote to his sister Alice, 'If the Irish settlement really succeeds, it will make an immense difference to American politics: but I cannot help feeling a little uneasy about Ulster- I trust without good reason.'[7] There were, of course, substantial reasons for unease. Policies advocated by Balfour and the Unionists in 1910–14 frustrated 45 years of efforts to resolve the Irish Question through parliamentary means, and certainly had a role in the re-introduction of the physical force tradition by Carson and the Ulster leaders, a situation which proved contagious. As J.B. Armour, the Presbyterian Home Ruler from Antrim wrote during the chaos and turmoil in the north in 1923:

> Carson came to break all laws and he arranged for bringing in arms into Larne not for shooting crows but for shooting the King's soldiers unless they took his side. The Sinn Féiners took a leaf out of his book with a result which is apparent on every hand.[8]

The 1920 six county settlement, did not solve the problem of Hibernia Irredenta, and instead produced a constant source of anxiety and instability within the northern state.

The partitionist policy proved ineffective in guaranteeing the long term fiscal stability in the north, and, ironically, not long after its establishment the northern Irish state, whose citizen's Balfour had hailed for their industriousness, became dependent upon the same Treasury subsidies he had opposed for the allegedly feckless southerners. Moreover, by dividing off the industrial and Protestant north from the twenty-six counties, partition effectively accentuated the Catholic, Gaelic and rural features of southern Irish society that Balfour had decried. The social and cultural differences between north and south deepened and became more institutionalized over the next fifty years, partially because of the homogeneity of the Catholic population. Thus the worst fears that Parnell expressed in his 1891 Belfast speech had materialized. The periodic revival by the Irish Republican Army of guerrilla warfare during this same era was a product both of the political and economic ostracism experienced by the northern Catholic minority and the irredentist views that many southerners harboured toward Ulster.

In conclusion then, there was a fundamental ambivalence in Balfour's Unionism that made it difficult to accept the possibility or indeed desirability of the fully integrated partnership that the Act of Union theoretically intended. As early as 1887, this ambivalence was reflected in Balfour's private observation on Home Rule, 'After all when it comes I shall not be sorry. Only let us have separation as well as Home Rule. England cannot go on with Irishmen in her Parliament. She must govern herself too.' Poverty, rural disorder, and the character of Irish Catholicism as well as rabid sectarianism repelled Balfour and caused him to view Ireland not as a sister kingdom but more as a subservient colony whose stability depended on Britain exerting a supervisory presence. In 1889, when he was Chief-Secretary, Balfour denied the popular Nationalist contention that he was 'forging chains for their enslavement...where in truth I am merely doing my best to prevent them picking each other's pockets and cutting each other's throats.' Likewise, implicit in his exposition of the two-nations theory regarding Ulster, was the assumption that it was only a paternalistic British Imperial authority that could effectively neutralize sectarian antagonism and preserve communal peace. This condescension made a real union of hearts difficult, but the reality of close economic links, geographical proximity and the political connections forged over centuries made purely colonial approaches such as were adopted towards Canada and India inappropriate if not impossible. This ambivalence regarding the exact nature of Ireland's relationship to England was common to many English Unionists, and was a large factor in hindering a consistently constructive and generous policy based on an objective assessment of Ireland's immediate and long range needs. Similarly, indifference, con-

descension to all Irishmen, Catholic and Protestant, and an unwilling-
ness to objectively examine the long-range needs of Northern Ireland
or to treat it as an equal part of the United Kingdom has been noted by
scholars as persistent and significant factors in the failure of British
policy in the north from 1922 until very recent days. To the extent that
the present tragedy of Northern Ireland is a product of the strategies
and patterns of political support established in 1912–14 and the Government of Ireland Act, Arthur Balfour continues to exercise an influence on twentieth-century Ireland.

THE GOLDEN MOMENT.

ERIN (*to Mr. REDMOND and Sir EDWARD CARSON*). "COME, MY FRIENDS, YOU'RE BOTH IRISHMEN; WHY NOT BURY THE HATCHET——IN THE VITALS OF THE COMMON ENEMY?"

Punch cartoon of Erin urgung reconciliation between Edward Carson (on left) and John Redmond (on right) after 1916 Rising *Punch*, 24 May 1916

CHAPTER THREE

Irish Unionism, 1905–21
by
Alvin Jackson

Between 1905 and 1920 Unionism ceased to be a unified movement claiming to cover the whole island of Ireland. Between 1905 and 1920 Unionism ceased to have an exclusively parliamentary focus, and instead developed a local base and a paramilitary strength. By 1920 Unionism had shed some – though not all – of its landed leadership: in the years after 1905 the original leaders of Unionism, the survivors of 1886 and 1893, died away, leaving a new generation to exercise command. By 1920 Unionism was a more organised and a comparatively more representative movement. By 1920 Unionism had become more partitionist and more parochial. Between 1905 and 1920 Irish Unionism became Ulster Unionism, and Ulster Unionism became a six counties Unionism; Unionists – in so far as they accepted the Northern Ireland Parliament, became devolutionist and partitionist. Irish Unionists had evolved into Northern Irish Home Rulers. Unionism had become democratised, militarised, and localised.[1]

How can one justify these suggestions of rapid change in a movement more frequently associated with stasis? Three aspects of Unionism in the early twentieth century may be isolated and dissected for evidence of both continuity and instability. These three features are the leadership and the institutions of Unionism, and Unionist ideology. The emphasis in this essay is therefore on formal, organised politics. But it is also possible to pursue these arguments in the area of informal political behaviour – beyond the confines of party organisation.[2]

The four leaders of Unionism between 1905 and 1920–1 were Colonel Edward Saunderson, Walter Long, and, most conspicuous of all, Edward Carson. James Craig succeeded Carson in January 1921.[3] This transition in leaders reflected a variety of paradoxes and developments inside Unionism. Saunderson, though from County Cavan, and though a colonel in the Irish militia, was essentially an all-Ireland Unionist, and essentially a parliamentary politician. Walter Long, though connected on both sides of his family with Ireland and with the British Army, was

35

essentially an English Unionist and parliamentarian. Edward Carson, though a Dubliner, a distinguished lawyer and junior minister, revealed himself as a pragmatic Ulster Unionist and as a military commander. James Craig, a junior minister in Lloyd George's post-war coalition, and an effective operator inside the House of Commons, emerged as a peculiarly Irish politician, sensitive and responsive to local pressures. A battle-hardened soldier (in South Africa) and businessman, he combined his skills and experience in plotting the armed defiance by the Ulster Unionists of Asquith's Government in 1912–14.

Edward Saunderson founded a separate Irish Unionist Parliamentary Party in 1886, and commanded his creation until 1906, the year of his death. He was an Anglo-Irish landowner, who – like Parnell – had spent his formative years out of Ireland. Like Parnell he became increasingly entrapped within the House of Commons, and increasingly out of touch with local, Irish realities.[4] As a passionate defender of the landed interest he built up a network of well-placed allies within English Toryism – but, equally, by 1900 he had alienated parts of the electorally crucial farming community in Ulster. These farmers were orchestrated and commanded in 1900–05 by a radical Unionist, Thomas Wallace Russell, who caustically condemned the landed sympathies and the inefficiency of the Irish Unionist Parliamentary Party under Saunderson's leadership. Saunderson was too old, too ill and too limited to offer any adequate response to Russell, and to Russell's farmer support. The leadership of Unionism therefore fell into the hands of a younger and more socially diverse generation of loyalist leaders. When he died, in October 1906, Saunderson was a political anachronism.[5] He had been a landlord, a parliamentarian, and an Irish Unionist – an Irish politician whose life revolved around the sessions of the House of Commons. He was anti-populist, and in certain respects heedless of democratic values. He knew little about the condition of the Protestant urban working classes, and had little sympathy for Belfast Unionism. He embodied a late nineteenth century vision of Irish politics which was increasingly out of touch with the nature of Unionism in the early twentieth century.

His friend and successor, Walter Long, was fundamentally a similar figure. Like Saunderson, Long was a landowner with an extended family tradition of political and parliamentary involvement. Like Saunderson, he was strongly connected with northern Unionism, and yet utterly perplexed by the tougher aspects of populist Ulster Unionism. Even more than Saunderson, he was an Irish Unionist, representing a southern constituency (South County Dublin) at Westminster between 1906 and 1910. But he was also an Englishman whose interest in Ireland, though sincere, was ultimately marginal to other, English concerns. For Walter Long, who had extensive ministerial experience in a succession of Tory administrations, Irish Unionism represented only one of several power bases inside Conservative politics at Westminster. Irish Unionism was, therefore, a means to an end, and not always the end or goal itself. Unionism helped to consolidate Walter Long's position on the right wing of the Conservative Party, and to strengthen his claims on the Tory leadership. When, in 1908, a safe English constituency became available for Long, regretfully and predictably he announced his decision to leave South Dublin, and to resign from the chairmanship of the Irish Unionist Parliamentary Party.[6]

The ending of Long's brief reign in 1910 represented a fundamental break in the continuity of Unionist leadership and strategy. Long had helped to bind northern and southern Unionism at a time of drift between these two partners. He had encouraged the creation of the Joint Committee of the Unionist Associations of Ireland in 1908 – a body designed to unite northern and southern Unionists in English campaign work. His own Union Defence League (of 1907), unlike later English bodies of loyalist sympathisers, was intended to promote the interests of all Irish Unionists, and not simply the northern variety. [7] Though Edward Carson was born a Dubliner, he showed less practical concern for southern Unionism than Long had done; indeed after 1918 Carson chose to represent a Belfast constituency rather than the Trinity seat which he had held since 1892. Long's departure from Ireland helped, therefore, to create opportunities for a widening of the regional division inside Unionism. A semblance of unity between the Unionisms, northern and southern, was preserved until 1912–13, but thereafter the break was profound and irreparable.

Drift characterised another aspect of the relationship between Ulster Unionism and the rest of British and Irish politics – and here, again, Walter Long's leadership was significant. Long was the quintessential English Tory squire, and his command of Irish Unionism helped to sustain the often fragile link binding the two parties, Conservative and Unionist. Relations had been peculiarly strained between 1895 and 1905, and had nearly broken in 1905–06 when Ulster Unionists suspected and accused the outgoing Tory Government of plotting to foist a devolved administration onto Ireland.[8] Walter Long's succession to the loyalist leadership in 1906 helped to limit Ulster Unionist distrust to George Wyndham and his immediate circle; but Long merely presided over a temporary period of tranquillity – peace after the war, perhaps, but a peace born of exhaustion. Long's departure created the possibility of further division. It is important not to be deceived by the superficially perfect relationship between Toryism and loyalism in 1912–14, or to be puzzled by the apparent break-down in that relationship by 1918–20.[9]

Long had temporarily mended a scarred relationship, but the healing
had been far from complete. Despite the public unity of Tory and
loyalist in 1912–14, Ulster Unionists were pursuing an independent and
local political strategy. This reflected not simply frustration at parliamentary procedures, but also a profound scepticism concerning the
abilities, strength and conviction of the Tories.

Edward Carson presided over the more localised, the more militant
and the more independent strategies of 1912–14. His choice as leader
and his accession in February 1910 reflected an altered and a comparatively more representative and bourgeois, Unionism. He was the first
middle class leader of Ulster Unionism, and this was perhaps a more
significant feature of his background than his origins in Dublin as a
southern Unionist.[10] Carson was the first leader of Unionism to have
been selected after prolonged discussion among the elders of the Irish
Unionist Parliamentary Party, who were themselves, by 1910, largely
middle class in origin. He was the first practising lawyer and advocate to
lead the Ulster Unionists.

The paradox of Carson's record is of course that, as a man who had
spent his working life committed to legal niceties, he appeared curiously willing to swap judicial arbitration for violence. By 1910 he had
served for 18 years in the House of Commons, and had acted as Solici-
tor General for Ireland and for England. He had been offered senior
judicial office in 1905. He was both a British and Irish Privy Counsellor.
Yet he preached armed defiance of the King's Government in 1912–14.
He threatened to call out the paramilitary UVF as late as 1919.[11]
Throughout 1912–14 he also sustained a constitutional strategy, arguing
his case in parliament, and negotiating with Asquith through the winter
of 1913–14. He and Craig were at the Buckingham Palace conference in
July 1914 and, of course, he conscientiously served as a minister (Attor-
ney General in 1915, First Lord of the Admiralty in 1916–17, Minister
without Portfolio in 1917–18) under Asquith and Lloyd George. In 1916
and again in 1918 he was offered the Lord Chancellorship, and the
opportunity to head the English judiciary.[12] How does one explain these
swings and apparent contradictions in Carson's loyalties and in his
behaviour?

There are a variety of possible perspectives on Carson's shifting
attitudes. He was a tough lawyer, a convinced Unionist who at first
knew little about the North, and who relied heavily on James Craig for
local guidance. He was moody, hypochondriacal, and inclined to depression, to swings of temper. All these personal circumstances may
help to explain Carson's shifts of tone between 1911–12 and 1914. On
the whole he was more militant in 1912 than in 1914, and comparatively
more militant before audiences in Ireland than in England. In private

he swiftly emerged as a moderating influence on the hardliners of the Ulster Unionist Council. In general he was more conciliatory behind closed doors than in public.[13]

There are other, broader perspectives on these shifts. Unionist rhetoric had always been militant and threatening, but the threats had never developed into action because the Home Rule Bills of 1886 and 1893 had been swiftly laid to rest. Carson was by nature an emotional and hardhitting speaker, but he had also been in the House of Commons in 1893, and therefore knew about the form of Ulster Unionist rhetoric. Carson's bluster not only fitted into a long tradition of loyalist oratory, it also reflected the difficulties of Unionism in 1912, in the aftermath of the Parliament Act of 1911. As the Home Rule crisis of 1912–14 developed, Carson came under pressure to prove that his rhetoric and the stage-army which he had helped to create were more than empty threats and shadows. As the reality of violence came closer, and as his options narrowed in 1913–14, Carson grew perceptibly more cautious. His interests, and the interests of his movement, did not rest with violence, but they did rest with the threat of violence. Carson pursued every possible constitutional strategy in 1913–14 hence his comparative caution in 1914 and the fact that the young bloods of the UVF did not fight the Irish battles which had been promised to them.[14]

Carson, unlike Parnell, had a good knowledge of Irish history, and he and Craig evolved a strategy which may well have been based upon their reading of Anglo-Irish relations in the nineteenth century, and upon their view of the historical relationship between Irish Protestants and British Government. The historical relationship between the settler population and Royal Government had been seen as limited or contractual – a system of interrelated, mutually dependent obligations: the King would be accepted and his ministers obeyed for as long as he maintained faith with his peoples. Although a nominal loyalty to the Crown remained a central commitment of 'loyalism', certain radical Presbyterians in the eighteenth century were attracted by the notion that Government had a moral dimension and a popular responsibility, and that tyrannical Government could and should be overthrown. This thinking was close to the logic of Presbyterian United Irishmen of Belfast in the 1790s. In the twentieth century Carson and Craig shared the intellectual bequest of these Belfast radicals with other Irish politicians, including, ironically, Irish Republicans.[15] A tyrannical Government – and Asquith's administration was seen as such – had to be rejected as a matter of constitutional principle. Tactical advantage and a historical sense of political morality helped, therefore, to dictate Carson and Craig's attitudes in 1912–14.

There were other historical influences on the men of 1912, however.

The history of Anglo-Irish relations from the late eighteenth century onwards suggested that the British Government would only be moved by Irish grievance if the threat of force were liberally applied. From the Volunteers' campaigns for Free Trade and legislative independence between 1778 and 1782 through the campaign for Catholic relief, Fenianism and Parnellism, the British Government apparently responded only to the prospect of a violent and ungovernable Ireland. O'Connell and Parnell, essentially pacific and constitutional politicians, appeared from the perspective of Westminster to have influence over the most militant forces in Irish society. They were each certainly violent orators – but British governments only occasionally dared to call their bluff (as with O'Connell and Clontarf in 1843). The Ulster Volunteers bore a more than superficial similarity to the Volunteers of the 1780s and Carson appeared, like Parnell, to be a politician with whom the British could do business as well as a politician with influence over the more violent elements of his community. So it was not solely the unconstitutional behaviour of Unionists in 1912–14 which was so effective, but rather the combination of constitutional and unconstitutional, lawful and unlawful. Here again a historical perspective helped to condition Carson and Craig's plans.[16]

James Craig's Unionism is explored with skill elsewhere in this volume – but a swift appraisal is offered here in order to provide a logical conclusion to the section on leadership, and to clinch some of the earlier arguments.[17] Craig came to prominence inside the Edwardian Unionist movement as one of a number of younger loyalists who sought to reconstruct the unity of the movement after a period of division. He represented a younger, a more thoroughly middle class, and a more thoroughly northern generation of leader – a group impatient with the perceived failings of the earlier landlord leaders, and a group with comparatively little emotional sympathy for southern Unionism. Craig, born in County Down, and employed in Belfast, represented the northeastern heartland of Unionism where his predecessors as leader had sprung from the periphery of northern politics, or, indeed from within southern loyalism. Craig's networks in the north – Orange, commercial, Conservative, social – were effectively worked in 1912–14, and were a vital influence in the organisation of a distinctive Ulster Unionism in these years. As a junior minister in the post-war Coalition, when Carson was out of office, Craig was the most important Ulster Unionist influence over the emergence of the Government of Ireland Bill. In particular he pressed, and with little compunction, for a six-county Northern Ireland: indirectly he succeeded in having the Lloyd George Cabinet vote for six counties after its own sub-committee had recommended a nine-county partition scheme.[18] Craig's influence was therefore formidable, as befitted a politician of long parliamentary experience and ministerial standing. An easterner and a businessman, he decisively contributed to the evolution of an Ulster Unionism, and to the definition of a political territory which reflected this creed and these origins.

Unionist organisation developed rapidly and radically after 1905, and, in doing so, modified the nature of the movement itself. From a Unionism on the defensive at the turn of the century, a movement beset by internal and external difficulties, a rather more formidable institution had emerged by 1911–12. A threatened and fragmented Unionism in 1900 had matured by 1920 into the governing creed and party of Northern Ireland. Unionist organisation had swelled with each Home Rule challenge, but the resulting body, though extensive, was neither well-regulated nor economically efficient. The first and second Home Rule crises had thrown up a host of competing loyalist organisations which often withered away very speedily. Only in the south did one preeminent organisation emerge and survive – the Irish Loyal and Patriotic Union of 1885, renamed as the Irish Unionist Alliance in 1891.[19] In the north, especially after the defeat of the second Home Rule Bill in 1893, Unionist organisation fell into disrepair and political control could be exercised with ease by small numbers of wealthy activists. Landlords, in particular, despite a general political and economic decline, clung onto local influence.

Although the absence of an effective Home Rule challenge in the 1890s had a disastrous impact upon Unionist organisation and motivation, this did not mean that the Unionist leadership was without criticism. On the contrary, the slighter the challenge from Home Rule, the more noisy the opposition became from within Unionism. Some Presbyterian Unionists, some working class Unionists in Belfast, and farming Unionists, united in protest against the unrepresentativeness and inefficiency of Unionist democracy. Mainstream Unionists lost seats to dissidents in North Down (October 1900), East Down (February 1902) and North Fermanagh (March 1903). Against able and well-marshalled opponents, the feeble nature of much Unionist organisation was exposed and crushed. In particular the farmers' leader, T.W. Russell, proved an unrelenting and highly effective critic of Unionist failure. And it was partly to meet the challenge mounted by Russell's agitation that a younger, emergent generation of Unionist, including James Craig, proposed a fundamental reconstruction of Ulster Unionism. From this initiative emerged, in March 1905, the Ulster Unionist Council.[20]

The UUC comprised 100 representatives of Ulster Unionist constituency associations, 50 representatives of the Orange Order and 50 co-opted members. It elected 20 members of a 30 strong standing committee:

the remainder were appointed by the chairman of the Irish Unionist Parliamentary Party.[21] The Council represented the most democratic and representative forum that Ulster Unionism had ever inspired. It institutionalised the bond with the Orange Order, and with the more militant traditions of Irish Protestantism. The Council inspired a broader reorganisation of Unionism: the reactivation of defunct local associations and wider participation inside the movement. The Council provided the central structures of Unionist defiance in 1912–14. It helped to foster a partitionist mentality, representing, as it did, only Northern Unionism. Arguably, it was a prototype of the northern parliament which opened in Belfast in June 1921: it certainly provided members, schooled in partisanship and in the arcana of representative institutions, to the new parliament.

With the creation of the Council, and the spread of its influence, an era of haphazard, landlord-dominated electoral management came to an end. By the time of the third Home Rule Bill much had been done to reconstruct the crumbling facade of late nineteenth century Unionism. Constituency bodies in North Armagh and North Fermanagh had been reactivated in 1906; similar resuscitation was applied in East Donegal, North Monaghan, Newry and Mid Tyrone by 1909. Belfast Unionism was fundamentally revised in 1909. That Ulster Unionism had comparatively sound local foundations in 1912–14, and after, owed much to this mid-Edwardian revival.[22] The Council itself expanded both in numbers and in the authority which it claimed. In 1911 the membership of the Council was raised to 370, and now included the Apprentice Boys of Derry, and representatives of the Unionist Clubs movement. By 1918 the total membership had crept up to 432, with the inclusion, for the first time, of women Unionists.[23] Further restructuring and expansion followed in the 1920s. What was emerging from these revisions was a comparatively more democratic Unionism – a Unionism more fully, if still inadequately, representative of Ulster loyalism.

More important, these extensions created a Council which could give a quasi-democratic authority to the radical initiatives of the Unionist leaders in 1912–14. The outline plans for a provisional Government of Ulster were laid down and endorsed at a meeting of the UUC in September 1911. A more detailed scheme of resistance to Home Rule was approved by the Council on 24 September 1913. Sub-committees of the Council administered both the complex finances of Unionist resistances and the military preparations. Since late 1910 and early 1911 the Council had helped to import weapons into Ireland. The Standing Committee of the Council oversaw the formation of the Ulster Volunteer Force at the end of 1912.[24] In initiating and endorsing militant strategies, the Council risked creating a monster beyond its control. In fashioning the UVF, the middle class Unionists of the Council risked ushering paramilitary bosses into the commanding role once exercised by the Ulster gentry. In theory this risk was great, and apparently became greater through 1913 and into 1914. During these months weapons trickled into Ulster, and to the UVF, creatively disguised as 'carbide' or 'high class electrical plant', and smuggled in packs and crates. Although there were occasional disasters (such as the seizure of weapons at Hammersmith in June 1913), the memory of these was erased by the spectacular gun-running escapade of April 1914.[25] And recruitment continued apace: the numbers joining the UVF rose to between 90,000 and 100,000 by early 1914. Its military skills were sharpened in training camps and drill halls. Any threat however, of paramilitary ascendancy over the Council stumbled decisively on the obtrusive bureaucracy and discipline of the UVF. The UVF was a rigidly hierarchical and centralised institution whose commanders were old professional soldiers, accustomed to political authority, and on good terms with the luminaries of the Council; they were uniformly and excessively respectful of Carson. Considerably more energy was spent by these officers on tightening discipline than on preparing a strategy to fight any British or Irish enemy. Considerably more anxiety was lavished by the Unionist political leaders on the challenge posed by the UVF than on the challenge of John Redmond's Volunteers. Like the entrepreneurs that they were, the men of the Council had staked their own independence and the credibility of their cause in sanctioning the UVF. And, like good businessmen, they had calculated the odds wisely.[26]

In these ways the Council helped to create both a more representative, an 'Ulsterised' and a more militant Unionism. Reflecting the Unionist population with greater accuracy, the Council reflected the geographical distribution of Unionism and the militancy of its grass-roots. The Council was dominated by Belfast and by eastern Ulster, and it gave full representation to the more extreme Orange tradition inside northern Protestantism. The existence of the Council, and its growth in power and prestige, meant that Unionist politicians were, for the first time effectively accountable to a local authority. In this way the Council created a Unionism which not only excluded the south of Ireland, but which also, paradoxically, excluded England. Unionism was, by 1914, more fully local in form. The Tories were apparently sympathetic allies, and Westminster still played a role in Unionist strategy. But, fundamentally, the focus of Unionist activity in 1912–14 was in eastern Ulster. More particularly, the focus of Unionist activity was in Belfast, and within the intricate committee structure of the Ulster Unionist Council.

If the development of Unionist organisation prepared the way for partition in 1920, then the development of Unionist thought in the period had also partitionist implications. Unionism, like Nationalism, and despite appearances to the contrary, has not been a static creed. At the end of the twentieth century an Ulster Unionist political identity is associated with a British national identity, and Ulster Unionism is bound to an unshakeable faith in the necessity for partition. Yet the 'partitionism' and the 'Britishness' of Unionism have been aspects of the faith which have only comparatively recently emerged as predominant. In these ideological respects, as in so much else, Unionism was in flux between 1905 and 1920.[27]

When Unionism emerged in a coherent form in the 1880s and 1890s it was an essentially Irish political faith, which justified its existence in terms of the condition of the whole of Ireland. Unionism in Ulster was, institutionally, merely one fragment of a greater whole. Ideologically, Unionism was concerned with all of Ireland, and not merely with the northern province. If there were divisions in Ireland, then these were less a matter of geography than of morality: the division between 'loyal' and 'disloyal', between 'loyalty' and 'treason'. Edward Saunderson's political commentary on the early 1880s saw Ulster, not as a potential nation state, but as a focus of loyalty and of political morality – as a source of salvation – for all of Ireland. Division was not along national or racial lines, 'British' versus 'Irish' or 'Ulster-British' versus 'Irish', but rather along moral lines (Irish 'loyalty' versus Irish 'disloyalty'). The very title of Saunderson's pamphlet conveyed the integral Irishness of his perspectives: Two Irelands: Loyalty versus Treason.[28]

Ulster, like other parts of Ireland, had a strong regional identity, an identity strengthened by the historic associations between eastern Ulster and Scotland, and by the plantation of parts of the province. This provincial identity was gradually consolidated and refined through the course of the Home Rule era, so that 'Ulster' shifted from being an element of Irishness to being a form of counterweight to Irishness, or the antithesis of Irishness. Unionists looked to Britain and the Empire in 1886 and 1893 professedly as Irish people (or as Ulstermen and Ulsterwomen who also happened to be Irish people). But, as has been demonstrated, the importance of northern Unionism inside Irish Unionism was increasing. And, equally, Nationalism was emerging as a religiously and culturally more exclusivist phenomenon. The targeting by the Parnellites of the northern province helped to stimulate northern organisation.[29] Mass displays such as the Ulster Convention (of June 1892) or the Ulster Unionist Council (of 1905) were landmarks in the trek towards Ulster Unionist ascendancy within Unionism as a whole. The overwhelmingly northern nature of the campaign against the third Home Rule Bill confirmed this ascendancy. For Unionists 'Ulster' was not only becoming more important than 'Ireland' – 'Ulster' was becoming institutionally and ideologically an alternative both to Ireland and, indeed, to Britain.

The organisation of Ulster Unionism – especially after 1905, built upon a more ancient regional identity, and contributed to an ideological and strategic shift. The emergence of an ascendant and distinctive Ulster Unionism meant that the arguments against Home Rule focused even more on northern loyalist opposition in 1912 than in 1893, or in 1886: Unionist principle mattered less, and 'Ulster' mattered more in 1912. Once Unionism had become geographically more specific, once it abandoned its claim to reject Home Rule for all of Ireland, the opportunity emerged to recognise through a political border the emotional and institutional boundary which already divided Ulster Unionists from southern Unionists and from most Irish Nationalists. The organisation of Unionism in the North indirectly exposed the weakness of southern Unionism, and made Ulster Unionists more receptive both to the idea of a distinctive northern loyalist character and community, and to the British offer of partition. Partition became a probable component of a Home Rule settlement from the moment Carson and the Ulster Unionist MPs agreed to support T.G. Agar-Robartes in June 1912.[30] Political developments during, and immediately following, the First World War (the Lloyd George proposals of 1916, the Irish Convention, the Government of Ireland Bill) confirmed the distance between, on the one hand, Ulster Unionists, and, on the other, southern Unionists and British Tories. Partition, which may well have been a merely tactical stand in 1912 had become, by 1920, the only logical response from northern loyalists to their political isolation.

Ulster Unionists had become partitionist, and isolationist, because of the nature of their political relationships – both with Britain and within Ireland. Separated from Irish Nationalism, and even from southern Unionism, from British Liberalism and even from British Toryism, Ulster Unionism found consolation in withdrawal – in local political organisation, and, increasingly, in a localised political creed. Their perception of their own distinctive tradition, combined with these shifting relationships, meant that Ulster Unionists – who had once seen themselves as Irish (if in an imperial context) – increasingly emphasised their Ulster identity. For loyalists 'Ulster' became the geographical corollary of being 'Unionist'. Arguably it was only the limited nature of devolved government in Northern Ireland, and the sustained financial dependence of Stormont on Westminster, which prevented the Unionist party from propagating its own micro-government. As it was, Unionist identity after 1920 reflected the ambiguities of Northern Ireland's political position, resting uneasily between a strong provincial sense, and a wider British commitment. 'Irishness' was an unavoidable but uncomfortable element of the Unionist heritage, and was consigned after 1920 to a mental and constitutional quarantine.

CHAPTER FOUR

Nationalist Ireland 1912–1922: Aspects of Continuity and Change
by
Gearóid Ó Tuathaigh

The approach adopted in this essay will be selective and discursive. Four main themes relating to Nationalist Ireland have been selected for discussion. No attempt will be made to provide a detailed narrative of events, it being assumed that readers will be familiar with the principal historical events in Ireland during this period. Such narrative detail as will be provided is meant to supply the necessary contextual information for a useful discussion of the points of argument and interpretation advanced in the essay.[1]

In referring to 'Nationalist Ireland' we are not referring to a specific geographical unit. We are, rather, referring to a community, a community of common or shared political sentiment. In 1912 Nationalist Ireland seemed poised to receive an historic concession from the Imperial Parliament in Westminster, namely, the conferring of limited self-government on Ireland in the form of Home Rule. Whatever about the details of the scheme on offer, and irrespective of the degrees of enthusiasm (or lack of it) which individual Nationalists or particular groups of Nationalists may have felt about the precise measure of autonomy to be conferred, the critical emotional factor for Nationalists was that Home Rule could be taken as a symbol of the formal acknowledgement of Ireland's distinct sense of nationhood. This emotional satisfaction was an important factor in enabling the Home Rule party (the Irish Parliamentary Party led by John Redmond) to effectively mobilise Nationalist opinion at elections.It was, therefore, less the details than the symbolic significance of Home Rule which enabled a broad consensus of Nationalist opinion to share in a sense of satisfaction in 1912, and even to allow certain Nationalists, who themselves had far more radical, far more extensive, far more advanced projects in mind for an independent Irish state, to feel that the proposed Home Rule 'settlement' ought to be given a chance.These included people like

47

Patrick Pearse, who as late as 1913 was reconciled to the fact that Home Rule would have to be given a chance because it did, in fact, represent a major concesssion to Irish Nationalist sentiment and enjoyed, moreover, a broad measure of support throughout Nationalist Ireland.[2] Given the deep-rooted and complex historic sense of grievance which had sustained and nurtured Irish Nationalist sentiment since the seventeenth century, one may wonder whether, indeed, the Home Rule offer of 1912 was likely to provide a final and full redress of Irish Nationalism's charge against British 'oppression'. But the rhetoric of Redmond and the elected spokesmen of Nationalist Ireland certainly glowed with the language of 'a final settlement' of a long-standing issue of dispute between the peoples of two neighbouring islands.

There are a number of points which need emphasis in relation to that historic moment in 1912, when the Third Home Rule Bill was ready to begin its final rounds of debate on its way to the statute book. Firstly, the territory assumed in the discussion of Home Rule Ireland was the whole island of Ireland.This was unquestionably the case so far as Redmond and the spokesmen of Nationalist Ireland were concerned. Secondly, the settlement of this historic issue was finally to be arrived at by *agreement.* It was to be the peaceful and agreed outcome of a protracted political debate which, in the specific case of a Home Rule scheme, had taken place in the full light of British constitutional politics over the previous thirty or more years. Elections had been contested, public opinion had been 'educated', and the voters in Britain and in Ireland had given their views on the subject of Irish Home Rule at regular intervals from the 1880s. Accordingly, the proposal to grant Home Rule to Ireland in 1912 had emerged through the appropriate system of public and parliamentary debate by which major constitutional questions were resolved within the British parliamentary tradition. Even allowing for the limited parliamentary franchise of early 20th century Britain, the House of Commons within which Home Rule was to be proposed and debated was taken to broadly reflect public opinion on the major issues of the day.[3] The third feature of the Home Rule offer of 1912 worthy of close attention was the actual *degree of sovereignty* which it proposed to offer Ireland, a degree of sovereignty which, in many respects, was quite limited.The assembly to be established in Dublin would clearly be a subsidiary parliament with limited jurisdiction over certain local matters. In this respect, Home Rule for Ireland may have signified an acknowledgement of Irish Nationalism's historic sense of nationhood, but it was an acknowledgement which would have to be accomodated within (and be compatible with the interests of) a larger British polity. The British imperial context remained the paramount consideration for British statesmen and politicians. Michael

Laffan, in his admirably concise study of the making of Partition, summarises the limitations of the Home Rule offer of 1912 :

> The range of powers and responsibilities to be witheld from the Irish Parliament's control was enormous and included, among much else, the Crown, peace and war, naval and military affairs, treaties and foreign affairs, treason, navigation, merchant shipping, land purchase, trade marks, copyrights, patents, lighthouses, old-age pensions, national insurance and post office savings banks.

This formidable list of matters was to be excluded from the jurisdiction of the proposed parliament in Dublin. Laffan goes on to quote Arthur Griffith's caustic comment on the draft bill, that 'if this is liberty, the lexicographers have deceived us'.[4] But, of course, it wasn't meant to be 'liberty'. It was meant merely to be a measure of limited self-government for Ireland within a larger British imperial polity.

The fourth major aspect of Nationalist Ireland during 1912–22 which will concern us in this essay is the *ideological character of its leadership;* the dominant cultural attitudes and disposition of the Nationalist leadership of Redmond's Ireland, and the changing character of the leadership of Nationalist Ireland between 1912 and 1922. In general terms, the leaders of the Nationalist Home Rule movement were comfortable with an Irish identity which could find institutional expression in a parliamentary assembly in Dublin ('having the old parliament back in College Green'); an identity which combined a strong sense of patriotism and pride in membership of an ancient historic nation with an easy acceptance of Ireland's place in the larger family of the British Empire. They could, of course, resort to fiery speeches denouncing England's perfidy or treachery, when the occasion demanded, and many of them were able exponents of what Roy Foster has described as 'literary Fenianism'. But, in truth, few, if any, of them had any rooted aversion to 'British civilisation' as such. Most of the leaders of the party were, by 1912, experienced parliamentarians, seasoned House of Commons men. Many had lived parts of their lives, or followed their careers, in Britain. For many of the Home Rule leaders, their religious loyalty and the strong historic sense of Ireland's troubled past were probably the main ingredients of their sense of Irish identity.

Indeed, this was probably true not only of Redmond and his fellow leaders of the parliamentary party but also, for the most part, of the kind of people (professional and commercial middle class and comfortable farmers) who provided the local leadership of the party at home.[5] It would be easy to find exceptions to these generalisations. But, in the main, this general profile does not, I believe, greatly distort the general character of the Nationalist leadership at the moment when it seemed poised to receive the long-coveted prize of limited self-government in 1912. Having looked, therefore, at these four key aspects of the predicament of Nationalist Ireland – its expectations and, as it seemed, its destiny – on the eve of the crisis of the third Home Rule Bill, let us now move forward a decade and see how the political landscape looked from the Nationalist perspective in 1922. There was established in 1922 an Irish national state, as a result of negogtiations conducted between the British Government of the day and the leaders of the dominant Irish Nationalist movement, now a new political movement styling itself Sinn Féin and operating from the base of an elected secessionist assembly styling itself Dáil Eireann.[6] Even the new nomenclature suggests that some significant change had occurred. Considering the four main aspects of the Nationalist position that we discussed for 1912, what was the position in 1922?

Firstly, while a national state is indeed established in 1922 – Saorstát Éireann or the Irish Free State – the territory over which the new Irish state was to exercise jurisdiction was not the whole island of Ireland, but 26 counties of it. Secondly, the settlement of 1922 was not arrived at exclusively as the result of negotiations, the friendly persuasion of the parliamentary debate, the lobby or the hustings. It followed, and to a degree was the product of, a protracted armed conflict between British Crown forces and various armed groups of Irish Nationalists. Thirdly, the precise measure of sovereignty to be enjoyed by the new Irish Free State was to be 'dominion status', similar to that enjoyed by Canada, Australia, New Zealand and South Africa. This was a substantial advance on anything that had been on offer in earlier Home Rule bills, and yet it fell short of the aspirations and expectations of a large number of the elected representatives of Nationalist Ireland in 1922. It was reluctantly accepted, even by some of those who had negotiated the settlement terms, as an increment of Irish independence. But, more fatefully, it fell so far short of what a sizeable segment of the Nationalist movement was now proclaiming as the irreducible minimum (or, perhaps more accurately, the undilutable measure) of Irish sovereignty, that the Sinn Féin movement split and a bitter civil war followed on the contested basis of the precise degree and form of sovereignty necessary to satisfy the demands and the rights of the 'historic Irish nation'. Fourthly, and finally, in comparing the 'ideological character' of the Sinn Féin leadership of 1921–22 with the Home Rule leaders of 1912, we are struck by some interesting evidence of change. If we look at even the rhetoric and public trappings of the new Irish Free State in 1922 – at its symbols, its official version of itself, its statement of national culture, its particular construct of a sense of 'Irishness' designed to bond the citizens in loyalty to the state – we find that, at the very least, it seems to emphasise the Gaelic element in Irish ethnicity or nationhood in a way which was nowhere near as prominent in 1912. The status given to the Irish language in the constitution of the new state was a symbol of the understanding of Irish national identity which an influential group of the leaders of the new Free State had acquired in their years as members of the Gaelic League.[7] The supporters of the new Government of the Free State included many who had neither affection or regard for the symbols or glories of the British Empire. But this was especially true of those members of the Sinn Féin popular front of 1917–21 who had refused to accept the terms of the 1921 settlement, who contested the legitimacy of the new state, and who, under the banner of Sinn Féin and, after 1926, under De Valera's new Fianna Fáil party continued to assert not only the demand for an Irish Republic but also a version of Irish national identity that was to a degree, perhaps, Anglophobic, but was certainly anti-imperial and totally alien to the kind of easy fellowship within the larger British 'family' of the Empire that had characterised John Redmond and many of his followers in the Home Rule leadership early in the century.[8] These, then, are some of the more striking aspects of change in the political condition, as it were, of Nationalist Ireland between 1912 and 1922. The remainder of this essay will look, in turn, at each of the four main aspects under consideration, with a view to suggesting some reasons or possible explanations for the changes which had occurred in the predicament of Nationalist Ireland during this most eventful decade.

Turning, in the first instance, to the matter of national territory, we may remind ourselves at the outset that the electoral map of Ireland remained remarkably stable and consistent between 1885 and 1910.[9] Throughout that period, even allowing for the internal rows and convulsions within Nationalist Ireland after the fall of Parnell, roughly eighty per cent of the Irish seats were retained by Irish Nationalist representatives, that is to say, 80 or more of the 103 Irish seats at Westminster. At times of particular excitement or when organisation and discipline were especially good, this figure could rise to 85 seats (as it did in 1885) ; but it still stood at just over 80 after the Home Rule Party substantially reunited under Redmond after 1900. What this meant was that more than eighty per cent of Ireland's MPs throughout this period were in favour of some measure of Home Rule for Ireland, a national assembly in Dublin with certain specified powers and responsibilities. The remaining twenty per cent were opposed to such a development and wished full constitutional jurisdiction to remain firmly at Westminster. However, the geographical distribution of this divided political opinion was, of course, the real problem. On the specific matter of political opinion in Ulster, Patrick Buckland's essay in this collection will provide the main commentary. But it is important to stress that the 'problem' with Ulster was not that Ulster was uniformly and solidly different from the rest of the country; the problem was that Ulster was politically evenly divided within the province. Had there been a clear and uniform distinction of political sentiment on the 'National Question' between Ulster and the other three provinces, the solution to the Ulster problem would probably have been far less bitter and intractable than turned out to be the case. The real problem was that Ulster was divided, and fairly evenly divided, at that. True, there were broad geographical features of political divisions within Ulster (a contrast between the east and the west of the province); but these were by no means tidy or uniform. Of the 33 Ulster seats the balance of advantage never swung too heavily in either direction throughout the period 1885–1914. As late as 1913, after a by-election success in Derry city, Nationalists held 17 of the 33 Ulster seats, the remaining 16 being held be Unionists. This, perhaps, was a distortion of the true state of political sentiment throughout the province as a whole, as there was a degree of under-representation of the industrial centres of Ulster compared with the more rural areas. But the basic point being made is that, electorally, the balance of advantage between Unionists and Nationalists remained quite tight over the 33 Ulster seats all throughout the period of the Home Rule debate, 1885–1914.[10]

The ways and the pace in which Unionist, and specifically Ulster Unionist, opposition to Home Rule gathered momentum in the years after 1910 need not be discussed in detail here.[11] What must be stressed is the fact that almost from the very outset of the Home Rule campaign, from the mid-1880s, and certainly from the moment of Gladstone's announced conversion to Home Rule in late 1885, the leadership of Nationalist Ireland chose, for the most part, either to ignore or to totally play down the intensity of Unionist opposition to Home Rule. This was true especially in the case of Ulster Unionist opposition, where the basis of the opposition, its extent and its intensity, and the possible political implications of its significant geographical concentration, were not addressed seriously or systematically at an early stage of the debate. The Nationalist leaders assumed, or pretended to assume, that the Ulster threats were merely bluster. Indeed, the different groups of Nationalists, with very few exceptions, continued to insist right up to late 1913 that the Ulster Unionist furore was no more than fabricated hysteria, that the threats being issued should not be taken seriously. It was repeatedly asserted that, once a Home Rule assembly had been given sufficient time to prove that the declared fears of the Ulster Unionists were unfounded, then the hysteria and militancy would quieten down and the Irish assembly could set about its business in an orderly and efficient way in the interests of all the people of Ireland.

Indeed, Nationalist leaders in some respects seemed less exercised by the intrinsic nature of the Ulster opposition to Home Rule than by the political forces at play among the parties at Westminster. Nationalist anger and indignation was directed at the opportunism of the Conservative party, and at the dangerous game being played by its leaders, a game which refused to acknowledge the established rules of the parliamentary game. Nationalists strongly denounced those who were irresponsibly whipping up what would otherwise be a manageable local problem within an all-Ireland Home Rule context. There seemed to be far less attention devoted to the intrinsic nature of the Ulster problem, or, more particularly, to its implications for the kind of overall settlement that might eventually be arrived at. Instead, therefore, of systematically undermining the Ulster Unionist position, or moving immediately to negotiate directly with it, the Nationalist leadership, and Redmond in particular, placed its full reliance on the resolve and nerve of the Liberal Government. Redmond depended upon, and continuously exhorted, the ministers to stand firm. Of course, the passing of Home Rule did, ultimately, depend upon the disposition of the Liberal Government of Asquith. But, nevertheless, it was remarkable how Redmond placed all the Nationalist eggs in the basket of the Government, relying on the political constancy, the firmness of intention, and the basic nerve of the Government to face down the challenge of the Ulster Unionists and their Conservative allies. It was very late in the day when the specific problem of Ulster and the actual list of suggested solutions to the problem began to be addressed seriously as matters for political negotiation. This is not to say that Redmond and his fellow Nationalist leaders had not referred in their speeches or in their private political correspondence to the Ulster Question. They had indeed acknowledged the Ulster difficulty; they could scarcely have done otherwise as the political atmosphere became increasingly high-charged from 1911 onwards. But expressions of outrage at any proposed 'mutilation' of Ireland, or passionate denunciations of the extra-constitutional words and actions of cynical Conservatives, were no substitute for the kind of systematic, hard-headed appraisal of political options which the mounting crisis over Ulster demanded.[12]

There is a sense, therefore, in which the Nationalist leadership in general, and Redmond in particular, may be seen as a passive rather than a drastic element in the Home Rule crisis of 1911–1914. The drastic elements, those who were making the running, shaping the crisis, were Carson, the Ulster Unionists and the more active opportunists on the Conservative side of the Conservative-Unionist alliance. As the Liberal Government began to worry and to waver, as concerns began to focus on Ulster Unionism's real intentions and how to deal with them, the Nationalist leadership found itself almost invariably reacting to events, responding to shifts in the Government's position, rather than taking the initiative in shaping the agenda. It may be appropriate, at this point, to make some further comment on Redmond, before moving on to other considerations.[13]

Redmond did eventually come to realize that the Ulster Question would have to be addressed in the terms in which it was beginning to be defined by the Government and by other main actors in the drama, namely, in terms of a proposed 'exclusion zone' from the jurisdiction of the Home Rule assembly. This was a bitter pill for Redmond to swallow. But when it became clear to him that, notwithstanding the continuing claims of Unionist spokesmen (including Carson) that their aim was to save all of Ireland from the dire fate of a Home Rule Parliament, in reality the name of the game by 1913 was how to manage an acceptable 'exclusion zone' for the Ulster Unionists. His actions from this point forward may be seen as having at least the merit of consistency and honour, if not being particularly shrewd or tactically exciting.[14]

He sought to offer safeguards to the minority, that is, to the Ulster Unionists. His intentions were honorable, but such offers were probably beside the point by 1913. It is hard to imagine any safeguards or guarantees which a Nationalist leader could have offered to the Ulster Unionists in the highly-charged political atmosphere of 1913 which would have softened their opposition to a Home Rule settlement being 'imposed' on them. Certainly, so long as they could rely on Conservative backing for their stand they had no incentive to re-assess their position. As for Redmond, given the terms in which Home Rule had been denounced as the thin edge of the Nationalist wedge leading ultimately to full separation, his actions when war broke out in 1914 are understandable and have a degree of political logic to them. Pledging Nationalist Ireland's firm support for the Empire, committing the Irish Volunteers to the fighting line, as far as it extended; these promises, in Redmond's case, combined personal convictions with tactical advantage, the intention being to prove that Nationalist Ireland was committed to a genuine 'union of hearts' with the rest of the British Empire at a time of crisis, contrary to what Ulster Unionists had claimed in their denunciation of the slippery slope of Home Rule.

Redmond's promises of 1914 may ultimately have cost him dearly in terms of his standing in Nationalist Ireland in the years after 1914. But one must take care not to surrender perspective totally to the advantages of hindsight. Viewed from Redmond's perspective in the late summer of 1914, with the terms of the Home Rule settlement as it related to Ulster still to play for, with a Home Rule Act 'on ice', and with the prospect (confidently predicted on all sides) of a short war and an early resumption of negotiations on Ulster, what Redmond actually did was consistent with his instincts and his honour, and also with his desire to strengthen the hand of Nationalist Ireland in its bargaining on the Ulster Question at war's end. Nationalist Ireland's participation in the war effort would establish an unshakable moral claim for its bona fides in the post-war negotiations. Indeed, Redmond might have gone further and taken a place in government when invited. Joseph Lee is among the historians who have suggested that he might have joined the Government, to be consistent in his strategy and to gain the best possible advantage from his support of the war effort.[15] By so doing, it is claimed, he would have been in a position to safeguard the Nationalist interest on the inside, just as Carson sought to do for the Ulster Unionists when he joined the war Government. However, it is questionable whether Redmond's joining the Government would, in fact, have made any decisive difference to the final outcome of events. Given the changing configuration of British party politics under the pressure of war, it is probable that the balance of influence would probably have been against Redmond anyway on the issue of Partition. But, given the fact that Redmond played by the parliamentary rules throughout the crisis (it is a criticism made of him that, like Neville Chamberlain, he always played by the rules, and always lost), it may be said in his defence that he did all that he could, within these rules, to avert Partition and to enhance the moral claims of the Irish Nationalists on the support of the Government in 1914.

If, however, it was not going to prove possible to prevent partition and the establishment of an exclusion zone in Ulster, then it may be argued that for a Nationalist leader in Redmond's predicament, the next best option was to achieve the highest possible degree of damage limitation, while continuing to refuse to concede the principle of partition. This might have meant concentrating on limiting the territory of the exclusion zone to an absolute minimum, or attaching the most stringent conditions achievable to the size and administrative structure of the zone to be excluded. Viewed dispassionately, some combination of these options ought to have informed the Nationalist leader's exercise in damage limitation. For, despite the agonising of Carson and the anxious demands from Unionists in those areas of Ulster where they were a local minority that they should not be abandoned, it became clear very soon after the idea of an exclusion zone came under serious consideration that the area to be excluded was unlikely to be the whole province of Ulster. Of course, Unionist leaders (and Carson in particular) were in a real dilemma when it came to acknowledging in public that this would be the case. After all, if the prospect of a Home Rule assembly was so horrific, then how could any self-respecting Ulster Unionist contemplate deserting any section of their fellow-Unionists to the horrors of a Dublin parliament. But, the reality was that a unit of territory less than the full nine county province of Ulster was going to be the unit that would eventually form the exclusion zone.

From Redmond's position, therefore, the vital question ought to have been what were the criteria which would determine the exclusion zone, and what were the criteria which would best suit his purposes. Arguably, either 'county option' or the units of the parliamentary constituencies would have given Nationalists a stronger hand to play when it came to finally determining a zone, even under protest. County option would have suited in the case of five counties of the nine, and Derry city was being discussed as a special problem area also. But, while Redmond did support 'county option' as the basis for any proposed partition, he did not succeed in making it a condition for any proposed exclusion zone. It may be argued, of course, that he simply was not in a position to make 'conditions' even for Asquith's pre-war ministry. Moreover, if Carson and the Ulster Unionist leaders faced a dilemma in publicly admitting that any Ulster Unionists would be 'abandoned', Redmond likewise could not take too firm a line on a system of partition which, however drawn, would have 'abandoned' communities of Nationalists. However, whatever view we take of Redmond's bargaining position, it cannot seriously be claimed that he succeeded in limiting the territorial unit of 'excluded Ulster' to six counties, as distinct from the full nine of the province as a whole. The Nationalist leaders from first to last, from 1912 right down to the failure of the Boundary Commission in 1925, played no decisive or active role in drawing or redrawing the boundaries within Ulster and Ireland. Redmond argued for county option in negotiations with Asquith right up to March 1914, at which time the discussions were centering on four counties to be excluded and Derry as a problem still to be resolved.

The issue remained unresolved when war broke out. Thereafter Redmond's influence and bargaining position, whatever they may have been before the war, progressively weakened. Certainly after the 1916 Rising, but arguably as early as the immediate aftermath of the split in the Irish Volunteers in 1914, Redmond's standing can be seen to be weakening; not only in relation to Carson, after the latter became a member of the Government, but within Nationalist Ireland, as the focus of interest shifts from Parliament to the war front, as the Irish Parliamentary Party marks time, and as rival claimants for the support and loyalty of Nationalist Ireland begin to make their play. In sum, therefore, in assessing the Home Rule Party's record on the matter of territory, we may conclude that the party failed to anticipate the seriousness of the threat to the territorial integrity of the Home Rule state that they were waiting for Westminster to deliver in 1912, like a ripe apple ready to fall from the tree. The Nationalist party leadership did not assess correctly the intensity of Ulster Unionist opposition to Home Rule, nor the lengths to which it would be pushed. The implications of its regional concentration for a 'partition' settlement were not faced up to until relatively late in the day. When eventually the threat was realized, there was a degree of consistency, as well as honour, in Redmond's conduct, but it did not have a decisive impact on the unfolding of events.

Some intriguing questions remain. If it was not within the power of Nationalist Ireland's leaders in 1912–14 to re-assure or convince Ulster Unionists as to their future well-being in a Home Rule Ireland (as I am inclined to believe that it was not) then what alternative strategies were left to the Nationalist Party? They could try to out-manoeuvre the Ulster Unionists. The outcome demonstrates that they were unable to do so. Whatever about Carson's complex response to having to settle for partition when he had played for the defeat of Home Rule *tout court*, the final terms of partition were far more a victory for Craig and the Unionists than for Redmond and his successors in the Nationalist leadership. Likewise, on the vital question of whether the exclusion was to be temporary or permanent, an understandable revulsion at Lloyd George's duplicity and deception can not alter the fact that here also the Nationalist leadership lost the game.

The most difficult question to resolve is what other options were open to the Nationalist leaders in the prevailing political circumstances? Specifically, what exactly would have been required to 'face down' the Ulster Unionists in 1913? The Ulster Unionists themselves spoke of their determination to resist any attempt to 'coerce' them. Whose business was it to 'coerce' them into accepting the decision of a majority in the House of Commons, and how was it to be done? The responsibility for enforcing the law – any law – clearly rested with the Government. The Curragh incident gave a worrying indication of how uncertain might be the consequences of requiring the army to move to confront the Ulster revolt (in the form of illegal drilling by armed volunteers).[16] Was there a serious intention at any stage of the crisis to move to disarm the Ulster Volunteers? It is hard to avoid the conclusion that there was not. Evidence is lacking, therefore, of a clear resolve on the part of the Government to 'coerce' Ulster. Who else could or would undertake the task of 'facing down' the Ulster Unionists? One would be tempted to look closely at the Irish Volunteers. But what exactly was John Redmond's understanding of the role of the Irish Volunteers after the end of 1913?

Apart from being a status symbol, in the same way as the Ulster Volunteers were a status symbol at this stage of the seriousness of purpose of the Unionist leaders in the north, what else were the Irish Volunteers meant to be doing? It may be unfair to ask this question of Redmond; after all, the force was not his idea or his creation. But, apart from providing evidence of earnestness of purpose, what practical role was envisaged for the Irish Volunteers? It cannot have been defensive in any simple sense; by 1913 nobody was seriously suggesting that Home Rule was to be snatched away from Ireland. But neither Redmond nor anybody else suggested that the role of the Irish Volunteers was to be aggressive, to 'face down' the Ulster Unionist threat, to call their bluff. There remains a question mark therefore over whether Redmond had any clear understanding of the possible role which the Irish Volunteers might serve. In any case, by the time Redmond had gone through the nightmare of the fruitless rounds of talks after the 1916 Rising (and through the Irish Convention up to his death in March 1918) the issue of the territory of the Irish national parliament and the extent of the exclusion zone in Ulster were matters over which the Irish Nationalist leadership had very little control or influence. This was certainly the case when Redmond's party gave way to Sinn Féin as the elected voice of Nationalist Ireland in 1918.

Turning briefly to the position of Redmond's successors, it is hard to find evidence that Sinn Féin had learned any lessons or were better equipped tactically than the Home Rule Nationalists in respect of the issue of the territory as distinct from the constitutional status of the Irish state to-be. For example, if one traces the development of De Valera's position on this issue (as John Bowman has done), one is hard put to detect any advance in terms of an understanding of the actual conditions obtaining throughout Ulster and of their implications for political solutions to the 'Ulster problem'.[17] De Valera began, picking up where the 1916 Proclamation had left off, by maintaining that the divisions between Irishmen living in Ireland had been carefully created and continued to be fomented by British politicians for their own purposes. British imperial imperatives – resting on the old imperial ploy of divide and conquer – were the root cause of divisions between Irishmen. But, having stated the problem, what was to be done about it? De Valera began with a touch of bravado; if Ulster was the obstacle blocking the road to a settlement of Ireland's national claims, then the obstacle must be removed from the road. But how was this to be done? No more than Redmond before him, De Valera had no stomach for the actual use of the kind of force that would have been required to 'coerce' the Ulster Unionists. As Sinn Féin emerged as the dominant political force in Nationalist Ireland at the 1918 election, and as its leaders realised that they were now real, serious political actors, playing for high stakes in a post-war Europe in which new national states were being created and large parts of the map of Europe redrawn, it was only to be expected that they would have to formulate positions and tactics to deal with the political realities in Ireland (including Ulster) and in Britain. De Valera's was not the only political mind active and articulate in Sinn Féin at this time; but he was the movement's leader and figurehead. Between 1918 and 1922 he was forced to formulate a more flexible position in relation to the Ulster Unionists than the simple demand that the obstacle which blocked the road to Irish self-determination be promptly removed. His tone became more conciliatory, even as he continued to insist that the Ulster Unionists had no right to remove a portion of Ireland from the jurisdiction of the Irish people as a whole: geography, history and justice demanded that Ulster be an integral part of any Irish national state.

By 1921, on the eve of the Treaty negotiations, he was prepared to concede to the Ulster Unionists a substantial measue of autonomy or 'Home Rule', within the context of an all-Ireland national state. This was the crucial issue, however. Ulster Unionists were being offered a measure of self-government within a post-British, all-Ireland context, in place of the measure of self-government which they now enjoyed, under the 1920 Government of Ireland Act, under the constitutional umbrella of the United Kingdom. If De Valera saw this as a generous concession by Nationalist Ireland, the Ulster Unionists saw it as no choice at all. The elaboration of this position by De Valera in his 'Document No.2', as an alternative to the Treaty proposals, indicates the absence of any grounds for optimism that the advanced wing of Sinn Féin was going to make any new breakthrough in resolving (from a Nationalist point of view) the problem of Ulster and of partition. So far as the Treaty proposals were concerned, and these were adopted by a majority in the Dáil and later at elections in the 26 counties, the issue of partition was relegated to the deliberations of a Boundary Commission which was to be established to review and, as appropriate, make recommendations for the revision of the partition boundary.[18] Notwithstanding the fact that De Valera had advised the delegates that if the Treaty negotiations had to be terminated they should 'break' on the question of Ulster, the most notable feature of the lengthy and passionate debate on the Treaty terms in Dáil Éireann is the almost total absence of reference to the issue of partition.[19]

In short, there is little to suggest that the Sinn Féin consensus of Nationalist Ireland between 1918 and 1922 was able to do any better than its Home Rule predecessors in terms of thinking or of tactics in relation to the territorial 'integrity' of an Irish national state and in terms of dealing with the demands of Ulster Unionists for an exclusion zone. It must be conceded that the Sinn Féin leaders were in a less favourable position, in many respects, than Redmond's party in seeking to exercise influence on this particular issue. During the period in which the reconstructed Sinn Féin was obliged to formulate a position on Ulster (i.e.1917–22), it did not have the same negotiating status as Redmond had.Its leading members attended a secessionist assembly which was not recognised by the British Government as having any legal status. Many of the leaders were heavily involved in a military campaign against the authority of the Crown forces in many parts of Ireland. The deliberations of the Sinn Féin leadership were made difficult by the fact that De Valera was absent for a long interlude during a U.S. tour, that many of the leaders of the movement were, from time to time, on the run, in hiding, or in prison, and that the allegiance given after 1919 by Sinn Féin elected deputies to Dáil Éireann as the assembly of an independent Irish Republic meant that Sinn Féin was never represented at Westminster. Indeed, in the debates leading up to the passing of the Government of Ireland Act in 1920, the voice of Nationalist Ireland was notable by its absence from the House of Commons debates.

Furthermore, the fact that in 1918 and in 1920 the old Home Rule Nationalist Party continued to enjoy considerable support from Nationalists in Ulster and prevented Sinn Féin from making the gains among Nationalist voters that it had gained in the other three provinces, diminished further the likelihood that Sinn Féin would produce a major initiative for solving the 'Ulster Question' where the old Nationalist party had failed. In the light of historical events since 1920 some may question whether the territorial settlement eventually decided upon in 1920 was the wisest option from the point of view of the Ulster Unionists themselves. But that is not an issue which calls for adjudication here. What can be said is that from the perspective of Nationalist Ireland the balance of advantage, in the effort to retain the territorial integrity of Ireland in the establishment of some form of autonomous Irish state, was moving relentlessly against the Nationalists throughout the turbulent decade of 1912–1922.

Turning now to our second major theme, the means through which Nationalist Ireland eventually achieved its national state, the issue which will concern us here is *the militarisation of political disagreement* in Ireland in the period 1912–1922. In 1912 it was generally expected that the settlement of the Irish Home Rule issue would be achieved exclusively through peaceful, constitutional methods; by patient advocacy, parliamentary and public debate, by the arts of persuasion and negotiation sanctioned by the parliamentary tradition. The settlements which were eventually made during 1920–1922 were, however, achieved only after a considerable degree of violence, bloodshed and armed conflict, with the threat of even more serious violence as a key determinant of one part of the solution finally arrived at. The question which must be asked is what are the critical factors which led to this militarisation of political disagreement in Ireland, and what implications has the answer for developments after 1922.

In addressing this question, it is customary to echo what Eoin MacNeill wrote in the famous article in which he proposed the setting up of the Irish Volunteers, namely, that 'The North Began'.[20] And certainly, in the specific context of the Home Rule crisis of 1910–14, it is unquestionably the case that the first moves to militarise political positions were taken by the Ulster Unionists. That is to say, the first mobilisation of popular support along military lines to resist a political proposal sanctioned by a parliamentary majority in the House of Commons (and by a large majority of the MPs of Ireland) was undertaken by leaders of the Ulster Unionists. It would, of course, be utterly wrong to imagine that this was the only evidence of a military disposition for the achievement of political objectives in early twentieth century Ireland. There existed within Irish Nationalism a conspiratorial, separatist and militarist strand dating in a continuous line from the Fenians (or, more properly, the Irish Republican Brotherhood), but with an ancestry going back much further than that.[21] This strand in the Irish Nationalist tradition rested on the belief that the use of force in the achievement of Irish political independence was not only justified, but would most likely be necessary (for some it may even have been the preferred way for achieving 'freedom').

The option of force was, therefore, an integral part of the IRB tradition within Irish Nationalism. But the point must be stressed that, despite undergoing a degree of re-organisation and renewal in the first decade of the century, the IRB was not at the centre of political developments within Nationalist Ireland in 1912. In many respects it was quite marginalised. Its leaders were looking on as the bulk of the Nationalist community seemed depressingly happy at the prospect of the imminent achievement of limited Home Rule. The IRB seemed powerless to prod that Nationalist community into making larger or more radical demands. By 1912 the IRB was very much an organisation whose opportunity had not come. Its opportunity for re-investing Irish Nationalism with a militaristic purpose and separatist programme seemed nowhere in sight. It may be the case, as some historians suggest, that the changed circumstances of 1912–1918, with the increasingly bellicose mood throughout Europe culminating in the outbreak of the war to end all wars, produced an atmosphere conducive to the valorisation of all kinds of military action, an atmosphere in which the advocates of military action (warming the good earth with blood shed in battle) were bound to prosper. But the specific militarisation of the Irish Home Rule crisis of 1911–1914 began with the formation of the Ulster Volunteer Force, their importation of arms, their drilling, and their statement of intent to resist the 'imposition' of Home Rule by the Westminster Parliament.

While some Nationalists may initially have responded to the Ulster mobilisation with a dose of ridicule and disbelief, by late 1913 there could be no doubting the seriousness of the situation which had arisen as a result of the Ulster mobilisation along military lines. Certain Nationalist voices were heard expressing admiration for the Ulster Unionists, on the grounds that at least they were demonstrating that they took themselves and their political demands seriously. The best known example of this complex attitude was Pearse's statement that though the drilling and martial postures of the Ulster Unionists may have had their comic side, nevertheless, an Orangeman with a rifle in his hand was less a figure of ridicule than a Nationalist without one. The new militancy seemed catching; James Connolly formed his Irish Citizens Army to protect striking workers.

The most significant, and most ominous, aspect of this new militancy, however, was the fact that it was increasingly being seen, not merely as a symbol of political earnestness and determination, but as an effective way of getting one's way in political argument. As the Government showed growing signs of wavering and weakness in dealing with the threats of the Ulster Unionists, and as the prospect of major concessions having to be made to the Unionists as a consequence of their militancy began to dawn on many Nationalists, there were predictable recriminations and reassessments. The militarist element within Irish Nationalism now had a better chance of being listened to. Even some moderate constitutional Nationalists were coming to the conclusion (as MacNeill's article testified) that in the changed climate of debate on Home Rule, the voice of Irish Nationalism seemed, in effect, weak and unable to assert itself because it did not have an armed force behind it as a earnest of its determination. This kind of talk was music to the ears of those in the IRB tradition who felt that Irish Nationalism was, as it were, 'undressed', if it did not have its soldiers in arms to assert its claims. Clearly, therefore, there was a significant escalation in the 'militarisation' of political disagreement by the end of 1913, as, inexorably, political results seemed to be more responsive to the argument of force (or the threat of it) than to the force of argument.

It is difficult to gauge how far these convictions had hardened by late 1913. It is difficult, for example, to assess just how 'available' the Irish Volunteers were for any kind of overt military action by early 1914. But the outbreak of war in the late summer of 1914 drastically altered the entire political landscape. Quite apart from creating, initially at least, a mood almost of euphoria, in which the spirit of courage and valour were invoked for the 'manly' art of soldiering, the outbreak of war created a kind of political vacuum in Ireland. This allowed the conspiratorial Fenian element within Irish Nationalism to take initiatives and to exercise an influence on the course of events which had not seemed possible in 1912. The war side-lined Redmond and his fellow parliamentary Nationalists; as it dragged on beyond the expected short sharp engagement, it made the Parliamentary Party seem increasingly irrelevant. As casualties mounted, the early encouragement to recruitment came under critical scrutiny. The normal political process of negotiation seemed frozen, at least so far as it related to progress on the Home Rule impasse, and the militarisation of Irish Nationalism began to proceed apace. What we may conclude, therefore, is that while a militant strain was present within Irish Nationalism long before 1912, and was not 'created' by the militancy of Ulster Unionism after 1911, nevertheless the events of 1911–1913 as they related to the Ulster crisis, and the lessons drawn from these events, strongly re-inforced the temptations and tendencies within Irish Nationalism to militarise itself, to become 'manly' (a favourite adjective in the rousing rhetoric of the time) in asserting its political position.

The outcome of this increased militarisation need not be narrated in detail here. The 1916 Rising was an IRB project (with Connolly's tiny Citizens' Army force incorporated for tactical reasons at the eleventh hour). The Rising, it is now clear, was conceived, planned and in large measure executed by 'a minority of a minority of a minority'. Even within the top echelons of the IRB some notable members were not consulted or kept informed at vital stages of the project.[22] It was a project which had high stakes. It was, in its immediate impact, a military failure. The Rising was put down by superior military force in a relatively short time. But it is arguable that in the immediate aftermath of the suppression of the Rising Redmond's political fate was sealed. In the light of the significant changes which had occurrred since the outbreak of the war (the sheer carnage and duration of the war itself, the changing political complexion of the Government, the absence of any political 'movement' on Ireland), Redmond was inevitably put in a cruel dilemma by the Rising and the Government's response to it. He had to condemn the Rising, of course. To do so was not only consistent with his instincts, but it also reflected his political judgement that this action was a stab in the back to all he had worked to create, a spirit of trust in which the claims of Home Rule could be seen as representing no threat or hostility to Britain's security and welfare.

Seen from Redmond's perspective, in which the granting of Home Rule depended entirely on the Government's keeping faith with its commitments at the end of the war, the Rising was a cruel betrayal of trust. After all, the vast majority of the Irish Volunteers in 1914 had heeded his advice; large numbers had gone off to fight in the war. For a small group within the residual minority of the Volunteers to have so dashed his guarantees of Irish loyalty and solidarity in the war effort, and to have given such a trump card to the Ulster Unionists, must have been depressing and galling to Redmond. But, on the other hand, Redmond had to reckon with the changing mood of Nationalist Ireland in the aftermath of the suppression of the Rising. By 1916 Carson was in Cabinet, the Ulster Volunteers had been granted recognition as a distinct unit in the British army (a recognition not given to the Irish Volunteers). The leaders of the Rising were executed, there were widespread arrests and reprisals. How could Redmond endorse the harshness of the reprisals after the Rising had been put down? The growing sense of unease that there seemed to be different sets of rules for dealing with different sets of rebels was potentially damaging for Redmond's credibility and standing. The timing and the manner of a change of attitude among Irish Nationalists to the 1916 Rising is a matter still in debate. It seems clear that initially the Rising (and those who launched it) provoked hostility among many Dubliners; one can easily appreciate why this was so. But this hostility was not universal, and it is not clear how long it lasted or how general it was outside of Dublin. It has been pointed out that the non-publication of newspapers because of the disruption, the timing of the publication of provincial newspapers, the dearth of reliable information regarding the Rising, the imprecision and rumour which coloured many early accounts of what had happened: are all factors which must be taken into account in any assessment of Nationalist Ireland's early response to the Rising.[23] But there can be little doubt concerning the effects produced by aspects of the Government's response to the Rising.

The arrests (due to defective intelligence information) of many Nationalists who had no connection with the Rising, and the subsequent deportation of many of these to detention camps, caused anger. The long-drawn out series of executions of the leaders of the Rising caused widespread outrage and revulsion: it seemed vengeful and cruel. Moreover, as biographical details of the lives and conduct of the rebel leaders became more widely known, a wave of sympathy grew, and a kind of admiration for their courage, their self-sacrifice and their generally honourable conduct during the Rising (even if many still felt the action itself to have been misguided or simply wrong). This wave of sympathy and admiration was fuelled by poets and skillfully manipulated for

propaganda purposes by various political activists. As if creating martyrs and politicising numbers of moderate Nationalists through reprisals and wrongful arrests were not a sufficient litany of Government
mistakes and miscalculations in the aftermath of the Rising, the incor-
rect description of the Rising as 'the Sinn Féin rebellion' gave prominence, and ultimately the political kiss of life, to a small Nationalist
movement which didn't seem to be going anywhere by 1914. By incor-
rectly calling the Rising the Sinn Féin rebellion the Government succeeded in puffing out the sails of a small Nationalist grouping, in the
sense that 'Sinn Féin' soon became a kind of flag of convenience to
describe all those who were expressing sympathy or admiration (however qualified) for the executed rebels of 1916 and for their ideals. This
was potentially important for a change not only in the mood of Nationalist Ireland, but also in its political demands and structures.

None of these developments boded well for Redmond. His advice to
ministers seemed to go unheeded. The changing shape of the Government seemed to leave him increasingly marginalised and with diminishing influence. The failures of political initiatives in 1916 and in the Irish
Convention of 1917–18 seemed to suggest a kind of paralysis in constitutional politics when it came to resolving the Irish/Ulster Questions.
For Redmond, the growing realisation of his limited influence, the
frustrations of advice ignored and of warnings unheeded, must have
been profoundly depressing. By 1917 the over-riding impression, not
only with regard to Redmond but with regard to his party also, is of a
diminishing authority and relevance. The conscription crisis came near
to providing the coup de grace. when the initiative for a popular campaign among the Nationalist community was seized by the new (post-
1917) re-vamped Sinn Féin on its way to becoming the new, authentic
'voice' of Nationalist Ireland by the end of 1918.

However, it is not only the personal decline of Redmond's influence
or the eventual collapse of his party which merit attention in this
examination of the impact of 'militarisation', but the fate of the kind of
politics that he represented and that he practised. Redmond was a
dedicated parliamentarian. He led his party in the firm conviction that
political objectives were to be achieved by patient persuasion and
flexible negotiation within the rules of liberal democracy. He was un-
sure and uncomfortable when the formation of the Irish Volunteers
intruded a new and, for him, unwelcome note of military mobilisation
into his Home Rule movement in 1913. He never came to terms satisfactorily with what exactly the role and function of a (partially) armed
Volunteer movement ought to be in a movement led by him. In assessing the crisis of Redmondism, therefore, one is reminded of George
Dangerfield's view that British Liberalism was decisively undermined

by the growing militancy of elements within British domestic politics before 1914, and was ultimately to collapse under the demands and challenges of the great war. The resolution of internal or international disputes by force of arms was anathema to liberal values.[24] In this context, it is tempting to see Redmond's failure in Dangerfield's terms, and to see the decline of Redmondism or of the old Home Rule movement as an integral part of the crisis of pre-war British Liberalism, both unable or unfitted to deal with the growing militarisation of political disagreements.

Turning to the Sinn Féin popular front of 1917–21, it may seem at first sight that this particular Nationalist movement would not be as unsettled as Redmond's party had been by the intrusion of military methods. Sinn Féin's position differed from Redmond's in a number of fundamental respects. The post-1917 Sinn Féin leadership claimed their *imprimatur* from the leaders of the 1916 Rising, and its declared demand was for a fully independent Irish Republic. These factors, among others, ensured that it would be difficult to control or to stand down those more enthusiastic militarists in the Nationalist camp who could claim that in resorting to arms to achieve the Republic they were following the example of the 1916 leaders. It also meant that for as long as the British Government had no intention of entertaining the demand for a fully sovereign Irish Republic, the establishment of realistic negotiating positions would prove to be very difficult. It is worth emphasing, however, that from early 1919 to the final split on the Treaty terms in late 1921 the Sinn Féin movement experienced constant and serious tensions between, broadly speaking, militarist and constitutionalist tendencies.

As Sinn Féin became the broadly-based, catch-all movement of Nationalist Ireland from late 1918, it covered a broad spectrum of views and sentiments on both the acceptable form of Irish independence and on the methods appropriate to its achievement. There were even varieties of militarists, or degrees of militarism, in the Sinn Féin of these years: there were militarists by instinct and inclination, militarists by calculation (holding the view that the use of force would probably be necessary to achieve independence), and there were militarists in theory (those who insisted that armed struggle for national independence was justified, but who made every effort to avoid having to resort to arms if any alternative methods were available for securing the desired political ends). Apart from a minority of die-hard militarists, the distinctions between these other categories were neither clear nor constant. Moreover, as Sinn Féin became a broad-based movement it was supported by many who had faithfully supported Redmond's Home Rule Party in its day and whose instincts and inclinations were firmly constitutionalist.[25] The Sinn Féin popular front of 1918–21 was never simply the political front or handmaiden of the IRB There were IRB men in influential positions in Sinn Féin and in the reconstituted Irish Volunteers (increasingly described as the Irish Republican Army), but the military activists were at all times during 1919–21 in a minority within the broad Nationalist movement.

The sources of tension between constitutionalist and militarist tendencies within Sinn Féin can be easily illustrated: the difficult relationship between the authority of Dáil Eireann over the Volunteers and the actual conduct of the Anglo-Irish war of 1919–21; the potential confusion or conflict of interests and priorities inherent in the holding of multiple offices (political office under the Dáil, military office in the volunteer army, and, perhaps, military office also in the clandestine I.R.B) by leaders such as Collins; the degree of real autonomy exercised by volunteer leaders at local level in the difficult military conditions imposed by the conduct of a guerilla war. De Valera's lengthy absence in the U.S.A. from June 1919 to late December 1921 may have given the President of the Dáil the platform to elaborate political positions and to engage in long-distance diplomatic soundings, but it meant that a major portion of the Anglo-Irish guerrilla war was conducted without any direct involvement by the titular head of the Irish Nationalist political movement. Not surprisingly, perhaps, throughout the course of the war (indeed largely because of the conduct of it) the balance of influence within the Nationalist movement seemed to many observers (including British ministers) to lie with those in control of the military campaign. It was their endeavours, as it seemed, which would be crucial in determining whether or not the legitimacy and authority of Dáil Eireann, the assembly of the Irish Republic, would be recognized, both within Ireland and by others (most crucially the British Government). It was this primacy of military considerations (and the associated status and mystique attaching to various military leaders) during the war of independence which made it such a difficult matter getting back to the politics of negotiation and compromise during 1921–22.

The fact that Britain's conduct of the Anglo-Irish war (notably the use of the Black and Tans and Auxilliaries) had caused such revulsion throughout the Nationalist community in general served to further complicate the move towards fresh negotiations. In the light of the pervasive militarisation of political action in the years since 1913, the problem posed for the Sinn Fein leadership as it entered into negotiations with the British ministers in 1921 becomes easier to understand. It was the attempt to re-assert the primacy of political negotiation and compromise over the relative simplicity (and ideological purity) of the military 'struggle for independence', and to do so without splitting the unity of the Sinn Féin national movement, that produced De Valera's tortuous manoeuvres during 1921–22. The same challenge faced those actually entrusted with the final negotiations. The composition of delegations and negotiating teams was a matter of vital importance: they had to include members with high standing and credibility among the militarists.The suspicious, not to say contemptuous, attitude shown by revolutionaries towards conventional, constitutional politics was not an exclusively Irish phenomenon; it has been noted by political scientists interested in the mentalité of young revolutionary elites in many countries.[26] For the young revolutionary idealists in many national liberation struggles of modern times 'politics' meant opportunism and careerism, as distinct from the morally-pure idealism of the revolutionary activists themselves. The return to 'normalcy', it was feared, would signal a return to compromise and corruption.This high-minded but dangerously elitist idealism of young revolutionaries was to produce very mixed consequences in the political history of many European states in the first half of the twentieth century.

In the case of Nationalist Ireland, the final outcome of the negotiations between the Sinn Féin delegates and the British ministers did not produce terms acceptable to all sections of the Sinn Féin movement, and a split and Civil War followed.While De Valera was to find himself among the substantial minority (in the Dáil and among the electorate) who rejected the Treaty terms, it is most likely that even had De Valera, for all his authority and persuasiveness, been able to recommend acceptance, a split and armed conflict would have occurred when the moment for compromise eventually came.There was a core of Republican idealists within Sinn Féin who, come what may, would accept nothing less than a fully sovereign Irish Republic.[27] And such was not available through negotiation with the British Government in 1921 (as De Valera realised). The Irish Free State began its life, therefore, with the bitter baptism of a civil war. But, beyond the immediate tragedy of that conflict, there remained on in the Irish Free State – as there certainly remained on in Northern Ireland after 1920– the legacy of that shift in political discourse during 1912–1922 in which there had occurred a decisive militarisation of the process of political disagreement and debate in Ireland. The problems left by that legacy were to prove enduring in both parts of Ireland.

Turning briefly to our third major theme – the degree of sovereignty demanded and achieved by Nationalist Ireland – the central issue here is fairly straightforward. In terms of sovereignty the Irish Free State, established in 1922 with dominion status, enjoyed substantially more powers than the Home Rule Parliament would have enjoyed if established under the terms of the 1912 bill. How did it happen, therefore, that such a considerable section of Nationalist opinion in Ireland in

1922 was deeply disappointed with the status of the new national state? This disappointment was not confined to the Republican separatists, who refused to accept the 'betrayal' of the Republic proclaimed by the 1916 leaders. Even those who negotiated the terms of the Treaty, and many more who gave it their support, confessed themselves disappointed that a better deal could not be achieved, if not full sovereign independence. How had the aspirations and expectations of Nationalist Ireland climbed so high from the relatively modest measure of self-government which had, it seemed, enjoyed a large consensus of Nationalist support in 1912?

A comprehensive answer to this question would require a level of detail and explorations of a psycho-historical kind which we will not attempt here. But some things are clear. The 1916 Rising and the proclamation of a Republic by the leaders, and their subsequent execution for their action, raised the stakes dramatically, in terms of what the appropriate constitutional expression of Ireland's historic claims to nationhood ought to be. The 'martyrs' of 1916 set the moral as well as the political claims for an Irish Republic very high indeed. Climbing down, even a little, from this high moral ground of 'the Republic and nothing but the Republic' was going to be a difficult task for any later Nationalist leader seeking broad popular support (even if such leaders had themselves participated in the Rising). There is a further point worth noting. The basis of the 1921 settlement (and therefore of the 1922 Constitution of the Irish Free State) was an act of the British Parliament, giving effect to the terms agreed in the Treaty. But the 1916 Proclamation, and the Sinn Féin policy, asserted that the basis for the legitmacy of any government in Ireland had to be the sovereignty of the Irish people.[28]

This emphasis on popular sovereignty as the basis for political legitimacy was to be a recurring feature of De Valera's complicated documentary journey to the 1937 Constitution, which was enacted not by any parliament (still less the British Parliament) but by the people in a referendum. Apart from these crucial factors in domestic Irish politics, it is likely that the great surge of new national states created at the end of the war in 1918–19 in accordance with the commitment to the principles of national self-determination further fuelled Irish Nationalist expectations that an independent Irish state was attainable. They failed to fully grasp, perhaps, that while most of the new national states in central and eastern Europe were being created out of the debris of defeated multi-national empires, the Irish were seeking to gain their independence from the one major empire which emerged from the war among the victor powers.

Turning, in conclusion, to the final theme selected for discussion, let us consider what change, if any, had taken place in the ideological character of the leadership of Nationalist Ireland between 1912 and 1922. To set the question of leadership in context, it may be useful to look at the general support-base of the Nationalist Party of 1912 and of Sinn Féin in 1918–21. When Sinn Féin replaced the old Irish Party as the dominant electoral voice of Nationalist Ireland in the 1918 election, did this mean that the voters who had supported Redmond's Home Rule Party (and, presumably, what it stood for) had switched their allegiance (and their political demands) *en masse?* Any attempt to answer this question must begin with an acknowledgement of the novel aspects of the 1918 election.

The electorate was greatly enlarged from what it had been at the last general election in 1910, as a result of the Franchise act of 1918. The new franchise, combined with war casualties, meant that perhaps as many as two out of every three voters entitled to vote in the 1918 election were first-time voters.[29] But, of course, the large number of uncontested seats, together with charges of intimidation and impersonation, make it difficult to draw neat conclusions from the Sinn Féin sweep of 73 seats in that election (as against a mere 6 for the old Home Rule Party and 26 for the Unionists). But is is clear that some former Redmondite supporters were switching to Sinn Féin. More importantly, as soon as it became clear that Sinn Féin had become the elected voice of Nationalist Ireland, and as it began to set to work (through the Dáil, the Sinn Féin courts, and in the local authorities) supplanting the organs of British Government and administration in Ireland and replacing them with structures of its own, the entire Nationalist community (and, outside of Ulster, the dispersed Unionists) began to make terms with it and began to seek to influence its policies and the ways in which they would be implemented. Specifically, the propertied classes, whatever their previous political disposition, began to seek reassurances that Sinn Féin would not preside over a campaign of spoliation, land-grabbing or anarchy.

The bulwarks of the old Redmondite party at local level found, perhaps to the surprise of many, that, in the main, they had no great cause for worry ; they could do business and, if necessary, give support to the new Sinn Féin popular front after 1918. As Redmond's old party began to disintegrate rapidly, 'people with a stake in the country' saw no reason to go down with a sinking ship. Many of them rallied to Sinn Féin in order to stabilise it and to ensure that it would not embark on adventures of a socially radical kind. The old Nationalist Party's local organisation had become moribund in many areas, the consequences of complacent neglect during the long interval when it ruled the electoral roost unopposed. As the organisational structure of Sinn Féin expanded, its social base broadened. It became, in effect, a populist, catch-all political movement bonded by national sentiment.[30] The leadership showed its determination to have the movement speak for all sections of the Nationalist community. No socially divisive issues would put this communal solidarity in jeopardy. The Dáil (and, under instruction, the Volunteers) dealt firmly with any attempts to take advantage of the war of independence and the general assault on the authority of the Crown forces (notably the police) in order to engage in land redistribution or the settling of local scores. Indeed, the long litany of pressing social and economic problems – agricultural depression following falling prices from 1920, the wage grievances of agricultural labourers and other workers, chronic housing problems in Dublin – would all have to wait for attention until the constitutional issue was resolved. The Sinn Féin leadership was determined that at a time when it was preparing to deal with the British Government as the de jure and de facto authority in an embryonic Irish state, it would not be embarrassed and its case would not be damaged by internal conflict within 'its community' on divisive social issues.[31]

This 'communal' commitment of Sinn Féin after 1918 reflected the broadening base of the movement's support. But it also reflected the ideas and aspirations of its leaders. One can identify certain differences between the Home Rule leadership of 1912 and the Sinn Féin leaders of 1918–21. In terms of social class, the Sinn Féin leadership overall was more weighted to the lower middle-class and skilled working class than their Home Rule predecessors – more teachers, public employees (civil servants, customs and excise officers and like occupations). Indeed, there is a certain irony in the number of prominent Sinn Féin leaders who were employees of the British state. Tom Garvin, in his perceptive study of the Sinn Féin leadership, has remarked that 'revolutionary Nationalism in Ireland was . . . radical in style and means, not in ends'. Turn of the century Ireland, Garvin points out, saw 'the rise of political movements of an often visionary and romantic character, commonly dominated by relatively well-educated young people from the middle reaches of society'; what prompted them to radical political activism was a sense that their political status was 'noticeably lower than their political capacity'. The Sinn Féin leadership drew many of its members from this kind of well-educated and idealistic lower middle-class whose opportunities for political leadership were severely limited under the old Redmondite, parliamentary dispensation. The revolution which most of them sought was a national not a social revolution (despite occasional genuflections towards the memory of Connolly). As Garvin concludes, they were intent on taking over the apparatus of state, not in destroying it or establishing a new social order.[32]

In one other notable respect the Sinn Féin leadership differed in character from Redmond's team. Sinn Fein included a significantly higher number of committed cultural Nationalists; cultural Nationalists who subscribed to the Gaelic League ideals, and specifically to the proposition that language was the single most important mark of national identity or ethnicity, and that Irish political Nationalism would be an empty shell, a fraud, if it didn't rest on a healthy sense of Irish nationality. Such a healthy sense of Irish nationality could only be guaranteed by the restoration of the Irish-language, the most indelible mark of separate nationhood, to a position as the main vernacular of the Irish people. The Gaelic League had, it is true, found sympathetic supporters among the ranks of Redmond's party (and indeed, to an extent, among Unionists).[33] But the commitment to a vigorous attempt at re-Gaelicisation, as part of the project of Irish national renewal, which was the cultural programme to which a substantial group of the Sinn Féin leadership was ardently committed, had no precedent in Redmond's programme. Not all Sinn Féiners were equally ardent in the Gaelic cause. But a sufficient number of the most educated among the Sinn Féin leaders were believers in the Gaelic League gospel, that the language was the essential authenticating mark of nationality to ensure that, even after the rupture and civil war of 1922–23, the new Irish state would see an energetic cultural policy pursued based on the desire to revive the Irish language as the national vernacular.

Finally, in comparing the 'condition' of Nationalist Ireland in 1922 with what it had been a decade earlier, there can be little argument with the claim that the main casualties of the political turbulence of the decade were the Irish Nationalists who found themselves within Northern Ireland after 1920. They were the main losers within Nationalist Ireland from the changes which the decade had brought about. In 1912 they were poised to share in the joy of the Nationalist majority in Ireland, as a Home Rule Parliament, a symbol, however limited its powers, of a sense of Irish nationhood, seemed destined to be granted at long last by the British Parliament. Ten years later they were lodged in a political unit – Northern Ireland – in which they were meant to remain a permanent minority, and a minority, moreover, whose symbols and signs of national identity were to find no acknowledged place in the organs or symbols of the state.

The Ulster Unionists may not have asked for a 'Home Rule' state in the exclusion zone (their concern was to remain in the Union, under the Crown); but when they got it they determined that it should proclaim and entrench in power their political and cultural identity, and theirs only. Moreover, as a consequence of the manner in which the partition settlement had eventually come about – the climate of 'militarisation' in which the Home Rule settlement had been scuttled – the Nationalists in Northern Ireland found themselves in a situation of political powerlessness in a community where suspicion and hostility had poisoned relations to a degree that would be very difficult to remedy. It was neither comfort nor satisfaction to them to know that many Unionists in the new Irish Free State (not exclusively in the three Ulster counties incorporated in the state) were feeling deep hurt, unease, and various degrees of cultural and political alienation from the new political arrangements in which they found themselves after 1922.[34] Neither would it have been a comfort to them to learn that, contrary to Churchill's famous lament for the unique integrity of the quarrels of Fermanagh and Tyrone, in the early 1920s large tracts of central and eastern Europe, from the Baltic to the Balkans, were littered with Fermanaghs and Tyrones, disputed border lands where ethnic conflict remained unresolved by the state-making of the statesmen in 1918–1919.Throughout Europe there were innumerable national minorities left on the 'wrong' side of national boundaries in the 1920s. Some of these unresolved issues of minority and majority communities locked together on disputed territories have continued to trouble the continent up to the present day. All of this may give us a comparative context for understanding the Northern Ireland problem of the past seventy years. But it cannot alter the fact that from the perspective of Nationalist Ireland the major losers of the dramatic political upheavals of 1912–22 in Ireland were the Nationalists in Northern Ireland, who found themselves after 1922 looking back in bewilderment and shock at what had happened to rob them of what in 1912 they had confidently expected to be their political future as part of the national majority in a Home Rule Ireland.

Platform party at Unionist demonstration in Ulster Hall, 27 September 1912.
Two figures standing are Edward Carson and, on the left, Lord Londonderry.
James Craig is seated behind Edward Carson (photograph by Alex Hogg)

CHAPTER FIVE

Carson, Craig and The Partition of Ireland, 1912–21
by
Patrick Buckland

It is Edward Carson who is commemorated in that dramatic monument outside the Parliamentary Buildings at Stormont. Yet, in fact, the partition of Ireland and establishment of Northern Ireland are more James Craig's achievements than those of Carson. Carson was the front man in Ulster's fight against Home Rule. It was Craig who did the basic planning that thwarted the Irish Nationalist demand for an Ireland completely free from British rule. It was Craig who made the 1920 Government of Ireland Act work in Northern Ireland.

Public men

Personally, Carson and Craig could not have been more different. 'King Carson' is how opponents sneeringly described him. His public face was set permanently in a scowl of righteous defiance. His height and powerful frame, his hatchet face, his gestures, all gave the impression of power and character, big in resistance. He is part of the Irish legend. He is either adored as the man who saved Ulster or reviled as a rebel who sabotaged his country's independence. Carson was born in Dublin on 9 February 1854, the second son of a modestly successful architect, and died on 3 June 1935. A member of the Church of Ireland, an Orangeman at 19 and educated at Trinity College, Dublin, he really had three careers. His main career was law. He came to prominence as Crown Prosecutor in Ireland during the 'Plan of Campaign' and then transferred to England where he became one of the leading advocates of his day before being appointed Lord of Appeal, 1921–29. His famous cases included the Oscar Wilde libel case, the Marconi case and the Archer Shee case. As member of Parliament for Trinity College, Dublin, and then for the Duncairn division of Belfast, he also held posts in various Unionist governments, with legal appointments in Ireland and then England. The high point of his ministerial career occurred during the First World War, when in various posts within and without the war

Cabinet he helped to bring a sense of purpose to the war effort, although he was less successful as a departmental minister. Finally, there
was 'King Carson', leader of the Irish Unionist Party, 1910–21, when he
spearheaded the spectacular campaign against the third Home Rule
Bill. It was in this campaign that he worked closely with Craig.

Craig was also physically a big man, but an Ulsterman through and
through. Craig means 'rock' and Craig was one of the rocks upon which
the Irish Nationalist claim for a united Ireland failed. As one of his
biographers wrote in conferring a public image on Craig:

> His countrymen believed . . . that James Craig was, under God, cho-
> sen to perform a task that must have baffled, if not defeated, any
> other person . . . James Craig, bone of their bone, and flesh of their
> flesh, alien to them neither in belief nor in birth, achieved what no
> other man could have achieved. Against that rock, the gates of the
> Eirean hell could not prevail.[1]

Craig was born in the Belfast suburb of Sydenham on 8 January 1871,
the seventh son of James Craig, a whiskey millionaire. He died on 24
November 1940. A Presbyterian and an Orangeman, he was educated
at Merchiston College, Edinburgh, did not go to University, but, like
Carson, had three careers. His initial career was stockbroking, after
leaving school at the age of seventeen. His father, although wealthy,
expected Craig to earn a living, starting at the bottom in a broking firm,
running messages and licking stamps. Craig was a reasonably successful
stockbroker, being a founder member of the Belfast Stock Exchange,
but he did not like it very much and he soon embarked on his second
career, the Army.

His army career was short-lived. He served, as a Captain, in the
South African or Boer War between 1900 and 1901, at one time being
Assistant Director of the Imperial Military Railways –a job for which he
trained himself by purchasing a model railway on which he practised
signalling. After the war he declined to make a career in the regular
army, and with the aid of a legacy from his father, he embarked upon his
third career. This third career was politics and fell into three parts.
Between 1906 and 1916 he was a backbencher. He first entered Parliament in 1906 as Unionist MP for East Down. It was during this phase
that he came to prominence, masterminding Ulster Unionist resistance
to the third Home Rule Bill. In the second part of his political career,
1916–21, Craig enjoyed junior ministerial office in Britain, his last post
being financial secretary to the Admiralty. This post he resigned on 7
June 1921 in order to begin the third and final part of his political career
as the first Prime Minister of Northern Ireland, from June 1921 until his

death in September 1940. In the first two years, 1921–22, he turned partition into a reality.

Private men

Both Carson and Craig had strong public images, but the private face was often strikingly different. Carson was famous for his scowl of righteous defiance and steely strength. William O'Brien spoke of him as 'a liverish young man, with the complexion of one fed on vinegar and with the features as inexpressive as a jagged hatchet.'[2] In many respects, Carson was a formidable figure and certainly a formidable opponent, largely, perhaps, as a result of his legal training and experience as a barrister in Ireland. He had physical and moral courage, as was shown by his vigorous prosecutions for the Crown during the agrarian agitation associated with the 'Plan of Campaign' in the later 1880s. Unlike other lawyers he refused to be intimidated by agrarian violence or threats to his own safety.

He was also devastatingly direct, disregarding irrelevancies and going straight to the hard core of questions. Unlike those other Irish barristers and politicians of his day, his speeches were relatively short and lucid, gaining strength from their apparent unstudied simplicity of style, short, clear, clipped sentences. He carried his courtroom style into Parliament, where he treated opponents as though they were in the dock, accused of unutterable crimes brought home by the inquiry and testimony of members of the Royal Irish Constabulary. These traits were also combined with a powerful sense of moral righteousness when his sympathies were engaged and by a flair for the dramatic gesture. At key moments he often left the courtroom or the House of Commons to underline his point out of a sense of the dramatic, not just petulance.

On the other hand, this was not the whole man. In many respects, his features libelled the real man, and in reality he was a vulnerable figure. There was nothing of the fanatic in his composition, and his mind was not narrow, religious intolerance he despised. A Liberal Unionist, he supported the abolition of capital punishment, of the political disabilities of women and of the connection between church and state. Above all, he wanted fair and equal treatment of Irish Catholics. On the Irish university question, for instance, he differed from many of his party in arguing that the Irish Catholics should be given the type of university education they wanted. One of the last pieces of advice he gave the Ulster Unionist Council when stepping down from the leadership in February 1921, just before the establishment of Northern Ireland, was this:

From the outset let us see that the Catholic minority have nothing to fear from the Protestant majority. Let us take care to win all that is best among those who have been opposed to us in the past. While maintaining intact our own religion let us give the same rights to the religion of our neighbours.[3]

Physically, too, there is a contradiction between appearance and reality. Behind the steely exterior was a man who worried continually about his health. His pale, saturnine features and deep-set eyes were the mirror of his hypochondria. He lived to be over eighty, but he never believed his health to be robust, and his letters to friends usually contained gloomy references to his ailments. Indeed, it could be plausibly argued that the whole of Carson's career can be explained in terms of his perception of his health. One of the reasons he did not press his claims for the leadership of the Conservative and Unionist Party in 1911 was ill health. He was going through a bad patch at the time, being frequently confined to bed and being urged by his doctor to try one treatment after another for his neuralgia.

Craig's public image was as a man of granite strength. In appearance, he was big, bluff and stolid in appearance, with a large, red, craggy face. Nor was he an original thinker. He read little and reflected opinion rather than created it. On the other hand, he was not the dour Ulsterman that people made him out to be. Indeed, he can best be summed up by that television advertisement for the Automobile Association, the one with 'a nice man, a very nice man.' That was James Craig. He was a straightforward, likeable man, with no side. What he said he meant. Political allies and opponents alike recognised this. Stanley Baldwin, the English Prime Minister, reckoned that Craigavon had no one who disliked or hated him, 'he was a lovable man'. This view was shared by one of the leaders of the Irish Free State, William T. Cosgrave (President, Executive Council of the Irish Free State, 1922–32). Recalling some difficult negotiations about Irish unity in 1924–25, Cosgrave said that 'Lord Craigavon improved on acquaintance ... we found him honourable and straightforward. I never knew him to finesse, and he never sought to break [off] a conference to his own advantage where he had the opportunity'.[4]

In this, Craig was a striking contrast to many of his contemporaries. Carson was a moody and magnificent hypochondriac, while Michael Collins was a passionate man of action who, certainly in respect of Northern Ireland, lacked judgement. With Craig, however, people knew where they were, as might have been expected from a Presbyterian, Co. Down stockbroker who had bought a model railway train set to help him organise military railways during the South African War. Craig was also a man of simple courage if he believed a course of action was right. This was clear during the Anglo-Irish war when, to the horror of his

Ulster Unionist colleagues he went south to meet Eamon De Valera and was driven to an unknown destination, as he told his wife, by 'three of the worst looking toughs I have ever seen'.[5]

Unionism and opposition to Home Rule

Carson and Craig shared a common Unionism and largely agreed on why the United Kingdom should be maintained. In their dedication to the Union and their opposition to Home Rule, they were no different from the other Irish Unionists, who were drawn mainly from the Protestants who made up some twenty-five per cent of the population of Ireland. The first reason they opposed Home Rule was satisfaction with the status quo, satisfaction with the Union. They believed that Ireland had prospered under the Union. They denied the Nationalist claim that the British connection was ruining Ireland culturally, economically and politically. Instead, they subscribed to an Irish Unionist version of Irish history, whereby Irish economic, social and political progress was dependent upon the Union, including, Carson told one audience in 1910, local self-government ... £150,000 a year in relief of taxation ... a system of education [with] every child trained in the religion of its parents (and discharged out of the Imperial taxation) ... University education ... land purchase.[6] According to this view, what Ireland needed was not new laws but the steady enforcement of existing ones. ·

Secondly, neither Carson nor Craig believed that Irish Nationalists and Irish Catholics were capable of governing Ireland competently and fairly. However, there was a difference in emphasis. Carson was more inclined to emphasise the lawlessness of Nationalism, influenced as he was by his experiences of prosecuting cases during the 'Plan of Campaign' in the late 1880s. He was particularly scathing about the role some Home Rule MPs had played in promoting the assassination of landlords or their agents. As Carson told the House of Commons in 1912, Nationalists were not to be trusted:

> Anyone who knows Ireland, or who knows the history of Ireland for the last twenty years, the methods of intimidation, the methods of persecution, the methods of the leagues, which, unfortunately, permeate the whole south and west of Ireland, knows the oppression and the cruelty which are the ordinary weapons of the Nationalists in Ireland and knows perfectly well that the only protection against these methods is the proper protection of the Executive power. ·

Craig was also wary of Irish Nationalists, reckoning that professional agitators were turning Irish people into 'beggars and mendicants'. How-

ever, he was more inclined than Carson to emphasise the power of the
Roman Catholic Church. Sharing the general Ulster Protestant distrust
of that Church, he once wrote,'At every stage in life from the cradle to
the grave, the Roman Catholic Church intervenes, exhorting and commanding her adherents to have no intercourse with Protestants . . .
Ireland was probably the most priest-ridden country in the world.'So
satisfaction with the Union and suspicion of Irish Nationalism and Irish
Catholicism made Craig and Carson into determined opponents of
Home Rule and staunch upholders of the Union. Home Rule would be
a 'a risk for Ulster', and, Craig asked, 'Why should Ulster be asked to
place in jeopardy the position she has manfully won for herself by
industry and enterprise, by patience and perseverance?'

This Ulster perspective set Craig slightly apart from Carson who had
a broader, southern Unionist, view of the value of the Imperial connection to Ireland. For men like Carson, the Union offered Irish people a
fuller and richer social life. It also enabled them to make a valuable
contribution to the common development of the two islands and of the
British Empire as a whole. If their Nationalist opponents accused them
of treachery to the Nationalist cause, men like Carson retorted that they
were fighting for larger loyalties against the onset of a stifling provin-
cialism. Carson wrote to his friend and confidante, Lady Londonderry
in February 1912, 'How I long to see Home Rule defeated – it is, I think,
a passion with me as I hate the degradation of Ireland being turned into
a province and our own splendid folk being put under in the race for
progress.'[10] Irish Unionists of Carson's ilk were all the more sure that
Ireland would be set back 'in the race for progress'. Not only would
Home Rule mean separation from Great Britain, it would also mean
the eclipse of the most intelligent and progressive elements in Irish life,
namely themselves. As one of Carson's southern Unionist friends put it,
the so-called English garrison in Ireland formed as a whole:

> oases of culture, of uprightness and of fair dealing, in what will
> otherwise be a desert of dead uniformity where the poor will have no
> one to appeal to except the Priest or the local Shopkeeper . . . whence
> the rich will fly and where lofty ideals, whether of social or Imperial
> interest, will be smothered in an atmosphere of superstition, greed
> and chicanery.

These Unionist objections to Home Rule were fundamental, because
underlying them was a refusal to accept that Ireland was a separate
nation. The third Home Rule bill had been introduced by Liberals and
Nationalists to satisfy the Irish nation, but Carson and Craig denied that
Ireland was a separate nation.

Fighting Home Rule

The determination of Carson and Craig to maintain the Union was underlined during their epic fight against the third Home Rule Bill. When the bill was introduced into the House of Commons in April 1912 by Asquith's Liberal Government, British Liberals and Irish Nationalists confidently looked forward to the speedy re-establishment of a Dublin Parliament and to a new, more harmonious relationship between Britain and Ireland.

Ulster Unionists, under the leadership of Carson and Craig had other ideas, however. They organised massive resistance to the Home Rule Bill, particularly in Ulster. The campaign included the signing of the Solemn League and Covenant in September 1912, the formation of the Ulster Volunteer Force, and 'the arming of Ulster' with the Larne gun-running in April 1914. By July 1914, the time that the Home Rule Bill had completed its parliamentary circuit, Ulster Unionists were in a position to resist its imposition on their province, with a Provisional Government, backed by a disciplined and armed volunteer force of some 100,000 men and women. In this resistance, Craig's contribution was decisive. At a most practical level he enabled Ulster Unionists to overcome the many problems facing their fight against Home Rule. He became, in fact, their masterly director of operations. Craig realised that efficiency and discipline were essential in this fight against Home Rule. He knew that unruly mobs could be intimidated, but it was harder to coerce a disciplined and organised community. He also knew that British Liberal and Irish Nationalist opinion dismissed lightly Ulster Unionist threats of resistance – mere 'Orangeade' was a favourite dismissal – and was determined that Ulster should be taken seriously.

He set about his task systematically and effectively. In Ulster he ensured that effective organisation would weld together the disparate elements that made up the Ulster Unionist movement and maintain discipline. This was one of the functions of the Ulster Volunteer Force: to provide a command structure to ensure that energies were not dissipated and to avoid a repetition of the sectarian rioting that had greeted the introduction of the first two Home Rule bills. He also ensured that Ulster had the best possible public image in Britain. What many English people regarded as the bigotry and intolerance of Ulster Protestants had long created an unfavourable impression in Britain. Ulster Unionists needed a leader with credibility in Britain, and thus it was that Craig persuaded Sir Edward Carson to head the Ulster Unionist resistance. As a famous barrister and leading member of the Conservative and Unionist hierarchy in Britain, Carson could lend credibility and dignity to the Ulster Unionist cause in Britain. But Carson had his doubts and needed to be convinced of Ulster Unionists' determination. As he told Craig in July 1911, 'What I am really anxious about is to satisfy myself that the people over there really mean to resist. I am not for a mere game of bluff, and, unless men are prepared to make great sacrifices which they clearly understand, the talk of resistance is no use.'[12]

Craig energetically set about convincing Carson. He did so not merely by arranging a series of dinners and luncheons, as he told his wife, but mainly by organising a massive demonstration in the grounds of his own home, Craigavon, on 25 September 1911. There Carson found himself addressing 50,000 men representing all parts of Ulster. It was a master-stroke. The Ulstermen popularly acclaimed Carson and he responded, going straight to their hearts by saying :

> I know the responsibility you are putting on me today. In your presence I cheerfully accept it, grave as it is, and I now enter into a compact with you, and every one of you, and with the help of God you and I joined together – I giving you the best I can, and you giving me all your strength behind me – we will yet defeat the most nefarious conspiracy that has ever been hatched against a free people.[13]

Carson evoked a loyal response from the Ulster Unionists, the Marquess of Londonderry even telling him, 'My dear Edward, if I was to lose everything in the world, I will go with you to the end'.[14] In return, Carson did Ulster Unionists proud. His directness, sense of drama and morality lent conviction to the cause both inside and outside Ulster, particularly on occasion in the House of Commons. One of his most effective statements on behalf of Ulster Unionists occurred in February 1914, when he told the Government:

> You have never tried to win over Ulster. You have never tried to understand her position. You have never alleged and never can allege that this Bill gives her one atom of advantage. No, you cannot deny that it takes away many advantages that she has as a constituent part of the United Kingdom. You cannot deny that in the past she has produced the most loyal and law-abiding part of the citizens of the United Kingdom ... (And turning to John Redmond) I say to the Leader of the Nationalist Party, if you want Ulster, go and take her, or go and win her. You never wanted her affections. You wanted her taxes.[15]

These charges were repudiated by Redmond, but the speech made such a deep impression on his Liberal allies that Prime Minister Asquith wrote to 'My Dear Carson' 'without prejudice', saying that 'your speech this afternoon impressed me more than anything I have heard in Parliament for many a long day'.[16]

This was a superb combination, the 'dream ticket', for Ulster Unionism – Carson and Craig. Each had what the other lacked. Carson's mercurial temperament and powers of oratory complimented Craig's stability and organising genius, which Carson so conspicuously lacked. Together they became a third, undeniable person. At times Carson's vanity and need for constant re-assurance could be trying, but Craig was tolerant and did not mind that, as Carson, himself admitted, 'It was James Craig who did most of the work, and I got most of the credit'.[17] Craig's contribution was generally recognised at the time and was nicely summed up in this contemporary postcard, entitled 'Ulster's Gallant Volunteer. Capt. Craig, MP'. It showed a uniformed Craig with a sword in his right hand, his left foot on a prostrate and wriggling John Redmond, the leader of the Nationalist Party, and his left hand holding aloft an aghast Herbert Henry Asquith, the Liberal Prime Minister. The verse beneath the picture read:

He who volunteered for England in her deadly Boer War
Is for Ulster volunteering a treason plot to mar;
By his voice in Britain's Parliament he has fought the deadly foe,
By his sword in loyal Ulster he'll lay treason mongers low,
Then hurrah for Craig and Ulster, with a hip, hip, hip hurray!
With men like him and Carson we're quite ready for the fray.[18]

Legitimacy of armed resistance

It is reasonable to ask how could such pillars of the establishment as Craig and Carson set out so deliberately to defy the Westminster Parliament. To ask this question, raises, of course, the whole paradox of Ulster Unionist loyalty. How could such a professedly loyal province as Ulster contemplate an act of defiance to the Parliament of the United Kingdom to which they and other Unionists were attached? It was a question which did worry Unionists at the time. How could they say that they were loyal on the one hand, and yet threaten armed resistance to an act of the parliament of the United Kingdom? In the end, however, they managed to reconcile defiance with loyalty by producing a series of arguments about the nature of democracy and loyalty.

First, Ulster Unionists had a particular view of 'loyalty' arising from their own notion of rights of governments and citizens. They held a contractual view of loyalty which distinguished between loyalty to the Crown and loyalty to any particular Government, and which also maintained that loyalty was a two-way street. Automatic loyalty was not owed to the state. Rather that loyalty must be earned. In this view, if the Government fails to protect its citizens then it is disloyal not to rebel. It was a view expressed most starkly by the Rev. Ian Paisley in 1975, when he said, 'If the Crown in Parliament decreed to put Ulster into a United Ireland, we would be disloyal to Her Majesty if we did not resist such a surrender to our enemies'.[19] It was a view which Carson thought would have found favour in Britain at the time of the third Home Rule Bill.As he later told Asquith, if he had been arrested for his activities in Ulster, he would have pleaded guilty and would have said:

> My Lord Judge and gentlemen of the jury: I was born under the British flag, a loyal subject of His Majesty the King. So much do I value this birthright that I was even prepared to rebel in order to defend it. If to fight, so as to remain, like yourselves, a loyal subject of His Majesty, be a crime, my Lord and gentlemen of the jury, I plead guilty.[20]

Secondly, Ulster Unionists argued that at the time of the third Home Rule Bill the constitution was in suspense and that they were, therefore, absolved from the normal constitutional conventions in their resistance to Home Rule. Home Rule was, according to this view, a nefarious conspiracy brought about by a corrupt bargain between Liberals and Nationalists and the clipping of the powers of the House of Lords by the 1911 Parliament Act. Thirdly, Ulster Unionists maintained that such apparent acts of defiance as the Solemn League and Covenant and the formation and drilling of the Ulster Volunteer Force served a useful social purpose by maintaining order and regulating sectarian and political tension in Ulster. As one Church of Ireland bishop wrote in 1914, 'It is certainly true that we should have had anarchy in Ulster long ago but for the splendid order and constant watchfulness of the Volunteer force. Their formation and the spirit which animates them have proved a blessing beyond all estimation'.[21]

The points were debated in public and in private, but underlying them was an often unspoken but smouldering mistrust of Westminster politicians. Ulster Unionists did not trust English politicians to take them seriously and were, as a consequence, determined to be masters of their own political destiny. It was this feeling that lay behind an angry exchange in the House of Commons in 1912 between Craig and the rather laid back and sceptical Irish Chief Secretary. The Chief Secretary had dismissed threats of resistance as 'Nonsense, my dear fellow, nonsense! Rubbish!', but Craig angrily accepted the challenge:

> We shall henceforth take the steps which may become necessary to

prove to the Government the sincerity of our people at home – that is not to submit to government by the Nationalist Party, under any circumstances whatever . . . No one can say what will happen at this crisis, except that there is a very strong and earnest determination on the part of Ulster to take action, and there is a movement already on foot to take it. If the right honourable gentleman has challenged this part of His Majesty's dominions to civil war, then the challenge is accepted.[22]

Partition of Ireland

Legitimate or not, the campaign against the third Home Rule Bill changed the nature of the debate over Home Rule. By late 1913 there was recognition of Ulster's special position. It was generally agreed that in the event of Home Rule for Ireland, special arrangements would have to be made for Ulster. Ulster was not to be coerced into accepting Home Rule or the authority of a Dublin Parliament. Furthermore, when the Union was eventually modified, the 1920 Government of Ireland Act made such special provision. Ireland was partitioned, with a government and parliament for Ulster Unionists in the six counties that now make up Northern Ireland, and a government and parliament in Dublin for Irish Nationalists, both subject to Westminster's sovereignty. The 1920 act was superseded in the twenty six counties by the Anglo-Irish Treaty of 1921, but for fifty years it provided the basis of government in Northern Ireland. It was at this point that Carson faded into the background and Craig made partition a reality by making Northern Ireland work. Craig's role was crucial in implementing the 1920 Government of Ireland Act in the six counties and establishing the Government and Parliament of Northern Ireland. His achievement was all the more remarkable in view of the many difficulties he faced from outside and from within.

Internally, with the aid of a few dedicated civil servants he created a new administration from scratch, at first addressing envelopes himself, while his wife sat on the floor sticking stamps on them. Moreover, when violence threatened to swamp the new state, he tried to avoid extremes with a Government which would only have in view 'the welfare of the people' and 'would be absolutely honest and fair in administering the law'.[23] Externally he resisted pressure from both Britain and Dublin to abandon Northern Ireland's new won status and accept Dublin's sovercignty. The pressure was all the more intense in that in Britain he had to face experienced politicians, skilled in negotiations, and anxious to 'keep the twenty-six counties in the Empire', while in the south tired and inexperienced leaders were fighting for their political lives as

opinion divided over accepting less than a Republic. The threat to
Northern Ireland's position was epitomised in the Anglo-Irish Treaty
which provided for a boundary commission to re-examine the border
between north and south. It was the confident expectation of Nationalists, north and south, that this commission would lead the way to a
united Ireland.

It was all very wearing dealing with 'all these twisters', as Lady Craig
put it, but Craig stood his ground.[24] He remained impervious to the
blandishments of the British Prime Minister, when Lloyd George turned
on the pathetic tap, saying that he might have to resign if the negotiations over the Anglo-Irish treaty broke down on the Ulster Question.
This is how Lady Craig recorded the episode,—L.[loyd] G.[eorge] said
to J.[ames] Craig. This may be a most historical meeting, as I may be
forced to resign. J.[ames] said unsympathetically, 'Is it not wonderful
how many great'men have come to grief over the eternal Irish Question?' [25] He was similarly courteously firm in dealing with the leaders of
the Free State. At the risk of alienating his own followers he met
southern leaders like Michael Collins since, he told his wife, 'No stone
ought to be left unturned to try and stop the murdering that is going on
in Ireland'.[26] As far as Craig was concerned, 'The question is so big that
I have determined to pursue a straight and steady course and to pay as
little attention as possible to those critics who – though well-meaning –
have not been trained in a wider outlook'.[27] He was duly rewarded for
pursuing this 'straight and steady course' for by 1925 the position of
Northern Ireland seemed secure. Peace reigned and the threat to Northern Ireland's borders was finally removed in 1925 when the Boundary
Commission was put to sleep and the Free State recognised the six-
county border. There was much rejoicing among Unionists in Northern
Ireland and Craig was presented by the Northern Ireland Parliament
with a silver Celtic cup, with the words 'Not an Inch' inscribed on the
plinth.

Success or failure

It may seem surprising even to question the success of two men who
challenged Westminster and apparently won – securing the partition of
Ireland and establishing Northern Ireland as a bastion for Ulster Unionists against rule from Dublin. Yet these successes can also be represented as failures when compared with what Craig and Carson had
originally wanted. Indeed the failure was threefold. The original aim
had been to maintain the Union in its entirety – to kill Home Rule
completely and to keep the whole of Ireland within the United Kingdom. For Carson, part of the reason for taking up the Ulster Question

was tactics – a means to defeat Home Rule altogether. He thought that Ulster was the weak point in the Unionist case and that without the economic and financial resources of the north a Home Rule Parliament would be unviable. At least that is how he tried to reassure anxious southern Unionists, 'If Ulster succeeds, Home Rule is dead. Home Rule is impossible for Ireland without Belfast and the surrounding parts as a portion of the scheme . . . In this fight Ulster is the key of the situation. With Ulster strong there need be no fear.'[28] .

The second failure was the fact that not only was Ireland partitioned, but so also was the historic province of Ulster. Unionists from three of the nine counties of the historic province of Ulster, which had sub-scribed to the Solemn League and Covenant, were excluded from Northern Ireland and forced to accept rule from Dublin. The Unionists of Cavan, Donegal, and Monaghan felt bitterly betrayed by the six-counties Unionists, who, they thought, had thrown them to the wolves in an unseemly rush to save themselves. A six-counties Northern Ire-land contained a safe, sixty-six per cent Unionist majority, whereas Unionists would be only fifty-seven per cent of the population in a nine-counties Northern Ireland – giving them only a small majority in Parlia-ment. This narrow margin was unacceptable to the six-counties Unionists. As Craig's brother, Charles, told the House of Commons in 1920, on the second reading of the 1920 Government of Ireland Bill:

No sane man would undertake to carry on a Parliament with [so slender a majority] . . . A couple of Members sick, or two or three Members absent for some accidental reason, might in one evening hand over the entire Ulster Parliament and the entire Ulster position [to the South] . . . A dreadful thing to contemplate.[29]

The third failure was that Ulster Unionists were themselves marginalised in the United Kingdom. It was ironic that having resisted Home Rule for so long, they were themselves obliged to accept a form of Home Rule, which meant that they were only indirectly governed from West-minster. They accepted this position because they knew they had few friends left at Westminster. They knew that if they continued to be ruled directly from Westminster they would be under constant pressure to join a united Ireland. As Charles Craig explained:

We would much prefer to remain part and parcel of the United Kingdom. We have prospered . . . under the Union . . . but we have made many enemies in this country, and we feel that an Ulster without a Parliament of its own would not be in nearly as strong a position as one in which a Parliament had been set up . . . and where

... the paraphernalia of Government was already in existence. We believe that so long as we were without a Parliament of our own constant attacks would be made upon us, and constant attempts would be made ... to draw us into a Dublin Parliament, and that is the last thing in the world that we desire to see happen ... We see our safety, therefore, in having a Parliament of our own ... we prefer to have a Parliament, although we do not want one of our own.[30]

Carson was very well aware of these failures. It is this sense of bitter failure that leaps out from his famous speech in the House of Lords in December 1921, condemning the Anglo-Irish Treaty and lashing out at former friends and colleagues:

> I did not know, as I know now, that I was a mere puppet in a political game. I was in earnest, I was not playing politics. I believed all this. I thought of the last thirty years, during which I was fighting with others, whose friendship and comradeship I hope I will lose from tonight, because I do not value any friendship that is not founded upon confidence and trust. I was in earnest. What a fool I was! I was only a puppet, and so was Ulster, and so was Ireland, in the political game that was to get the Conservative Party into power.[31]

This outburst not only reflected the bitterness of failure, but also the naivety of Carson's politics. Carson always maintained that he was a lawyer first and a politician afterwards, motivated only by a desire to maintain the Union. He disliked politics and in the end was disgusted by them as negating the very virtues on which he placed most value – loyalty, honesty, consistency and truthfulness. Politics for him could never be, as it could for Lloyd George, simply the art of the possible. Nor was the 1920 settlement a glorious triumph for Craig. He became the first Prime Minister of Northern Ireland out of a sense of duty rather than in anticipation of personal fulfilment. He had enjoyed junior office in the Imperial Government and probably would have achieved Cabinet rank, but he sacrificed these opportunities to return to Northern Ireland. His last day at the Admiralty, where he had been a very active financial secretary, was a sad one. In the evening Craig's wife had, 'never seen him so depressed', but he was a man of duty. As he told his wife:

> All my political career has been bound up with Ulster, and this [1920 Government of Ireland] Act is the culmination of all my humble efforts. Was I then to say, Take your Act, I will stay in London, and while you work the Act I will look on. If it was a success I would thank

God for it, but if it broke down and was a failure, after all the efforts of my colleagues and myself, I would go to my grave ashamed if I did not go down with the ship too.[32]

For Craig, too, there was a further failure. He had hoped to establish in Northern Ireland a model government working for all the people all of the time. Instead, Northern Ireland developed into a Protestant State for a Protestant people and today Northern Ireland continues to suffer the consequences of the failure to establish equitable government there. Craig must bear some responsibility for this. Exhausted by his efforts in resisting Home Rule and then defending Northern Ireland against initial onslaughts, he was content to let Northern Ireland drift with no sense of direction and to let the minority question fester. The achievement of Craig and Carson was that they won partition as a way of securing at least part of Ireland for the Union and Unionists, but Craig ultimately failed to do his utmost to ensure the stability and continued existence of the Government and Parliament he in particular had done so much to create.

DIRECT ACTION LAB

SANKEY REPORT

PROFITEERING

IRISH QUESTION

THE SOLUTION.

MR. LLOYD GEORGE. "'DIRECT ACTION'? BY JOVE, THAT'S AN IDEA!"

Punch cartoon of Lloyd George at work on the Irish Question
and other matters, *Punch*, 30 July, 1919.

CHAPTER SIX

British Politics and the Irish Question, 1912–1922
by
George Boyce

Before the introduction of the third Home Rule Bill in April 1912, and the foundation of the Irish Free State in 1922, Irish politics underwent revolutionary changes. One Nationalist political party was replaced by another; southern Unionism disappeared as an effective political force; Ulster Unionism found itself obliged to abandon its battle against Home Rule for the whole of Ireland, and even accept Home Rule for six counties of Ulster; Ireland was portioned. All this is clear. Yet what is often neglected are the changes – which might without exaggeration be called 'revolutionary' – which took place in British politics at the same time, which altered the political landscape of Great Britain, and had important consequences for Ireland as well.This essay traces the connections between developments in British politics and the changing character of the Irish Question; for these British developments helped move the Irish Question from the pre-war political impasse to the settlement of 1922.

Ireland was not always a major preoccupation of British parties. The great excitement of the first Home Rule crisis of 1886, the passionate commitment of W. E. Gladstone to Irish Home Rule, the split in the Liberal Party, and Gladstone's second – and for him, final – attempt to give 'justice to Ireland' in 1893, was followed by a period when the British Conservative and Unionist Party seemed secure in its Irish goals (reform but not Home Rule in Ireland), and when the Liberals were anxious not to find themselves labelled as a 'single issue' party. The decline in Irish interest in Home Rule seemed to offer an opportunity for a different approach to the Irish Question.In 1904 the Conservative/ Unionist Government considered a scheme drawn up by Sir Anthony MacDonnell, the Under-Secretary at Dublin Castle, and Lord Dunraven, to extend the idea of cooperation (which had led to the 'Round Table' conference on the land question in 1903) to politics, through a plan of 'devolution'. This envisaged the creation of a central Irish Council endowed with local autonomy, but was abandoned under fierce Irish

Unionist protest. But the mood of conciliation was abroad, and was reinforced by the desire of the other major British party, the Liberals, to shake off the dead hand of Gladstonian Home Rule. In 1906–7 the Liberals introduced an Irish Councils Bill which was designed to increase Irish participation in local government and administration. But they too met opposition, in their case from the Home Rule Party which held that this was an attempt to deprive Ireland of her rights as a 'nation once again'.[1] Both British parties found themselves damaged by their excursion into the politics of conciliation, yet neither wanted to place Ireland in the forefront of their programmes. In any case the Conservative/Unionists were divided over the tariff reform question, which one of their number described as 'a revolutionary new departure'.[2] And the Liberals, while bearing the burden of Home Rule, made but little mention of it in the general election of 1906.

The crisis over the 'People's Budget' and the reform of the House of Lords between 1909 and 1911 altered the whole atmosphere of British politics. The Conservative/Unionists emerged embittered and betrayed by the Liberal Government's passing of the budget, and still more by the Liberal alliance with the Irish Home Rulers, which, Conservatives held, was a 'corrupt bargain'. Moreover, while Conservatives were prepared to consider a comprehensive reform of the Lords, covering its membership as well as its relationship with the Lower House, they held that the Liberal's removal of the Lords' veto on Commons' legislation was a breach of the constitution: now England had a 'single chamber' tyrannical Government, and one, moreover, that was determined to bring about another major constitutional change – Home Rule – without further reference to the electorate. In these circumstances the Conservatives held that they were released from the usual niceties of British parliamentary life, and when the Liberals introduced their Home Rule Bill in 1912, the Opposition held that it was confronted by a revolutionary Government which aimed at the dismemberment of the United Kingdom. But some Conservatives were uncertain about how this would be received in the country at large. In May 1912 J.S. Sandars, A. J. Balfour's private secretary, noted in his diary that:

> There is no sign of any considerable feeling against the Bill in the country. Welsh disestablishment seems more unpopular. Such are the reports we get. My personal experience rather shows that there is a feeling against Home Rule. We badly want another by-election of two in which we have a chance.[3]

The Conservative Party's uncertainties were revealed in its varying tactics when it sought to play the 'Orange Card'; in the suburbs they stressed the importance of Ireland to the British Empire; in Cornwall and Devon – areas where Methodism was strongly rooted – they stressed the danger of 'Rome'; in the Lancashire cotton districts they warned of the dangers of an Irish Home Rule Parliament erecting customs barriers against English goods.[4] There were also problems for both parties of defining their goals with regard to Ireland. Of course, Conservative/Unionists were defenders of the Union, that was at the root of their identity. Liberals were the inheritors of the Gladstonian Home Rule legacy; that was, whether they liked it or not, central to their identity. But Unionists were divided in what they conceived their central task to be: some wanted to defend the Union, complete and entire; some held that they must place the defence of Unionist Ulster to the fore; others mentioned obligations of honour to the southern Irish Unionists; and there was in the party a federalist group, which argued that the question was wrongly defined as an Irish one, and was really one concerning the reorganisation of the whole United Kingdom on federal lines which would lay the foundations for a federation of the whole British Empire. Moreover, Andrew Bonar Law, who replaced A. J. Balfour as leader of the Conservatives in 1911, was a compromise choice, emerging as leader as the result of a conflict between Walter Long and Austen Chamberlain. Long was a leader of uncompromising language and sharp attacking style, but he led a divided party, and was the unexpected beneficiary of the leadership contest. Much of his career was dedicated to retaining mastery of a factious and divided party, he was, therefore, not in a position to make easy compromises. Asquith, for the Liberals, was unquestioned leader; but not all Liberals were enthusiastic Home Rulers and not all of them wanted to risk serious conflict if some compromise – perhaps over Ulster – might be found. Yet they too were committed to the party battle, had donned their political plumage, and were publicly arrayed in battle against the 'evil' of Conservative/Unionism. The political cartoons of the time spoke volumes: the leading political actors were depicted, according to political taste, as prisoners of the Irish Unionist and Nationalist parties, as men without honour or scruple, as destroyers of Ireland, the United Kingdom and the Empire.

The Conservative/Unionist Party and the Liberal Party joined battle, but meanwhile a new development was taking place which was, in the future, to have an important effect on their perception of how they would respond to the Irish Question. This was the gradual shifting of the centre of activity from Westminster to Ireland; the increasing determination of Ulster Unionists to organise, drill, arm and prepare to act for themselves; and the alarming signs that Westminster was losing control in Ireland, and could no longer be sure of mediating the question. 'The fact is', wrote one Conservative in March 1914, 'that neither the Nationalists nor the Ulstermen want to compromise'.[6] The extreme behaviour of the Conservatives, shown in such desperate moves as considering the amendment of the Annual Army Act (which would thereby deprive Parliament of control over the armed forces of the Crown), and their attack on the Liberals for their alleged 'plot against' Ulster in March 1914, when some regular officers declared their determination to resign rather than march to Ulster, hid a fear that such actions might in the end damage the Conservatives. 'Most of the Whips are against it' (amending the Army Act), wrote J.S. Sandars in March 1914 'and on the whole the feeling in the party is against it'. He added, however, that 'the one strong point is that it must force an election, and it is rather hard to see how to force one otherwise'.[7] The Curragh incident placed the party in ever deeper dilemmas. Here was a fine opportunity to accuse the Government of plotting to provoke conflict with the Ulster Unionists; yet the party 'did not approve' Law's reference to 'the right of soldiers under certain circumstances to disobey', because it 'gave the other side an opening'.[8]

The Liberal plight was equally real. In Parliament the Liberals seemed determined to hold steadily to the course of placing Home Rule on the statute book, and thus fulfilling the Gladstonian policy of ignoring any special consideration for Unionist Ulster. But the first tabled amendment to the bill, to exclude from its operation the counties of Armagh, Antrim, Down and Londonderry, came from a Liberal M.P., Agar-Robartes; yet the Government's decision to examine seriously possibilities of an exclusion option was taken too late, since the 1911 Parliament Act required Opposition agreement to any amendments in the last two parliamentary circuits. If the Government could not legislate to deal with the Ulster difficulty, then it might use the ultimate argument of force; but this – described by one usually fair minded Conservative peer as 'Russian methods', unacceptable to British public opinion[9] – was rendered impossible by the Curragh incident. Just as the Government forfeited its military option, the Ulster Volunteer Force found itself armed and ready to defy the Liberals' authority. So by May 1914 the Liberal Government was dependent for a settlement upon the Opposition's agreement; yet the Conservative/Unionist Opposition was in no mood to concede, since it was increasingly certain that it was driving the Liberals into the corner, where they must call an election, or risk civil war.[10]

On 25 May 1914 the Home Rule Bill, still in its original form, passed the third reading in the House of Commons. The position remained deadlocked. Yet there were Conservative/Unionists who thought that there must be a compromise, and that it must be made on Ulster. A.J. Balfour believed that this was the way forward; and Sir Edward Carson warned that even if the Unionists won a general election, they would find Ireland difficult to govern. The Duke of Devonshire suggested that if Home Rule were carried with the exclusion of Ulster, then the

southern Unionist would not suffer 'because the Home Rule Parliament would be on its good behaviour in order to induce Ulster to come
in eventually'.[11] But the party was equally anxious about the effect any
compromise would have on its morale and unity: 'The fear with our
people is as to the effect on our supporters in the country of anything
like abandonment of opposition to every sort of Home Rule'.[12] Austen
Chamberlain, for his part, thought that the exclusion of Ulster was
'almost the worst solution that is possible – certainly the worst solution
short of civil war', advocating instead a federal united Kingdom.[13]

On 23 June 1914 the Government introduced an Amending Bill to
the Home Rule Bill in the House of Commons, offering the option for
any of the six Ulster Counties which now form Northern Ireland to opt
out of the Bill's operation (an offer first made on 9 March). This might
form the basis of negotiation; but it would require the Opposition's
assent, and from 21 to 24 July 1914 the Government and Opposition
entered a last minute conference to explore the possibility of a negotiated settlement. The Buckingham Palace Conference failed to resolve
the question of the area to be excluded; and there was in any event an
air of unreality about its deliberations, since neither party felt that it
could afford to compromise; and since their respective Irish allies certainly would not compromise. This sense of frustration was felt in some
Government circles, for on 22 July Winston Churchill and Lord Grey
urged that a 'British decision' be imposed on the two warring Irish
factions; but this would only open further dissent among the Liberals,
because many would feel that Redmond was being badly treated.[14] A
'British solution' would only come, if at all, when the British parties
were in a position to distance themselves from the Irish parties, abandon their bitter party strife, and feel sure that any such solution would
not jeopardise their own party unity still further.

The outbreak of war was greeted with some relief by Asquith, for at
least it meant that the Government would avoid civil war or a damaging
retreat from its Home Rule policy. But even then the struggle was not
over. On 3 August John Redmond made a pledge of Irish Nationalist
cooperation in the war. He was anxious that he should not find himself
compromised: 'I took great risks', he told Asquith, Lloyd George and
Churchill. 'If the Home Rule Bill is postponed my people will say they
are sold'.[15] Asquith felt that the Government must press on and meet
Redmond's demand that the Bill be made law, and he could now do so
in the growing certainty that the political balance was shifting to his
advantage. Ireland was a keen supporter of the war; Britain needed
Nationalist support for the war effort; and the Unionists were still
divided over what kind of compromise they would find acceptable: 'I
could never follow Bonar Law in accepting the present Government of

Ireland Bill with the complete exclusion of the six Ulster counties as a final settlement of the Irish constitutional question (even if I thought it would work, which I don't)', wrote Lord Selborne to Austen Chamberlain on 12 August, 'and I cannot conceive it possible that Redmond either should accept it as a final settlement'.[16] Moreover, Carson had always demanded the exclusion of the whole of Ulster; any abandonment of three counties now might split the Ulster Unionists and – more dangerously – the UVF, some of whose members would be left on the wrong side of the exclusion line.[17]

Asquith postponed his decision for as long as possible, but on 31 August he announced that the Home Rule Bill would be placed on the statute book, and an Amending Bill, dealing with the Ulster problem, would be considered as well. Unionists knew that to obstruct the passage of the Home Rule Bill would be to place them wholly in the wrong in the eyes of British public opinion and they would be branded as unpatriotic. They watched helplessly as Asquith moved towards his resolution of the dilemma. The Home Rule Bill would become law, there would be no specific exclusion of Ulster or of Ulster counties, but the Home Rule Bill would be suspended from operation and an amending bill dealing with Ulster in some unspecified way would accompany the Bill to the statute book. The Opposition was outraged and Carson warned that the battle against Home Rule would be joined again, when circumstances permitted. Asquith was accused of having used the war emergency to force through a policy would otherwise have been contested to the very end.[18]

The Home Rule Bill became law on 15 September 1914. And, while in retrospect it might seem but an empty victory for Redmond and Asquith, it was – as Unionists acknowledged – a major defeat for the Unionist cause. There could be no going back from the point now reached; there could be no realistic possibility of saving the Union from some kind of Irish self-government, however, qualified. The Liberals had fulfilled their Gladstonian destiny and they did so because they reckoned that it would be more costly for them to deny Redmond his prize than to seek a compromise with the Opposition. Britain needed Nationalist Ireland and Redmond took advantage of this stark truth to press home his demand. The cost was, however, considerable, for both British political parties went into the war convinced of each other's duplicity and insincerity.

II

Once this controversy died down, and normal political activity was suspended, the concentration of the Government, the Opposition and the whole United Kingdom was naturally directed towards winning the war. This was in the end to have a vital significance for Ireland, though at the time nothing seemed further from the British or Irish political horizons. In May 1915 Asquith, under increasing criticism for his unsatisfactory conduct of the war, felt obliged to offer the Unionist Opposition a place in a new Coalition Government. The Unionists were by no means certain of gaining any advantages from accepting such an arrangement, but once again, as in September 1914, they could not appear unpatriotic, and so must accept the Liberals' offer. Carson joined the Cabinet; Redmond was offered a place, but declined. This was a natural response of every Irish Nationalist leader since the heroic days of C.S. Parnell; political purity must be preserved. Yet it was to prove a costly mistake on Redmond's part, for he was soon to be in that most unenviable of positions: that of criticising the Government upon which he depended for the satisfaction of his demands. There were other important stresses in the apparently united front which the Government of the United Kingdom presented to the world. Coalition was not fusion; the parties were not blended, but merely yoked together. They were still deeply suspicious of each other's motives. And there was no issue more likely to lay bare this suspicion than the Irish Question which – quite against everyone's expectations – burst upon the British political world again, and in more acute form, in the Easter Rising of 1916.

The immediate reaction in the Government to the Rising was that it represented the 'usual Irish tragic comic opera', and that the feeble and discredited administration of Dublin Castle, headed by the 'scandalous' Augustine Birrell (the Irish Chief Secretary) must be reformed.[19] But the swift action of General Maxwell in rounding up and executing the rebel ringleaders pushed the Cabinet into further action. Asquith now saw what he believed was the chance to meet foreign, and especially American, criticism, of the execution of the Rebels, and turn the tide decisively against any recrudescence of Irish separatism. A settlement could be hammered out, and Asquith requested Lloyd George to undertake direct negotiations with Carson for the Unionists, and Redmond for the Nationalists, to produce a settlement. Lloyd George negotiated between 23 May and 8 June, seeing the respective Irish leaders separately, and drawing up a draft settlement which they each felt they could recommend to their parties. His plan was for the immediate implementation of the 1914 Home Rule Act, with an Amending Act to exclude the six counties which now form Northern Ireland. Irish MPs would continue to sit at Westminster, and an Imperial Conference would be called after the war to decide the final constitutional future of Ireland, considering in particular the question of final arrangements for the six counties. Lloyd George dealt with this delicate problem through a subtle use of words. On 29 May he assured Carson that 'we must make it clear that at the end of the provisional period Ulster does not, whether she wills it or not, merge in the rest of Ireland'. This was not a promise of permanent exclusion, but rather – if it was anything at all – it amounted to a promise of no automatic inclusion. The final settlement of the Ulster difficulty was still to be resolved. Redmond accepted this version of the arrangement; that exclusion was still to be settled. Carson placed more emphasis on the words 'Ulster . . . does not . . . merge in the rest of Ireland'. But the document drawn up by Lloyd George indicates that exclusion was indeed to be finally decided upon at the Imperial conference, when there would be 'the permanent settlement of all the great outstanding problems, such as the permanent position of the exempted counties, the question of finance and other problems'. This, indeed, was why Irish MPs must be retained at Westminster in their full strength, despite Ireland's having immediate Home Rule.[20] This plan was revealed to a small Cabinet committee, consisting of Asquith, Lord Crewe, Lord Lansdowne, and Walter Long on 1 June. Lansdowne and Long protested that it contradicted the Prime Minister's original opinion, expressed on 21 May, that there could be no immediate implementation of the 1914 Home Rule Act. But they did not yet press their opposition.[21]

Lloyd George, perhaps encouraged by their acceptance of his negotiations so far, pressed on to his idea of an immediate implementation of the Home Rule Act, and, moreover, appears to have given Redmond and Carson the impression that his plan was not approved by the Cabinet as a whole. When the scheme was made public, after 10 June, Long and Lansdowne began to concert their opposition to it, and were joined by Lord Selborne, but the plan was supported by Bonar Law, Balfour and F.E. Smith. The Southern Unionists roused themselves to thwart the settlement, with the Earl of Midleton urging Lord Selborne not to be 'a party to this fiasco. We shall fight it to the death'.[22] On 15 June 1916 Walter Long presented two long memoranda on the issue, claiming that Lloyd George had exceeded his brief, which did not involve the immediate implementation of Home Rule in Ireland.[23] But the Unionists were deeply divided over the plan, as a backbench meeting held on 22 June revealed, and there were those who held that the key issue was not the safeguarding of Ulster (Carson's chief aim), but the 'standpoint' of England.[24] With a divided Unionist Party, and a united Liberal Party, Asquith seemed on the verge of success. Law stood firm for the settlement; Selborne had resigned; Long and Lansdowne alone opposed the plan. In these circumstances, Asquith was prepared to make some concession to Unionist fears, and at a Cabinet meeting on 27 June it was agreed that a small sub-committee should be formed to examine the question of safeguards in military and naval matters. On 5 July the Cabinet as a whole accepted these safeguards, Redmond swallowed them as well. Asquith described the situation to the King as 'very satisfactory'.[25]

Agreement on the Lloyd George plan was destroyed by Lord Lansdowne's speech in Parliament on 11 July 1916. Lansdowne insisted that a bill to deal with safeguards and the Ulster Question would 'make structural alterations in the Home Rule Act of 1914', and would make exclusion of a 'permanent and enduring character'. This swept aside the ambiguity which both Carson and Redmond had lived with since negotiations were first undertaken by Lloyd George in May. On 19 July the Cabinet agreed that, 'Sir E. Carson's claim for the definitive exclusion of Ulster could not be resisted'.[26] Negotiations were finally abandoned on 27 July; they were destroyed, not by the partition question as such, but by Unionist opposition to the whole settlement plan, opposition which threatened the unity of the Unionist Party, and threatened therefore the Cabinet and the whole war effort. This, however, revealed how much the political landscape was moving on the Irish Question. Before the war, the battle was one of Unionist versus Liberal; now the battle was one of Unionist versus Unionist. If the battle could be resolved, then indeed there might be an agreed Irish settlement. For the moment an Irish settlement was the last thing the Government wanted to think about. The war must be won; Ireland must not stand in the way. But it soon became clear that if the war were to be won, then Ireland must be taken up again, and efforts made to settle it, or at least to indicate that the Government wanted a settlement. Separatist Nationalism was beginning to threaten John Redmond's grip on Ireland. The Dominions pressed Lloyd George for an initiative on Ireland and the American decision to enter the war, on the allied side in April 1917 forced the issue.

The idea of an Irish Convention which would allow the Irish parties to meet and reach agreement among themselves was an attractive one. It would split no British party; it would occupy no valuable Cabinet time. The idea had been around since the end of 1916, and Redmond, desperate for some movement on the issue, accepted the notion of a convention on 15 May. But the previous four months' confusion in Government policy – when the Cabinet threshed around for an Irish policy, now supporting the idea of an Imperial conference and now plumping for the old expedient of 'county option' – was hardly encouraging.[27] There was little sign of any move towards agreement among the Irish parties and, equally important, little sign that the Government really wanted to become deeply involved in Irish affairs, especially with its Unionist members of the Coalition still divided and sensitive after the failure of the 1916 negotiations.

While the Irish Convention sat, the Government could enjoy a welcome respite from Ireland. But when it began to move towards some kind of agreed plan, with southern Unionists and Irish Home Rulers working together, then the Government must again respond to the new developments. The problem was that British Unionists had to square two separate, but closely related problems. They had their allies in the north and south of Ireland, but if one set of allies broke with another – as they did in the Convention – then British Unionists had to redefine their response. At the same time, British Unionists had to consider their own party unity, always in jeopardy over Ireland, and of course the wider concerns of the war effort. Would an Irish settlement help or hinder the war? Was the risk acceptable, or would it prove too dangerous not only to the war but to the party?

These issues surfaced as soon as the southern Unionists and Redmondites seemed on the point of reaching agreement over Home Rule and a fiscal settlement whereby Dublin could have excise duties, but the more lucrative customs duties would remain with Westminster. Lloyd George now put pressure on the Ulster Unionists to seize the opportunity for an agreed solution. British Unionists found themselves in a dilemma once again, with the old fear of 'Ireland the enemy' aroused – an Ireland, moreover, with a Parliament and executive of its own. In their extremity, some Unionists now began to take up the idea of a federal United Kingdom, which had first been suggested before the war, and which now found increasing favour as a means of reconciling Irish Nationalists, Ulster Unionists, and the constitutional integrity of the United Kingdom. Carson was won over to the federal principle; the *Observer* newspaper, inspired by its editor J.L. Garvin, acted as the chief propagandist for the federalists, ably assisted by F.S. Oliver, a businessman and political pamphleteer. The federal discussion revealed that the British political world was indeed in the process of great change. Austen Chamberlain and Lord Selborne had always been favourably inclined towards a federal plan. But now they were joined by Walter Long, who enjoyed much support among Irish and British Unionists alike.[28]

The German offensive of March 1918, which threatened the collapse of the allied western front, revealed yet again that the Irish Question could act as a damaging and embittering influence on British politics. There had been rows amongst Unionists over the failure of the British Government to extend conscription to Ireland when it was first introduced into Great Britain in 1916. In January 1917 Lord Derby warned Lloyd George that, 'When we are putting all this pressure on English labour to find men for the Army, you are sure to get a cry as to why should England provide it, and Ireland not contribute its proper share'.[29]

When Lloyd George announced on 9 April 1918 that military conscription would be extended to Ireland by Order in Council, he declared also that the Government intended, as a result of the Convention majority vote in favour of Home Rule, to invite Parliament 'to pass or introduce a measure of self-government in Ireland'.[30] This only plunged the Coalition into deeper difficulties. Some Unionists, like Lord Robert Cecil, opposed Irish Home Rule, but acknowledged that 'its only chance of success would be to carry it with conscription by a rush as a war measure'.[31] But there were Unionists who held fast to the idea that Home Rule must not be conceded to a disaffected Ireland, and threatened to break the Government rather than the Unionist Party.[32]

The war Cabinet nonetheless decided to press forward with the conscription/Home Rule policy, but only encountered further dissension, with some Liberals, such as H.A.L.Fisher and Christopher Addison, objecting to Irish conscription.[33] Unionists remained divided, not only in the party but throughout the country, with much support for the Ulster Unionists being expressed.[34] It was small wonder, then, that the Government escaped from the consequences of its own policies by discovering a 'German plot' to assist another rebellion in Ireland. It abandoned Home Rule, and sought recruits from Ireland by the voluntary system, while warning Ireland that it still retained the power to impose conscription if all else failed. Meanwhile, Lord French was sent to Ireland to govern her by military means, which even the normally broad minded F.S. Oliver described as 'the way which had always suited her best'.[35]

British politics seemed then to stand in 1918 where they stood in 1914. There was no settlement of the Irish Question, no operation of the Home Rule Act, no resolution of the Ulster Question. And yet this was not really the case. The split in the Liberal Party between supporters of Lloyd George and those of Asquith (which had existed since Lloyd George replaced Asquith as Prime Minister in December 1916) was perpetuated in the spring of 1918 and the way was prepared for the wartime Coalition to campaign for its extension in a new appeal to the people. It was expected that this election would be held during the war, which it was believed would continue into 1919 or perhaps even 1920. The Unionists agreed to adhere to the Coalition; and this involved them in the purpose of the Coalition enterprise, which was to contain radical or 'bolshevik' movements in the United Kingdom, and to bring to bear on post war problems a combined political strategy. On 12 November 1918 Bonar Law told members of his party that the responsibility for dealing with Ireland lay with the Coalition Government of which the Unionists were full members.[36]

The way was cleared for the Irish Question to be taken out of the contentious field of party politics, and moved into the neutral ground of problem-solving administration. The 1918 general election resulted in the return to Parliament of 322 Coalition Unionists, 132 Coalition Liberals and 22 Labour MPs. In addition there were 52 sympathetic but 'non-coupon' Unionists, and 16 uncouponed Liberals, all of which gave Lloyd George's Government a possible total of 554 supporters.[37] The political security of the Coalition, combined with the new mood, and a recognition that certain pre-war issues must be wound up, so that new problems might be tackled, encouraged the Coalition to act in a non-partisan way when it came to Irish policy. The result was an extraordinary reversal of the pre-war political roles of, in particular, Conservative/ Unionist politicians. Walter Long chaired the Cabinet's Irish sub-committee, which produced a report advocating a Home Rule Parliament for Dublin and another for Belfast ('Southern' and 'Northern' Ireland respectively), with a Council of Ireland to act as a bridge between them to deal with matters of common concern, and, possibly eventual reunification. Bonar Law chaired the committee meeting on 17 February 1920 which originally advocated, not a six-county, but a nine-county Northern Ireland, because a six county state would be permanently divisive. Law hoped that the northern Parliament would act as an inducement to the south to work its own legislature, for when it began to function then the rest of Ireland would see 'the evidence that they can have the same self-government the moment they like', and then 'the motives of the south and west must be to get Ireland united'.[38]

There was an equally remarkable spectacle of a Cabinet led by a Liberal Prime Minister, and containing Liberal members, supporting, or acquiescing in, a policy of coercion of Nationalist Ireland to oblige Sinn Fein (the victors in the 1918 general election in most of Ireland) to accept and work the 1920 Government of Ireland Act. But Liberals had a tradition of meeting Irish violence with coercion, as Gladstone had met it in the 1880s: law and order must be restored and the constitutional principle asserted. It is certain that neither Gladstone nor his colleagues would have found themselves comfortable with the Black and Tans, yet they were meant to constitute a less repressive policy than full-blooded martial law, those 'methods' of Sir John French that S.S. Oliver had found acceptable in 1918. In his autobiography, published in 1940, H.A.L. Fisher noted that, while he assented to the Black and Tans only with 'cruel misgivings', it was a policy that frustrated the Irish Republican gunmen and made a 'powerful section' of them 'ready to treat', but it is more likely that the Liberals simply accepted the drift to half-hearted coercion,[39] and certainly by the time the campaign of violence was in full swing, Fisher, Edward Short, Edwin Montagu, and Christopher Addison were prepared to see the Nationalists offered something like dominion status with control of customs and income tax.[40]

When finally the British Government took the advantage of a conciliatory speech by the King on the occasion of the opening of the Northern Ireland Parliament on 22 June, the advantages of a non-partisan, cross-party approach to the Irish Questions were soon to be demonstrated. Lloyd George needed all his considerable negotiating skill to bring Sinn Féin to the conference table, and then to induce them to accept what he first offered in August (Dominion Status with safeguards). This formed the basis of the Anglo-Irish Treaty which he obliged the Irish plenipotentiaries to sign on 6 December 1921. But his hand was strengthened by his domestic political position, there would be no danger of the disaster of 1916, when the Unionists had divided. over his attempted settlement, and brought it to ruin.

There were still some stresses in Unionist ranks, which came to the surface when in November 1921 Lloyd George, having brought Arthur Griffith to the point of accepting the offer of dominion status with safeguards for British defence, began to bring pressure to bear on the Government of Northern Ireland to exchange the sovereignty of Westminster for that of Dublin. Craig seems to have at first accepted this in principle. On 8 November one Conservative/Unionist noted that, 'James Craig has been consulted and is ready to do what he can, but doubts whether his people will accept any such terms. If there is an absolute deadlock, the Government will resign'.[41] The evidence for Craig's attitude is inconclusive, but Craig's malleability in later negotiations with the British Government (in particular, in the 1938 Anglo-Irish Agreements) would seem to indicate that indeed he could be induced to see what British Government regarded as reason'.[42] When Craig's Cabinet and party indignantly repudiated the Lloyd George plan, then the Unionist Party seemed once again to be about to enter an Irish crisis. Bonar Law threatened to return to lead the 'diehards' in the Conservative/Unionist party who not only supported Ulster, but also disliked the whole principle of negotiations with Sinn Féin. But this latter turned out to be their weakness, rather than their strength. For while the Lloyd George pressure on Unionist Ulster might indeed provoke some British Unionists to recall the good old cause, the bulk of the party, and the country, did not want the Lloyd George negotiations to break down irrevocably. Moreover, the Conservative/Unionist Party rank and file were, many of them 'new men' who had not learnt their politics in the heat of the Irish Question, and had no wish to do so. Thomas Jones, Lloyd George's confidant reckoned that only about 80 Coalition members had sat in Parliament before 1910. 'We are dealing with a new House. They have not lived through the struggle; they are only concerned about finance and trade'.[43] The Conservative leadership, ably marshalled by Lord Birkenhead, were obliged to work hard behind the scenes to ensure that the Government's Irish policy received the approval of the party's annual conference held in Liverpool. The 'die hards' were persuaded to withdraw their resolutions, 'except a mild one' and the Government's supporters 'blessed' the Irish talks. 'Liverpool', wrote one Conservative, 'was a great success'. It was creditable to the Conservative Party. The speeches were not bitter, and all were most anxious to avoid a split'. On 8 December, two days after the Anglo-Irish Treaty was signed, the same diarist noted: 'Ireland squared and nearly everyone happy'.[44]

The 'nearly everyone' did not include Sir Edward Carson who, on 14 December 1921, made a brilliant but destructive attack on the Anglo-Irish Treaty. Carson's speech reflected, not only his disappointment at the break-up of the Union, but the changed circumstances in which Irish and Ulster Unionists were now living. His scorn was especially reserved for Lord Birkenhead, whom Carson dismissed as typical of the 'loathsome' politicians who used a cause to climb the ladder to power, and then kicked that ladder away once they had reached the top. This same Birkenhead had acted as Carson's Aide de Camp in a pre-war UVF review parade. Now he was describing the 'die-hards' as people whose time had come – and gone.[45] The Irish settlement was by no means popular with all rank and file Unionists, and the continuing violence in Ireland, the efforts of the Provisional Government of the Irish Free State to draft a more 'Republican' constitution, and the IRA challenge to the Treaty and its signatories, all put stresses and strains on the Coalition. But the Coalition was not to be dislodged from its adherence to the united front towards Ireland that it had managed to present in the Treaty negotiations. There was no going back to 1914, or 1916.

The 'bipartisan' approach of the Coalition was nowhere better illustrated than in its attitude to the new Northern Ireland state that it had established in 1920–21. From the moment the Government initiated talks with representatives of Sinn Féin, its policy towards the Northern Ireland Government became more ambivalent. This ambivalence was reflected in its attitude to the security and public order problem in the north. The British Government desperately wanted the Irish Free State to become stabilised, for the sake of the wider British and Imperial interest. Thus it wanted to avoid anything that would give Dublin an excuse for breaking the letter or the spirit of the Treaty. In any case, the contending parties in the south might reasonably hope to unite in their opposition to the Border. The Government, with a few notable exceptions, had little understanding of the difficulties facing the Unionist Government, and wished to distance itself as far as possible from

Northern Ireland's law and order problems – and solutions.[46] The connection between the Ulster problem and the desire of the British Government for the Free State to conform to the constitutional principles of the Treaty was revealed in May 1922. The new Free State constitution proved so unsatisfactory to the British in respect of acknowledgement of the Crown and membership of the Empire that the British even considered reimposing Crown Colony Government. But Lloyd George warned his Cabinet colleagues that the crisis required careful handling, because it coincided with an IRA incursion into the north in the 'Pettigo triangle', a narrow strip of land on the boundary between north and south. British troops were used to drive out the insurgents, but Lloyd George pointed out that the Cabinet must not break with the Free State Government over Ulster, because there would be:

> a shout of approval tomorrow if immediate action were taken, but . . . the shouters themselves would give the most trouble three months hence; their tenacity would ooze out, and they would turn to criticise the Government's methods and charge them with being too gentle here or blundering there . . . He strongly urged that they should take such steps as would eliminate the Ulster issue and leave a clean issue of 'Republic' versus British Empire.[47]

'Let us keep on the high ground of the Treaty – the Crown, the Empire', wrote Lloyd George to Churchill. 'There we are unassailable. But if you come down from that height and fight in the swamps of Lough Erne you will be overwhelmed'.[48] No wonder that Sir James Craig believed that his presence was needed in London, since 'after every conference [of Imperial ministers] with the members of the southern delegation, it is necessary for me to supply a corrective, otherwise action on our behalf is delayed'.[49]

In the event, the Free State produced a constitution acceptable to the British, and by the time it was incorporated into statute law, and received the Royal assent, on 5 December 1922, the Lloyd George Coalition had fallen, and Andrew Bonar Law was Prime Minister of a Conservative Government. It was symptomatic of the change that had taken place in British politics since 1914 that the transition occurred without in any way jeopardising the Anglo-Irish Treaty. The Coalition had disappeared, but the spirit that made its Irish policy between 1918 and 1921 remained, and, for that matter, continued into the foreseeable future. Thus it was appropriate that the 'revolution in Ireland' between 1914 and 1922 should begin, and end, with a British Act of Parliament, as the British parties managed, through the pressures first of war, and then of peace, to remove the Irish question and its damaging impact from domestic British politics.

Nationalist demonstration in Belfast, 1912 *Illustrated London News*, 11 February 1912

CHAPTER SEVEN

Northern Nationalists, Ulster Unionists and the Development of Partition 1900–21.
by
Eamon Phoenix

The re-emergence of Home Rule as a burning political question occurred at a time when Irish men and women, regardless of party outlook, were more highly politicised than ever before. The Third Reform Act of 1884 had extended the vote to the agricultural labourer and urban worker alike. This act was to pave the way for both an Orange and a Green political resurgence in Ireland.

Until the emergence of Home Rule as a live issue in the 1880s, Protestant voters in the north had been divided into supporters of the two main British political parties, Conservative and Liberal, while a small section of extreme loyalists identified with Orangeism. Most Ulster Catholics, on the other hand, tended to support the Home Rule Party of Charles Stewart Parnell, particularly from 1885 when Parnellites captured 17 of the province's 33 seats. But as the tar-barrels blazed in West Belfast and other Nationalist strongholds at this signal triumph, the mass of Ulster Protestants were determined to thwart any attempt by the Liberal Prime Minister, William Gladstone to grant Ireland self-government.

Parnell's dramatic electoral victory finally convinced the 'Grand Old Man' of the essential justness of the Home Rule cause. His first Home Rule Bill of 1886 failed, however, in the teeth of a combined 'Unionist' opposition in the House of Commons. A second bill in 1893 was thrown out by the Tory-dominated House of Lords which now became the greatest obstacle to Nationalist aspirations.

The more dramatic result of the Home Rule Crisis in the north of Ireland was the revival of the Orange Order. Formed in north Armagh in 1795 against a background of sectarian faction-fighting, the Order's sectarian overtones had tended to repel the better-off during the nineteenth century. From 1880s the gentry and middle-class returned to its banner, realising its potential as a powerful cross-class alliance against an all-Ireland Home Rule scheme. Led by the redoubtable Cavan landlord, and Unionist MP, Colonel Edward Saunderson, the Ulster Unionists declared their determination to use force rather than submit to 'Rome Rule'[1]. In their campaign against an Irish Parliament, the northern loyalists were assured of the powerful support of the British Conservative Party, now re-named the 'Unionist Party'.

From 1885, therefore, until the Treaty settlement of 1921, the 'Union' was the single dominating issue in Irish politics. Apart from a faithful band of Protestant Home Rulers centred around the fearless Presbyterian divine, Rev.J.B. Armour of Ballymoney, the mass of Ulster – and indeed Irish – Protestants took their stand against any form of Home Rule.[2]

The Parnellite Split of 1890–91 led to the break-up of the party he had welded into a disciplined phalanx. The next decade was to witness a bitter 'civil war' within the Home Rule movement. Such internecine feuding, together with the Conservatives' long ascendancy at Westminster (from 1895–1905) ensured that the Home Rule Question was placed firmly on the 'back burner' of British politics.

Conservative Governments, meanwhile, sought to undermine the popular groundswell for Home Rule by a policy of 'kindness'. The policy was always doomed to failure but two of its fruits deserve special mention. The Local Government Act of 1898 swept away the old landlord-oriented 'Grand Juries' and placed local power in the hands of the people. A second measure of revolutionary significance was the Wyndham Land Purchase Act of 1903. By enabling the tenants to buy out their farms, this measure amounted to a bloodless social revolution and finally solved the vexed Land Question.

The ending of the period of Conservative rule coincided with the reunification of the various strands of constitutional Nationalism under the chairmanship of John E.Redmond. Redmond, a Wexford barrister and unrepentant Parnellite, believed passionately in the concept of 'Home Rule within the Empire'. His early career as a clerk in the House of Commons had instilled in him a deep attachment to the British parliamentary tradition. As Dennis Gwynn has observed in the first sentence of his life of Redmond, 'John Redmond's entire life was centred in the House of Commons.'[3] As such, he was strongly opposed to the separatist stirrings which marked the dawn of the new century. The Gaelic League had from the 1890s steadily promoted the idea of a separate Irish cultural nation. Of a similar stamp was Arthur Griffith's tiny Sinn Féin party whose novel policy of an Anglo-Irish 'dual monarchy' even attracted some northern Protestants like the essayist Robert Lynd. In the background too flickered the 'Fenian Flame' of the militantly separatist Irish Republican Brotherhood.

The Irish Parliamentary Party, however, still reigned supreme.

Redmond's co-leaders in the regenerated movement were the astute John Dillon, former leader of the anti-Parnellites and the young Ulster barman turned journalist 'Wee Joe' Devlin. Devlin was the most significant Nationalist politician to emerge in the north during the first half of the Twentieth Century. Born in 1872 into a working-class family in West Belfast, he rose from humble beginnings as a pot-boy in a local public house to become a Home Rule MP and finally, in 1903, holder of the key post of general secretary of the United Irish League (UIL), the main organisation of the Irish Parliamentary Party. For the next thirty years, Devlin's name was synonymous with northern Catholic politics. Small and thick-set with a large head, coal-black hair and a deep resonant voice with the hard intonations of his native city, he had emerged in the strife-ridden 1890's as the leader of the Dillonite 'Irish National Federation' in Belfast and a superb organiser. He soon gained a reputation as a combative and captivating orator, skilled in the cut and thrust of political debate. Moreover as a later Sinn Féin critic put it, 'No man knew Nationalist Ulster, its conditions and particularly its prejudices better than Mr Devlin.'[4] His standing in the reunited Irish Parliamentary Party (IPP) was further enhanced by a series of fund-raising tours in the United States and Australasia during 1902–06. For some 12 years from 1904 till 1916, this 'pocket Demosthenes' (as his enemy T.M.Healy once dubbed him) dominated the Ulster Nationalist scene by the sheer weight of his personality and consummate political intellect.

Devlin was actuated by a fixed hatred of dissent within the Home Rule ranks. Along with John Dillon he was an opponent of the moderate Nationalist, William O'Brien's policy of conciliation towards the landlord element. Already in the early 1900s, he had shown a characteristic ruthlessness in crushing the 'Belfast Catholic Association', the political machine of the local bishop, Dr Henry Henry. His hostility to Henry's clericalist party was influenced by two factors: the first was the potential threat which such a 'factionist' vehicle posed to the official party in Belfast, but another was undoubtedly the close identification of Nationalism with Catholicism which the BCA seemed to portray.[5]

Devlin's growing ascendancy was cemented in 1906 when he captured the 'cock-pit' of West Belfast from the Conservatives by the narrow margin of 16 votes. His success in that election was partly due to an unwritten pact between Devlin, T.H.Sloan, the radical Independent Orange leader, and the Labourite William Walker. Devlin, always a populist, declared the Belfast contests 'a fight of the workers and toilers against intrigues, political machines and combinations'. Both Devlin and Sloan were elected in what was the greatest reverse ever sustained by official Unionism in the city.[6] It was this peculiar blend of populism and Nationalism which marked Devlin off from the rest of the Home Rule leadership and especially Dillon who feared that social innovation would undermine the demand for self-government.[7] Devlin's rise to power, however, was closely associated with the revival of the Ancient Order of Hibernians, a sectarian secret society which he converted into a personal power-base within the Home Rule movement after 1905.

The AOH traced its historical origins to the Defenders, an agrarian banditti which surfaced in Ulster in the 1790s as a sectarian corollary to Orangeism. As such it fed on the intrinsic religious bitterness which characterised rural parts of the province. It saw its role as twofold -to give protection to both the Roman Catholic faith and the Roman Catholic population in Ireland. In a real sense therefore, the 'Hibs' claimed, 'to do for the Catholic community what the Orange Order claimed to do for the Protestants.'[8] Given the traditional importance of the religious factor in Ulster politics, the AOH provided Devlin with a potential power-base.The United Irish League, with its essentially agrarian programme, had little appeal in the industrial north-east. Devlin shrewdly realised that a revived AOH, firmly harnessed to the Home Rule movement, could provide the social cement that the IPP badly needed in Ulster.

In 1905, he established the Board of Erin as the controlling council of the organisation with himself as national president, a post he retained until his death in 1934. In his cultivation of the expanding order, Devlin was assisted by his close ally Bishop Patrick O'Donnell of Raphoe who succeeded in persuading the Hierarchy to lift its long standing ban on Hibernianism.The attraction of the AOH was partly increased by the National Insurance Act of 1911 and by 1915, it was strong within most 'chapel areas' particularly in Ulster and, with 122,000 members, formed the grassroots of the Nationalist Party in the north of Ireland. Devlin's control of the AOH, 'Molly Maguire's' to their Nationalist critics, has led to the somewhat distorted image of the Ulster Home Rule leader as a 'ghetto boss', assiduously cultivating an atavistic sectarian vote.This view however, is unfair to a politician who, despite his shortcomings, did much to improve the lot of the Catholic and Protestant working-classes of Belfast.

The truth is that he was, in some ways like his great adversaries, Craig and Carson, an enigmatic figure. As the leading Nationalist in Ulster during the period 1902-18, it was inevitable that his speciality should be in organising and 'getting out' the Catholic vote, especially in West Belfast, which, after 1906, became 'virtually his own little kingdom'. This role however, which is really a reflection of his strong sense of political pragmatism, given the realities of the time, does not detract from his deep-seated hostility to every form of religious intolerance.

His own humble origins, his personal experience of the bitter sectarian rioting in Belfast in 1886, and the leavening effect of his travels in America and Australasia had convinced him of the common interests of the Protestant and Catholic working-classes. Moreover, his proletarian apprenticeship left its imprint in a sharpened social conscience, which did not go unregarded amongst sections of the Belfast Protestant working-classes. Devlin was not a Socialist but he inveighed against the social evils of unemployment, sweated labour and insanitary housing conditions, and saw state intervention as the only solution. His successful exposure of the sweated conditions in the Belfast linen mills resulted in the application of the Trade Boards Act to the industry with a consequent improvement in the lot of the workers.[9] Indeed, it was a criterion of his uniqueness in Irish politics in the twentieth century, that he evoked a genuine affection and admiration that transcended class or creed. He was a tireless worker for all the Belfast working-classes, and was remembered for his total accessibility to supporters of every party. In the words of his political adversary, James Craig, with whom he had a good personal rapport, 'he was ... an outstanding figure beyond politics in the way in which he strove unremittingly for the underdog ... throughout the Ulster area.'[10]

How then, does this image of Devlin as the champion of working-class harmony and the enemy of religious intolerance square with his reorganisation of a sectarian, semi-secret society? For Devlin, the answer was a simple one: there was no contradiction between his egalitarian principles and his *alter ego* as 'Grand Master' of the Board of Erin; he had demonstrated his antipathy to the sectarianisation of Nationalist politics by his wilful destruction of the 'Catholic Association' in 1905. As a fervent Catholic, Devlin could find nothing objectionable in the professed objects of Hibernianism. Indeed, he could argue that by gaining control of such an unpredictable body, he had salvaged it from the morass of sectarianism: by connecting it with the UIL, he had secured its firm support for an organisation which contained Protestants, and which lent its support to a Parliamentary Party, with Protestant MPs in its ranks. But in this defence, Devlin was, arguably, too simplistic. He failed to comprehend the exaggerated image of an insidious Catholic power which his reinvigorated AOH conjured up in the minds of Ulster Unionists. Apart from its sectarian nature, Hibernianism became associated with machine politics in the 'Tammany Hall' mould, fuelling the hatred of both James Connolly and the separatists. Moreover, its clandestine nature continued to incur the censure of the Catholic Primate, Cardinal Logue.

By the advent of the Third Home Rule Bill, Devlin was at the high-point of his political power in Ireland. Lovat Frazer, an astute observer

from the *London Times* who heard the northern Home Rule leader
address a great Nationalist demonstration in Limerick in 1913, informed his editor: 'One thing struck me very much indeed. Devlin had a
distinctly bigger reception than Redmond. He woke up the people
more, although his speech was very brief . . . It was most instructive to
mark his effect upon the people. He is evidently the coming man, and
even here, the Ancient Order of Hibernians was more in evidence than
the United Irish League.'[11]

The Liberal landslide in the British general election of 1905 and the
subsequent constitutional crisis in Britain over the powers of the House
of Lords conspired by 1911 to bring Redmond, Dillon and Devlin
within sight of the promised land. The Liberals' failure to win an
outright majority in the two general elections of 1910 forced the Prime
Minister, Herbert Asquith, back to the 1886 position of reliance on the
votes of the Irish Nationalists. One immediate result was the 1911
Parliament Act which effectively removed the veto power of the House
of Lords. With this, the last constitutional obstacle to Irish self-government now removed, the much-heralded third Home Rule Bill was
introduced in the House of Commons in April 1912. Nationalist Ireland
confidently predicted that 1914 would be the 'Home Rule Year' and
that John Redmond would preside over an all-Ireland Parliament in
Dublin's College Green. But the wheel of political fortune had not yet
come to rest and the two years between the introduction of the third
Home Rule Bill and the outbreak of the Great War in August 1914
were to see the emergence of determined Unionist resistance to the
Liberals' policy.

The leaders of Ulster Unionism at that time were Sir Edward Carson,
a Dublin lawyer and compelling orator and Capt. James Craig, a Belfast
stockbroker who, in his massive, blunt features seemed to personify 'the
soul of Ulster intransigence'. Carson's aim was not to get special treatment for the Protestant north, but rather to maintain intact the Union
of Great Britain and Ireland. He hoped to use the solid resistance of
almost 900,000 Ulster Protestants as a weapon in this battle, convinced
– wrongly as it turned out – that 'Home Rule without Ulster would be
impossible'. Craig, however, had one idea, to preserve the character
and integrity of the province he knew and loved. From the outset the
Unionist campaign was supported by powerful interests in British society, in the Conservative Party, (now led by Bonar Law, a ruthless
political antagonist and the son of an Ulster Presbyterian minister), in
the army, the aristocracy and big business. 'There are things stronger
than parliamentary majorities', declared Law darkly at Blenheim Palace in 1912, underlining the extra-parliamentary nature of the Unionist
campaign.

Tension rose in Ulster with the introduction of the Third Home Rule
Bill in April 1912. It seemed virtually certain that Home Rule would be
enforced by 1914. The climax and supreme demonstration of Ulster
Protestant feeling was the public signing by over 200,000 loyalists of the
Solemn League and Covenant in September 1912 at various centres
throughout the north.This document pledged its signatories, 'humbly
relying on God' to use 'all means which may be found necessary to
defeat the present conspiracy to set up a Home Rule Parliament in
Ireland'. The Covenant was signed by the Presbyterian Moderator, the
northern Church of Ireland bishops and leading Methodist clergy. The
Moderator, Dr. Montgomery, had appointed the previous Sunday as as
day of 'humiliation before God and supplication for deliverance'. But
prayer, he insisted, did not mean 'discarding of the sword'. Indeed, the
leading Presbyterian journal, The Witness declared that resistance to
Home Rule, even in arms, was 'a sacred duty'.[12]

Against this backdrop of mounting rhetorical violence, groups of
Orangemen throughout the north had commenced drilling with dummy
rifles in halls or in the estates of sympathetic landowners. In January
1913, the Ulster Unionist Council decided to weld all these strands into
a single disciplined force. This 'citizens' army' was to be known as the
Ulster Volunteer Force. It was to be limited to 100,000 men who had
signed the Covenant. Committees were set up in each of the nine
counties of Ulster, and drilling and semi-military exercises became the
norm.

At first, the UVF was dismissed by the Home Rulers as 'Carson's
Comic Circus', while the Belfast *Irish News* ridiculed the claim of the
Unionists' Provisional Government to 'conquer Ulster', a feat which
even 'that brawny and valiant warrior', John de Courcy had failed to
achieve in Anglo-Norman times.[13] Yet the decision of the Ulster Unionist Standing Committee in December 1912 to abate their opposition to
Home Rule for all Ireland and Carson's subsequent demand on 1
January 1913 to exclude the whole province of Ulster from the operation of the act marked a significant watershed. Government concern at
the turn of events in Ulster in the autumn of 1913 was increased by
disturbing reports of disaffection within the armed forces. Devlin, for
his part, assured Ministers that the danger of bloodshed was 'gro-
tesquely exaggerated' and regarded by the northern Home Rulers 'with
absolute contempt'.[14] But – never a Gladstonian Home Ruler – Asquith
was unconvinced and warned Redmond in October 1913 of the need for
a compromise to defuse the deepening crisis. The Nationalist leaders
reluctantly acquiesced 'as the price of peace'.

The upshot was the 'County Option Scheme', drawn up by Lloyd
George and unveiled in February 1914. The proposals allowed any

Ulster county to obtain, by means of a plebiscite of it electors, the right to be excluded from Home Rule for a six-year period. The Nationalists had little difficulty in securing the necessary local and episcopal support for such a measure since it would have ensured the inclusion of Fermanagh, Tyrone and Derry City under a Dublin Parliament while virtually guaranteeing that the expected 'four county bloc' would be forced to merge with Home Rule Ireland at the end of the statutory period. Carson's outright rejection of such a 'stay of execution' ended any hopes of a settlement. Lloyd George had, however, succeeded in introducing the idea of partition – or 'exclusion' as it was then known – into the public debate. A precedent had been created which would be built upon in the years ahead.

From the moment Carson spurned 'temporary exclusion', the whole of Ireland began a lurch into anarchy that was only arrested by the onset of the Great War in August 1914. The Larne gun-running of April 1914, together with such coincidental factors as 'the Curragh Incident' and the weakness of the Asquith Government, led to a radical change in the balance of power in Ireland. Military supremacy now lay with 'Carson's Army'. This factor, more than any other, was to ensure that the British Government would introduce some form of partition to deal with the Ulster problem. The impact of the UVF was no less dramatic on Irish Nationalism, however. As one historian has put it, by blatantly challenging the authority of the sovereign Parliament and by re-introducing the gun as the final arbiter in Irish politics, 'Carson rekindled the Fenian flame'.[15] The revolutionary Irish Republican Brotherhood, watching in the wings, was quick to take advantage of Carson's Army and by late 1913, had called into existence a Nationalist counterweight in the shape of the Irish Volunteers. Patrick Pearse, who saw war as a means of national redemption, found an Orangeman with a rifle, 'a much less ridiculous figure than a Nationalist without one'.

By the eve of the Great War, the IVF – now under Redmond's nominal control – had mushroomed to some 170,000 men, a quarter of them concentrated in the north. The Nationalist army's main concern was to ensure the implementation of all-Ireland Home Rule. The mood of the Nationalist majorities west of the Bann in the midst of the crisis was captured by the RIC County Inspector for Tyrone in his report for March 1914: 'The Nationalists are disquieted by recent events and think they must have an army of their own . . . It is alleged that the Catholic clergy have sanctioned the movement and . . . it is likely to spread.'[16]

Meanwhile, the Home Rule Bill had undergone drastic amendment in the Lords, so as to exclude the whole province without either plebiscite or time-limit. In a final effort to break the *impasse,* the Government convened the abortive Buckingham Palace Conference on 21–24

July 1914. This involved Redmond and Dillon in protracted negotiations with Asquith and Lloyd George, for the Government, Bonar Law
and Landsdowne, and Carson and Craig, representing the Ulster Unionists. In this event, the discussion focussed on the question of 'acre-
age' and the more critical issue of 'temporary v permanent exclusion'
was never addressed.

It was, perhaps, too much to have expected agreement on the Ulster
Question at such a juncture. Arguably, feelings were running too high
for either of the Irish protagonists to make the necessary concessions.
Redmond, straining under pressure from the restive anti-exclusionists
of west Ulster, took his stand on 'county option'. To have settled for less
would have drastically undermined his credibility in Nationalist Ireland. Carson's hands were similarly tied with his pledges to the scat-
tered 'Covenanters' of Cavan, Monaghan and Donegal compelling him
to demand the 'clean cut'. Between these two entrenched positions, the
quest for a compromise seemed futile. For Nationalists, Carson's argument that the exclusion of the whole province, with its large Catholic
minority, was the best guarantee of eventual Irish unity, had much to
recommend it. Practical politics, however, dictated otherwise.

As a result, much of the conference became bogged down in what
Churchill termed, 'the muddy by-ways of Fermanagh and Tyrone'. In
an effort to define the 'excluded area', Carson revealed his 'irreducible
minimum': the proposition that a six-county *bloc* – the area which was
later to comprise Northern Ireland – should be precluded from the
operation of the Home Rule Act.[17] Though firmly repudiated by the
Nationalist leaders, this was a portentous development in the evolution
of the partition debate. Amongst Ulster Unionists, it marked the beginning of a rethink which, in subordinating principle to pragmatism,
sought to salvage the maximum possible area from the operation of
Home Rule, whilst projecting an image of 'reasonableness' in the eyes
of the British public.

The outbreak of war was marked by what the RIC termed 'a mutual
cessation of political strife' in Ireland as both Redmond and Carson
pledged unequivocal support for Britain's war effort.[18] As the storm
clouds gathered, the Irish leader's success in forcing a reluctant Asquith
to place the Home Rule Act on the Statute Book proved something of a
hollow victory. Not only was its operation suspended for the duration of
the war, but Asquith made it clear that any final settlement must
include partition. In a desperate effort to win British goodwill for the
future, Redmond was to make his great mistake in September 1914 in
urging Irishmen to enlist in the British Army. In advocating such a
course, the Home Rule leader – ever the imperialist – revealed his lack
of touch with grassroots opinions which remained deeply mistrustful of

the British Government. The immediate effect of Redmond's speech was to split the Irish Volunteers. A small radical section – by far the most active military – broke away under Professor Eoin MacNeill, Antrim Glensman and Gaelic Leaguer. This element now passed into the hands of the IRB which was to use it as the strike-force of the Rising it was determined to stage before the end of the war. Thousands of Irish Volunteers joined the rush to the colours in the first two years of the war and fought bravely alongside their former UVF adversaries on the battlefields of Europe. Amongst the Irish contingent were several thousand members of Devlin's National Volunteers from West Belfast. 'We have succeeded in making national self-government the law of the land', Devlin assured them as they marched off to the front in November 1914. James Connolly, the leader of the Irish Citizen Army and a supporter of a separatist uprising expressed a rather different view, however, in his paper, the *Worker's Republic*:

> Full steam ahead, John Redmond said,
> And everything is well chum.
> Home Rule will come when we are dead
> And buried out in Belgium.[19]

Redmond's political standing was further weakened in May 1915 when the Liberal administration was replaced by a War Coalition which included such Nationalist *béte noires* as Carson and Bonar Law. In such circumstances, it required only the 'blood sacrifice' of the Easter Rising and the crop of martyrs it produced to seal the Home Rule Party's fate. The Rising was the climax of careful planning by the Supreme Council of the IRB. It had been originally intended as a successful national revolt by the anti-war Volunteers and the small, but *élite,* Irish Citizen Army, formed by the Ulster Protestant 'misfit', Captain Jack White during the 1913 lock-out. But, in the event, with the struggle narrowed to Dublin, Pearse and the secret cadre of revolutionaries realised that they had no prospect of military success. However, they calculated that an armed stand – however futile – would almost certainly provoke the British into harsh reprisals; by their 'martyrdom', they might give their cause – an Irish Republic instead of anaemic Home Rule – its elixir of life.

The insurgents judged accurately. The Rising had at first engendered feelings of strong hostility among Irish Nationalists, many of whose relatives were fighting on the Western Front. Redmond's hasty condemnation of the Rising as a 'wicked German plot' reflected the characteristic reaction of middle-class conservative Nationalism. It was faithfully echoed by the *Irish News*, a paper closely controlled by Devlin. On 1

May 1916, the paper rejoiced that an attempt by 'German agents' to create a diversion had been thwarted. 'Happily', the editor observed, 'the Irish people were not duped. We say nothing of the unhappy instruments of Teutonic duplicity who have fought Germany's battle in the capital of this country'.

The insurrection's aftermath, however, internment, martial law, and above all, the execution of 16 of the leaders, worked a sea-change in Irish public opinion. As one observer, Colonel Maurice Moore, the Inspector-General of the Redmondite National Volunteers, wrote: 'A few unknown men, shot in a barrack yard, had embittered a whole nation'. Unionist opinion, on the other hand, was bitter at what was seen as 'a stab in the back' and 'a sample of what might be expected if Home Rule came into being', as the Belfast RIC Commissioner put it.[20]

In a final effort to salvage the Home Rule Act, the Nationalist leaders allowed themselves to be stampeded in May 1916 into the disastrous Lloyd George scheme for six-county partition. The resourceful 'Welsh Wizard' led Redmond to understand that the 'exclusion' would be temporary. Home Rule would apply immediately in 'five-sixths of Ireland'; there would be no 'Orange Parliament' in Belfast while the interests of the northern Catholics would be safeguarded by the continual presence of eighty Irish Nationalist MPs at Westminster.[21] To Carson, however, Lloyd George gave a contrasting written guarantee that partition would be permanent, a factor which helped ensure the support of the pragmatic 'six-county' Unionists. For the first time, however, Redmond and Devlin found themselves confronted by the virulent hostility of the Ulster Catholic bishops, whose fears for the future of Catholic education in the north-east was only matched by a desire to avoid – in Logue's phrase – 'going down to posterity as the destroyers of the country'.[22]

The proposals fell through in July 1916, sabotaged by the southern Unionists in the cabinet, but not before the Home Rulers, and Devlin in particular, had become tarred by the brush of partition in the Irish Nationalist mind. The 'Black Friday' conference in St. Mary's Hall, Belfast, which endorsed the Lloyd George scheme in June 1916, was to split northern Nationalism irrevocably and paved the way for the rise of the anti-partitionist 'Irish Nation League' with a major power base in Tyrone, Fermanagh and Derry City. Beginning as a reformed Nationalist party, the new league gradually became separatist, finally merging with Sinn Féin in the middle of 1917. As such it provided the bulk of the revolutionary movement's northern leadership. Rev. Philip O'Doherty P.P., a leading Ulster Sinn Féin cleric, attacked the beleaguered IPP leadership for 'abandoning the Catholics of the six counties to . . . their unsleeping and relentless hereditary enemies.' [23] As a result of the

Nationalists' endorsement of the Lloyd George scheme and charges that Devlin had 'packed' the Belfast Conference, the traditional AOH and IPP machinery in Ulster began to disintegrate while, as in the south, many of the younger clergy identified themselves with the advanced Nationalists. Only in east Ulster, where Devlin's influence remained strong, and amongst the older generation, did the Home Rule movement retain a substantial following.

Support for the insurgents and their cause soon crystalised around the new republican Sinn Féin party, embracing Griffithites, Republicans and National Leaguers and dedicated to a policy of abstention from the British Parliament. Its president from 1917 was Eamon De Valera, a young mathematics teacher and the sole surviving commandant of the Easter Rising. The new movement's growing popularity was reflected in a series of by-election triumphs in the south. In the north, however, the burning issue for Nationalists remained partition rather than 'Home Rule v Republic'. Many Ulster Catholics opposed the abstentionist tactic, arguing, with much force, that such a policy would make the 'naked deformity of partition' more likely. This fear on the part of Ulster Nationalists largely explains the decisive victories of Home Rulers over Sinn Féin in the South Armagh and East Tyrone by-elections held in January and April 1918, respectively. They may also have hoped that the Irish Convention, which the IPP had attended, might yet produce a workable all-Ireland solution.

Events during the last months of the war and particularly the British Government's threat to impose conscription in April 1918 brought an accession of strength to the revolutionary party. All over the country, tens of thousands declared their defiance to this 'blood tax' by signing the strongly-worded Anti-Conscription pledge, issued by Cardinal Logue. The fictitious German plot of May 1918 merely consolidated Sinn Féin's ascendancy over Nationalist Ireland. Though it brought de Valera and John Dillon (Redmond had died in March) together in temporary alliance, the conscription crisis enabled Sinn Féin to project itself as the champion of Nationalist Ireland. As Dillon wryly put it, 'the Sinn Féin tiger emerged from the conference with the constitutional party inside.'[24]

This was the background to the post-war general election of 1918. Sinn Fein, campaigning on a policy of abstentionism and an all-Ireland Republic, swept 73 of the 105 Irish seats. The old Home Rule party was reduced to half a dozen seats in Ulster thanks to a 'Green Pact' with Sinn Féin to avert the dangers of a split vote.[25] Edward Carson, pledged to a policy of partition for the north-east, and assisted by a redistribution, now led the largest Irish grouping at Westminster with 26 seats. Joe Devlin humiliated the Sinn Féin leader, De Valera, by a margin of almost three to one. It was a slight which the Republican leader would never forgive.

Few periods in modern Irish history have been as momentous as the three years which elapsed between the 'Khaki Election' of 1918 and the Anglo-Irish Treaty of 1921. This short time-span was to witness the setting up of Dáil Éireann as the effective Government of much of the south, the Anglo-Irish War, partition and the conferring of Dominion Status on 26 Irish counties. In accordance with their election manifesto, the Sinn Féin M.P.s ignored Westminster and met in Dublin as Dáil Éireann ('The Assembly of Ireland'). Amongst other things, the new assembly reaffirmed the declaration of an Irish Republic 'in arms' in 1916, appointed delegates to the post-war Paris Peace Conference and set up an alternative Government to that of Dublin Castle, headed by President De Valera. But while the new Cabinet achieved striking success in several areas, its hopes of raising the question of Irish self-determination at Versailles came to nought. As the peace strategy faded, an astute Devlin could predict gloomily in May 1919: 'Things must come to a fierce conflict between the Government and Sinn Féin'.[26]

Indeed that conflict had already erupted at Soloheadbeg in what slowly crystalised into an Anglo-Irish War between the Volunteers, re-styled the IRA and the RIC, soon to be reinforced by the notorious 'Counter-Terror' forces, the Auxiliaries and Black and Tans. Though the relationship between the Dáil and IRA was a confused one, the Volunteers might claim a certain legitimacy as the military arm of a democratically-elected order. The struggle between the IRA and the RIC and Crown Forces was to continue with accelerating ferocity until the Truce in July 1921.

In Britain, meanwhile, the return of a Coalition Government, headed by Lloyd George, ensured that Partition would become a 'fixed idea' of British policy. In a joint manifesto issued on 21 November 1918, Lloyd George and Bonar Law firmly rejected both Irish separation and the 'forcible coercion of the six-counties of north-east Ulster to a Home Rule Parliament against their will.'[27] Sinn Féin's 'blessed abstention' from Westminster – to borrow Churchill's phrase – meant that the balance of power now shifted from Irish Nationalists to the Ulster Unionists. Joe Devlin and his tiny band counted for little in the over-whelmingly Tory House of Commons. Craig and Carson were, there-fore, well-placed to influence the shape of the forthcoming Home Rule Act – the only one to be even partially enforced.

The Cabinet Committee which drew up the 'Partition Act' in late 1919 was tempted to include the historic nine-county province in the new 'Northern Ireland'. Liberals argued that the large Catholic popula-tion (43%) might make eventual Irish unity more probable. In the end, however, the Lloyd George Cabinet gave way to Craig's pragmatic view that a six-county *bloc* would provide a more 'viable area for permanent Unionist control'.[28]

The Government of Ireland Act (1920), as finally passed, divided Ireland into two areas, each having its own regional Parliament and Government with control over domestic affairs. At the same time, the measure seemed to envisage Irish unity by providing 'a bond of union' in the shape of a low-powered Council of Ireland. The 1920 Act represented a major triumph for the Ulster Unionists. In the words of James Craig's brother, Captain Charles Craig, MP, it placed them 'in a position of absolute security, for the future'.[29]

On the Nationalist side, only Devlin, a solitary figure at Westminster, saw the dangers of the 'Partition Act'. He railed against it as portending both 'permanent partition' and 'permanent minority status' for northern Catholics.[30] Not without justification, the West Belfast MP attacked the glaring lack of safeguards in the act for the minority. In particular, he railed against the Government's failure to provide Nationalists with weighted representation in the northern Senate and contrasted this with the treatment of the southern Unionists who were to enjoy the protection of a strong effective voice in the Dublin Senate. The need for such safeguards, he told the Commons, was underlined by the tragic sectarian bloodshed in north-east Ulster in the summer of 1920 against the backcloth of the Anglo-Irish War. The worst episode occurred in Belfast in July 1920 when the assassination of a northern-born RIC officer in Cork resulted in the mass expulsion of some 8,000 Catholic workers from the shipyards and other industries.[31] These events were a foretaste of the serious sectarian disturbances which were to scar the face of Belfast and other northern towns during the next two years. In Lisburn, the assassination of District Inspector Swanzy by the IRA in August 1920 was the signal for what the police described as 'a crusade against all members of the Catholic faith'.[32] The effect of these 'pogroms' as Catholic church leaders described them, was ultimately to create a strong anti-Unionist feeling in Britain where the Liberal and Labour Press represented them as a sectarian assault upon defenceless people by those who claimed Home Rule would lead to persecution.[33] The Dáil responded to northern Nationalist pressure with the 'Belfast Boycott' but this tended merely to reinforce the incipient border. It was not until late 1922 that murder, arson and expulsion from homes ceased to be a daily occurrence. Over 450 people, the majority of them members of the minority community, died violently during the black days of 1920–1922. In a reference to these events, and the failure to prevent their monotonous recurrence, Lloyd George was to admit to Churchill: 'Our Ulster case is not a good one'.[34]

The upsurge of violence had two important effects. First, it seemed to confirm Nationalist fears of being subjected to the rule of the Unionist majority in a separate state. Secondly, the mounting unrest led Lloyd George to endorse Craig's scheme for a new auxiliary police force. Formed in October 1920, the Ulster Special Constabulary – formed largely from ex-UVF members – was to play a crucial role in the creation of the new Irish border. In Nationalist eyes, however, this sectarian force was viewed – in the words of a British official – 'with a bitterness exceeding that which the Black and Tans inspired in the South'.[35]

In May 1921, following elections in the six counties, the new northern Parliament was established with Sir James Craig as its first Prime Minister. 'From that moment', wrote Churchill perceptively, 'Ulster's position was unassailable'. The Nationalists and Sinn Féin, cooperating on a platform of anti-partition and abstention from the 'Partition Parliament', secured a total of 12 of the 52 seats and one third of the popular vote.[36]

In general during those vital years, the Sinn Féin leadership failed, in the words of one northern Sinn Féin leader, 'to grapple with the Ulster Question'.[37] The 'naked deformity of partition' came a poor second to National Status in the revolutionary scheme of things. This was certainly the case during the Treaty negotiations between Sinn Féin and a formidable British delegation in London in the fall of 1921. Arthur Griffith and Michael Collins, the leaders of the Irish delegation, tried to secure the 'essential unity' of Ireland but were forced in the end to settle for Dominion Status for the 26 counties. A Boundary Commission was to revise the 1920 border. The prospect of the Commission and the belief that it would so reduce the North's territory as to produce Irish unity to 'contraction' largely explains why Griffith and Collins signed the Treaty of December 6, 1921.[38]

Northern Nationalists were shocked and bitterly disappointed at the Treaty terms. Most supported them however, in the hope that some form of 'essential unity' might yet be achieved. For the border Nationalist majorities of Fermanagh, Tyrone, Derry City and South Armagh in particular, the Boundary Clause (Article 12) was the crucial article. The wording of the clause, however, was fatally flawed. The point here was that while it referred to 'the wishes of the inhabitants' – implying large-scale gains by the new Free State – this was made subject to 'economic and geographic conditions'. Four years later, in 1925, the much-vaunted Boundary Commission collapsed, leaving the Northern Ireland state intact and partition more deeply entrenched. For the northern Nationalists, the disunity and disenchantment of the Parnell Split had been replaced 30 years later by an even deeper sense of isolation and betrayal. For the Ulster Unionists, their new state had survived despite Nationalist non-recognition, IRA attacks and British pressure. The minority problem, however, remained unaddressed and would continue to fester in the years ahead.[39]

CHAPTER 8

Irish Labour and Politics in The Late Nineteenth and Early Twentieth Centuries
by
Peter Collins

In many respects this is an exercise in looking at why the Labour movement failed to rise to the prominence and power that it did in the island across the Irish Sea. Yet to write Irish Labour off as a failed entity is to greatly overstate the case, certainly in the period considered here, from 1881–1921. The Labour movement had a very prominent role, particularly in relation to the two main cities, not least in the two actions led by James Larkin in Belfast in 1907 and Dublin in 1913. In both cases he brought them to a standstill for months as epic struggles raged between men and masters, the latter supported by the civil authorities. However, although bitter defeat was the immediate outcome of these actions, the movement emerged eventually able to fight another day and indeed prepared to mount a political challenge to the status quo represented by the socially conservative mirror images of the Home Rule and Unionist parties.

This dominance of opposing nationalisms stood in the way of Labour's ultimate aim of forging an alternative which could could command the allegiance and look after the interests of all the workers of Ireland, be they Protestant or Catholic. The problem for Labour was that most Protestant workers were fiercely loyal to the Unionist party, while their Catholic contemporaries were no less wedded to the Irish Parliamentary Party. Without doubt for most workers the National Question took precedence over the Social Question. Particularly in the perception of northern Protestants their social and economic well-being depended on the maintenance of the link with Britain. The active members of the Labour movement including their leaders were no less susceptible to national aspirations. This will be seen clearly as our story unfolds.

Background

The Labour movement in Ireland grew rapidly in the last two decades of the nineteenth century.In this it emulated and indeed was part of the expansion of the British movement. In effect the writ of the British TUC ran throughout all Ireland. Only in 1894 did an Irish Trades Union Congress (ITUC) come into being, the year after the British Congress was held in Belfast. The ITUC did not see itself as a replacement of the TUC as the trade union centre for Ireland. Indeed its founders were at pains to stress that it was merely complementary to the British body. As for trades unionists themselves, most were members of branches of large British unions rather than those originating in Ireland. It was only after 1909 with the foundation of Larkin's Irish Transport and General Workers' Union (ITGWU) that this began to change, especially in the south. Belfast workers were much more attached to the British move- ment, not least because many shipyard workers had recently come over from Britain, bringing with them their union membership and recruit- ing many Belfast workers to their unions.

Industrial Belfast

Belfast was in its heyday at the turn of the century. In many ways it was a byword for industrial and commercial superlatives. It had the largest shipbuilding capacity in the world with two mammoth yards. It had the largest ropeworks in the world. Its tobacco manufacturing, dominated by the ebullient Ulsterman Thomas Gallaher, was world renowned. Irish linen, centred on the Lagan valley, had cornered the quality end of the world textile market and provided constant employment for many thousands in Belfast, particularly women. Textile engineering and foun- dries arising out of the linen industry also served manufacturers as far away as Catalonia and India. There were plenty of Belfast firms doing brisk business in many other areas of manufacturing, prominent among which were spirits and mineral waters, printing and box-making . It was a booming 'Brumagem' with a soaraway population. Incomers were attracted by its plentiful employment opportunities and, for those skilled workers who could afford it, housing superior to that available to them in most British cities . Yet the people of the city, especially the poor, paid the price of rapid industrial and population growth in terms of a despoiled environment, dreadful working conditions for the unskilled, and a death rate much higher than that of any comparable city in Britain. It is with British cities that Belfast should be compared rather than with the towns and villages of Ireland or even with Dublin.

Dublin

Dublin during the late 1800s was in decline from its zenith of the previous century. By the end of the nineteenth century, Belfast had a larger population than the capital city. In an industrial and commercial

sense, the 'Linenopolis' of the north had by then far outstripped its
southern counterpart. In effect Dublin was a commercial port and
administrative centre with little largescale manufacture. Most male
workers were either employed as casual labourers in the docks, in
building and in what are now called service industries. These were
largely casualised and only the Guinness brewery provided any large-
scale employment of a permanent reasonably paid nature. This scenario was in marked contrast to that prevailing in industrial Belfast. The
situation for employment for women was even worse. The vast majority
were in domestic service or worked in shops. The only manufacturing
jobs for women were in Jacob's Biscuits or in several other factories.
Partly because of this and the presence of a large garrison, Dublin had
prostitution on a scale never approached in Belfast. Another sense in
which the lot of the Dublin working-class was worse than in Belfast was
that their housing mainly consisted of tenements. These were in large
terraces around the city centre, long abandoned by the gentry in their
flight to the suburbs, and now under multi-occupancy by poor families.
They were the breeding-grounds for a militancy which would find
expression and leadership with the arrival of Larkin.

New unionism

The 1890s saw the rise of unions representing unskilled workers for the
first time in a significant way. Previously they were excluded from the
movement dominated by skilled unionists who feared that organisation
of the unskilled would lead to the erosion of differentials and a decline
in their own position. It would be a long time before this mutual
antipathy between artisan and labourer could be allayed to the extent
where they could come together with shared goals within the Labour
movement. The general unions of unskilled workers known as 'new' to
differentiate them from the existing skilled unions were much more
militant. Their leaders were generally involved in Labour politics, seeing their union work as part of the larger struggle to change society.
Both in Belfast and Dublin the British based new unions, such as the
National Amalgamated Union of Labourers (NAUL), the National
Union of Dock Labourers (NUDL) and the Gasworkers' union, found
large numbers of recruits among the masses of unskilled workers who
looked to them to win for them famous victories such as the London
docks strike of 1889.

Trades Councils

Trades councils were another development in the movement in Britain
which transferred to Ireland as a matter of course. Described somewhat

grandiosely as 'parliaments of labour', such councils were set up in Belfast in 1881 and Dublin in 1886 and had spread to most towns of any size by the turn of the century. The two big city trades councils came to represent labour in Ireland as a whole and for a long time they were more representative overall than the ITUC. 'In times of crisis, in a time of poor leadership, trades councils can react to developments faster than the national trade union or indeed political leadership'.[1]

Thus it is to developments within these two city trades councils that we must look for an understanding of the movement in general. It is only in the later part of our period that the ITUC comes to the fore. Politically the trades councils reflected the views of their largely artisan membership in the early period. Thus Dublin Trades Council was largely made up of supporters of the Irish Parliamentary Party with a small segment of Conservatives. After 1905 this was to change with some becoming members of the newly formed Sinn Fein. In Belfast most were either Conservatives or Liberal Unionists. However, members generally were loath to bring party politics into the Belfast Trades Council viewing it as a possible source of division and strife. Indeed such had been the case when the secretary Alexander Bowman was forced to resign for publicly supporting Home Rule in 1886.

The Independent Labour Party

A new political force emerged with the foundation of the Independent Labour Party (ILP). The holding of the TUC in Belfast in 1893 with most of the leading ILP members present was a tremendous filip to the fledgling branch in the city. It set about spreading the Socialist message with an evangelical fervour and was opposed by Protestant extremists who saw the ILP as dispensers of a lethal cocktail of atheism and disloyalty. In fact the Belfast members were opposed to Home Rule, unlike most of their party in Britain. In response to their loyalist critics the Belfast ILP developed a programme which combined Labour social and economic policies with a Unionist position on the National Question. The foremost exponent of this Labour Unionism was William Walker; so much so that it became known as Walkerism. In Dublin the arrival of the ILP was not the beginning of an immediate breakthrough for Labour politics. Indeed within a few years it had been transformed into the Dublin Socialist Society, in reality little more than a middle class discussion group. Nevertheless it was this group that invited James Connolly to Ireland in 1896.

Municipal Politics

In 1897 the first major Labour gains in an election in Ireland were made by municipal candidates put up by the Belfast Trades Council. Six councillors were elected, not on an ILP Socialist ticket but rather on a wave of revulsion against corrupt local government and support for the good work the Trades Council had been doing in trade union and municipal matters. However, it was an encouraging breakthrough for the movement throughout Ireland and was soon emulated in Dublin. There in the municipal elections in 1899, no less than eleven candidates, standing under the banner of the Labour Electoral Association, were elected, although this success soon turned to ashes due to internal bickering and the desertion of some Labour councillors to the National-ist camp. There was as yet, however, no Labour grouping with a candi-date strong enough to mount a credible challenge for a parliamentary seat in either city.

The Labour Representation Committee

The Labour Representation Committee was a merger in 1901, of the ILP and various Socialist sects with the trade unions, in the wake of punitive legal judgements such as the Taff Vale Decision. It aimed to get the election of Labour members of Parliament to oppose anti-union legislation. It was welcomed in Ireland particularly in Belfast and Dub-lin where the Trades Councils were prominent in setting up local LRCs. William Walker was particularly enthusiastic, not least as he saw him-self as a possible candidate. In Belfast the Trades Council and the LRC formed a working partnership with its own well-subscribed weekly paper *Belfast Labour Chronicle*. Walker was now the leading light in all of these groupings of Labour in Belfast.

Walkerism

Walkerism was based on the twin pillars of Unionism and Socialism. It was opposed to Irish Nationalism and stood for nationalisation of utilities such as gas, electric and the tramways. Indeed the epithet 'municipal socialism' described a good deal of what Walker and his colleagues stood and worked for. In its more extreme forms Walkerism, always very hostile to Nationalism, verged on anti-Catholicism and indeed contained traces of racism. *The Belfast Labour Chronicle*, edited by John Murphy, Walker's closest associate, to which Walker contrib-uted, contained many articles attacking Irish Nationalism. For example one such article entitled 'The language craze', attacking the revival of Gaelic, could be interpreted as close to racism. As a principle, National-ism was for them, '. . . dead or dying and imperialism is the transition stage to international union of the proletariat all the world over. The total separation of Ireland would be but a disintegrating influence on the people and can proceed from narrow views alone'.[2]

If Imperialism could be regarded as progressive, so Nationalism should have no place in the Socialist future. Rather it was a tool of capitalism to divide the workers:

> Class ties are stronger than those of race and the workers of all lands and climes have a common class interest. They are all units in the army of labour and they ought therefore to forget their differences of race, language and colour and stand shoulder to shoulder in order to withstand the attack of their common foe, Capitalism.[3]

Walkerism was also a reflection of the views of the Protestant workers of Belfast that their well-being lay in close links with Britain rather than the rest of Ireland.They broadly shared the view of Conservative businessmen, that a Nationalist run Ireland, would be one in which the industrial wealth of the north east would decay, either because it was subject to Governmental neglect from Dublin, or because it was cut off from the British economy, or both. It would be a state in which Catholic clerical and agrarian interests would predominate. Unionists of all classes shared an almost racist view of the inability of southerners to do well in industry. These considerations would come to the fore, during the reopening of the Home Rule question, in the years immediately preceding World War I.

During the almost year long carpenters' and joiners' strike, which he led in 1900, Walker clearly articulated this sense of separate identity and of superiority to the rest of Ireland:

> Whilst every other city in Great Britain, of like size to Belfast, can obtain substantial reductions in hours, with a corresponding increase of wages and generally improved conditions of labour, Belfast, simply because it happens to be in Ireland, is to model itself upon the provincial towns of Ireland both in wages and hours and not upon those cities with whom we are so proud to compare when speaking about our commercial prosperity.[4]

By 1904 Walker, already a city councillor, was waiting his chance to enter the parliamentary arena. That came in 1905 with a by-election in the North Belfast constituency. His opponent in this was the Conservative Sir Daniel Dixon who had been several times Lord Mayor. The auguries appeared good for Walker not least because his opponent was generally regarded as a weak candidate, a so-called 'dead-head'. He was tainted with the whiff of private scandal, and most importantly accused of corruption by selling land to the Corporation at vastly inflated prices.

His most persistent accuser in this was Walker in the *Belfast Labour Chronicle*.

In addition the Conservative Party machine at this time was unusually exposed to attack from Labour because both the party and the Orange Order were seriously split over what many of their erstwhile supporters regarded as the backsliding attitude of the Government towards the Catholic church and Nationalism in general. Most support for this view resided in the strongly Protestant working-class areas such the North Belfast constituency. Already Tom Sloan, a shipyard labourer and lunch-time evangelist, had won the South Belfast seat for the so-called 'Protestant democracy'. A breakaway Independent Orange Order had been set up with Sloan a prominent member and the Dubliner Lindsay Crawford, Grand Master. They saw themselves as the scourge of what they regarded as a plutocratic oligarchy at the head of the Conservative Party, which was well out of touch with Protestant grassroots feeling.

Crawford and Sloan were quite radical in their social attitudes. In fact Crawford made a speech, at the July celebrations in 1905, later published as the Magheramorne Manifesto, which showed him to be very close to the Labour position in social questions. Thus Walker had the support of the Sloanites and also the Belfast Protestant Association (BPA) led by Richard Braithwaite. They orchestrated rowdy disruption of Dixon's meetings. Walker, himself an excellent candidate, had the financial support of his union and was given Ramsay Macdonald as his election agent, as befitted a member of the LRC national executive. Dixon was running a lacklustre campaign, while Walker was addressing enthusiastic crowded meetings. However, just when he was on the verge of becoming Ireland's first Labour MP, he made a serious miscalculation which undoubtedly cost him the election.

The occasion of this was a questionnaire circulated to the candidates by the Belfast Protestant Association which was insulting to Catholics. Walker answered this to the satisfaction of the BPA because he needed still to establish his credibility with the 'Protestant democracy'. In fact he didn't find a lot to disagree with in it. It fitted in with the amalgam of Labour Unionism and his evangelical background. For instance in answer to the question 'Will you in all things place the interests of Protestantism before those of the party to which you are attached?', he replied, 'Protestantism means protesting against superstition and hence true Protestantism is synonymous with Labour'.[5]

His opponent wisely refused to answer the questionnaire and indeed had it and Walker's response circulated among the thousand or so Catholic electors in the constituency, who normally voted against the Conservatives. It undoubtedly had an effect as Dixon won by the narrow margin of 4440 votes to Walker's 3966. Ramsay Macdonald was furious and Walker was forced to defend himself before the LRC national executive. However, it would be a mistake to think that Walker had been the victim of an aberrant action. In fact his position reflected the essentially contradictory relationship between Labourism and Unionism in a city in which the 'National Question' dominated all spheres of political life. Nevertheless, Walker still maintained a high profile and when in the following year a general election was held he did even better against Dixon, polling 4616 to his opponent's 4907. It seemed only a matter of time before the seat would become Labour's first in Ireland. However, by the next contest, occasioned by Dixon's death in 1907 the situation had changed. Unionism had healed its divisions and the Unionist candidate George 'Orange' Clark, a shipyard owner and a much better candidate, trounced Walker with a majority of 1800. This was despite the fact that Walker again tried to establish his Unionist credentials, a matter in which he was easily outmanoeuvred by his opponent. This marked the end of any serious parliamentary challenge by Labour in Ireland for a long time.

Larkin and the 1907 Belfast Strike

In 1907 James Larkin came to Belfast as organiser of the local branch of the NUDL, the dockers' union which had gone into abeyance after a failed dispute in the 1890s, in which sectarianism had been used to split the men. Larkin also had a political agenda being an active member of the Labour party in Liverpool where he had been born to Irish Catholic parents. He had worked as a stevedore in Liverpool docks.Thus he was familiar with the problems facing the much exploited dockworkers and the sectarianism that divided the workers in his own city as well as in Belfast. He came to Belfast for the 1907 national conference of the British Labour Party, the only one ever to be held in Ireland. He stayed and within four months he had recruited around 4000 union members, Protestant and Catholic, and had affiliated to the Trades Council where he soon made his mark. However, he was not universally welcomed, as some, even in the Labour movement, regarded him as an extreme Nationalist and Socialist out to destabilise the industrial equilibrium and prosperity of Belfast. The charisma of Larkin on the Labour side was matched by an equally formidable leader of the employers of the city, Thomas Gallaher, tobacco magnate and chairman of the Belfast Steamship Company. Gallaher was determined that the brand of radical trade unionism espoused by Larkin would never get off the ground in Belfast. To that extent he rejected all communication with the union, refusing any meeting with Larkin.

Thus when a group of dockers refused to work alongside non-union men they were dismissed and although Larkin announced that a closed shop was not union policy the men were not reinstated. Larkin's offer to discuss the matter was simply ignored and reluctantly he had to bring out the rest of the men in support. So began a strike which was to last some seven months and involved most of the dockers and carters in the city and because of the knock-on of the lack of transport threw many others out of work. The strike was one of the most eventful in the history of the British Isles, attended by drama and incident that still resound today. The employers brought over 'blacklegs' from Britain. The strikers and their supporters took violent action against these. Police who were brought in to protect the 'blacklegs' themselves mutinied partly in sympathy with the the strikers but mainly in protest against their own appalling wages, hours and conditions. The shock of this galvanised the authorities into action, transferring some 300 mutineers and sacking the ringleaders, chief of whom was a constable Barrett.

With the police compromised, the Lord Mayor called the troops to the aid of the civil power. Soon the city centre resembled an armed camp, with soldiers on every corner. This situation brought with it its own tension especially when troops were sent up the Nationalist Falls Road. This was seen as an act of provocation and soon the troops were being engaged by rioting youths. Inevitably the army over-reacted and a youth and a girl, innocent bystanders, were shot dead by the military. A huge funeral for the two victims showed how high feelings were running among Nationalists. There was widespread belief that the whole scenario had been engineered to cause sectarian division in the ranks of the strikers whom Larkin had managed to band together. However the Conservative press was now in full cry after Larkin. Scurrilously, one paper stated that he was the son of one of the Manchester Martyrs. It was claimed that the whole strike had now been exposed as a Fenian conspiracy, inspired by jealousy, to destroy the prosperity of loyal Belfast and incite violence against the forces of the Crown.

The strike had by November almost run its course in terms of the ability of strikers and their families to continue it. They had fought and sacrificed long and hard but their personal reserves had been non-existent compared to the vast amounts available to the employers which allowed them to sit out the action indefinitely. Furthermore the strike was threatening to bankrupt the NUDL which was having to support the bulk of the strikers in strike pay. James Sexton, the General Secretary, was consequently looking an out. The General Federation of Trade Unions (GFTU) in England having promised to support the strikers financially was also seriously concerned. The pressure on Larkin from the national leadership to end the strike became stronger the longer it went on. Although Larkin, with his inspirational oratory and organising genius, was the strikers' greatest asset, he was persuaded to give up his sole control to a committee composed of Trades Council and national union leaders. While this committee was at first supportive and organised huge rallies in support of the strikers, it had become very uneasy about the outcome by the end of the summer. It was also afraid that the riots and press campaign would undermine the always fragile co-existence of Protestant and Catholic workers in the Labour movement in Belfast. The employers were obdurate and clearly determined to starve the workers into submission. It was at this stage that the strike committee and the national leaders accepted the invitation of the Lord Mayor to attend peace talks. The strike committee was represented at the talks by two English leaders of the GFTU, Allen Gee and Isaac Mitchell. The strike was by now dead on its feet, the carters having already capitulated and gone back to work. The GFTU men, backed by Sexton, settled over the heads of the strikers who had to return, literally cap in hand, on very unfavourable terms.

This was not only a defeat for Larkin and the strikers and their families who had sacrificed so much in vain, but it was also a major setback for the Labour movement throughout the British Isles, because they had been unable to use their overall strength to support the workers against a combination of employers. Larkin interpreted this as a sell-out and he determined never to put himself again in a position of reliance on the leadership of the English movement. He left Belfast almost immediately for Dublin where the following year he led dockers and carters to victory in a strike similar to the one in Belfast. This time he was able to put to use the lessons of Belfast, especially keeping to himself tight control on the strike and most especially not putting his trust in English unions. In 1909 he set up a separate union, not only for dockers but also the class of general workers, mainly unskilled, who remained outside union organisation. This was the Irish Transport Workers' Union. The *and General* was added shortly after, entitling it the Irish Transport and General Workers' Union (ITGWU). This union was to have a major impact on the industrial and political life of the country. Finally, 1907 had been a bitter defeat for the Belfast workers, most especially those employed in the docks. Indeed the Belfast dockers were only to get back their spirit with the arrival of James Connolly as Transport Union organiser in 1910.

Developments in the ITUC

So far the Belfast and Dublin Trades Councils had provided the focus for most of the developments in the Irish Labour movement with the

ITUC largely marginal to the bulk of union members. This was so for a number of reasons, one being the endemic suspicion of northern members of the political inclinations of the all Ireland body. Walker shared this attitude, although he had relaxed sufficiently to take on the job of President of Congress in 1904. By then he was urging the movement to affiliate to the LRC, of which he was a national executive member, in order to get Labour representation for Ireland in Parliament. The supporters of Redmond in the ITUC voted this down claiming that the Parliamentary Party already represented the interests of the workers. The attempt to get affiliation to British Labour became an annual feature at Congress, the closest to success being in 1909 when a resolution was passed urging support for the British body and calling on trades councils to put up candidates, but without setting up support machinery. In fact only Belfast put up a Labour candidate at the general election the following year.

By then the moment for latching on to British Labour had passed. The Irish movement was now coming under the control of elements with a different agenda which was both Nationalist and Socialist. A new coalition was emerging which was tilting the centre of ITUC power to the south. This resulted from the rise of Larkin's Transport union and an alliance of the socially progressive wing of Sinn Féin and the various Socialist groups in the Dublin area. They formed a bloc which had the industrial muscle of the ITGWU behind it and they now began to make all the running in the Labour movement nationally. By 1910, the Home Rule question was again on the parliamentary agenda, with the Liberal Government dependent on the Irish Parliamentary and Labour parties as a result of the two elections of that year. The possibility of a Home Rule Parliament in Dublin gave a vital shot in the arm to the campaign for a separate Irish Labour Party. Larkin was in favour of this and swung the growing power of the ITGWU behind it.

Socialist Politics

There already was a Socialist Party of Ireland (SPI) in existence. Although it was no larger than a sect, it had leading trades unionists as members giving it an influence greater than that merited by its numbers. It was the successor to the Irish Socialist Republican Party (ISRP) set up in 1896 by James Connolly. Connolly was born in Edinburgh in 1868, like Larkin the son of Irish Catholic migrants. He imbibed a tradition of Irish separatist Republicanism from a Fenian uncle. This he melded with the writings of Marx and other Socialist thinkers and honed it with his experience of deprivation in an Edinburgh slum. It was economic necessity that first brought him to Ireland, ironically in the uniform of a British soldier. His second visit was occasioned by an invitation from the Dublin Socialist Society, aware of his growing stature in the Labour movement in Scotland, to organise a Socialist party in the city. He did not make much headway in penetrating the core of Irish politics beyond establishing a reputation as a speaker, writer and organiser. In 1903, partly out of frustration at the lack of progress in Ireland, but also due to the need to support a growing family, he left for America. In the vibrant and cosmopolitan Socialist movement there Connolly was able to perfect the skills of a revolutionary which he would put to use in Ireland on his return in 1910.

Connolly in Belfast

The SPI prevailed upon Connolly to come back to Ireland as their organiser, having persuaded Larkin to give him the vacant job of Belfast organiser of the ITGWU. Connolly arrived in a city in which the Labour movement was only slowly recovering from the wounds of 1907, and a severe depression in the linen trade in the year that followed. He set about reorganising the shattered dockers' union, this time in the name of the ITGWU. He had an early success during a dispute in the port of Belfast winning an increase of an average of three shillings a week for the dockers, and their fellow strikers the sailors and firemen. This was the best propaganda for union recruitment. Membership increased and women linen workers asked him to organise them, during a strike in 1911, although there already was a union in existence. This brought charges against him in the Trades Council of poaching and resulted in an acrimonious debate in which Connolly was castigated not only for the matter in hand, but also for his advanced Socialist and Nationalist views, which did not accord with the prevailing Walkerism in the Belfast movement. Nevertheless the Council was split evenly and Connolly had supporters who were to join him in trying to win over the movement in the city to the more radical position of the SPI. Prominent among Connolly's new colleagues were D.R.Campbell, a Belfast Protestant, and Thomas Johnson who originated from Liverpool, both of whom were to become leaders in the local and national Labour movement. Danny McDevitt, whose tailor shop became a meeting place for Socialists and Republicans in the city, earning it the hostile epithet 'the bounders' college', made up the trio of Connolly's lieutenants.

Socialist Unity

Connolly set himself the task of weaning the movement in Belfast away from the influence of Walker and Labour Unionism. To this effect he

held joint education lectures with the Walkerite branches of the revived
Belfast ILP, during the winter of 1911–12. A unity conference called by
the SPI, was held at Easter 1912 in Dublin. It was attended by Connolly
and his Belfast colleagues and also by delegates from four out of the
five ILP branches. Only the Walkerite North Belfast branch let the
invitation to the conference 'lie on the table'. Out of this unity conference emerged the Independent Labour Party of Ireland [ILP (I)]. This
new radical alliance was soon to experience a baptism of fire in Belfast,
in the summer, in the heightened tension surrounding the introduction
of the Home Rule Bill.

The Congress Party

At the same time the radical elements surrounding Larkin and Connolly
were pushing the ITUC to set up an Irish Labour Party based on the
trades unions. For them Home Rule was now almost a *fait accompli,*
and this lent an urgency to establishing the party in order to make
inroads into Redmond's support before elections to any parliament in
Dublin. An added incentive was that the Irish Parliamentary Party
(IPP) was showing itself to be no friend of the workers in relation to the
Liberal social legislation. For example they voted against extending the
medical benefits of the National Insurance scheme to Ireland. At the
1911 Congress the attempt to set up an Irish Labour Party was narrowly
foiled by a combination of Walkerites and IPP supporters. Connolly
who had not attended the Congress wrote bitterly in the Scottish Socialist paper *Forward,* 'The unborn Labour Party of Ireland was strangled
in the womb by the ILPers' [6]. However, control of the ITUC executive
passed to the radicals who made assiduous preparations in the subsequent year to get the motion through. The 1912 Congress at Clonmel
resulted in a vote of 49 to 18 in favour of a motion from Connolly that
all affiliated bodies levy one shilling per annum per member for independent Labour representation on all public bodies. The main opposition had come from Belfast delegates and the result of the vote showed
how the balance of power had shifted to the southern radicals and the
small group around Connolly in Belfast, who were also playing a major
part in the new Congress regime. The resolution had not proposed
setting up actual machinery, but this was remedied at a meeting of the
ITUC executive in Dublin in September 1912, attended by Connolly
and Campbell. However it was not until after the 1913 Congress that
machinery for a new party, the Irish Trade Union Congress and Labour
Party (ITUC&LP), known as the Congress Party for short, was put into
motion. At that Congress there was no Belfast Trades Council representation, as that body was protesting at the Nationalist drift within the

ITUC, particularly in view of the difficulties this caused in a city now so violently split over the issue of Home Rule.

Dublin 1913

The Labour movement in Dublin in that year was preoccupied with a mammoth struggle of a different nature and which in many respects was one of life or death, namely the lock-out. In this twenty thousand workers of Dublin, marshalled by the ITGWU, and led by Larkin took on the employers' combine headed by William Martin Murphy, former Nationalist MP. He was Ireland's biggest employer, being the owner of the Dublin United Tramways Company and Independent Newspapers. Murphy and his colleagues in the Dublin Employers' Association demanded that their employees sign a declaration that they would refrain from membership of the Transport Union.They were primarily determined to break the industrial power of the union but perhaps another motive was to weaken the political power of Labour lest it pose a threat to the Nationalists after Home Rule became a reality. Many refused to sign the declaration and went on strike. The employers responded by closing down many businesses causing a mass lock-out. About twenty thousand workers and three hundred employers were involved in a struggle that was to last from August 1913 to early in 1914.

Ranged against the workers were the Catholic Hierarchy, the British administration and the press. Many intellectuals, the advanced Nationalists in the IRB, and progressive elements in Sinn Fein, though not Arthur Griffith, supported the workers. Although many of the leaders of the ITUC were also active in the Dublin movement, Congress took no active official role. Nor did the British TUC, although many unions in Britain were supportive and sent much needed support in money and goods. Leaders of the workers of Dublin, on speaking tours in Britain, addressed full and enthusiastic meetings. There was a groundswell of support for sympathetic strikes in Britain which the official movement sat on, fearful of the consequences of such action. Larkin and his lieutenant Connolly were bitter at the British leadership for curtailing a strategy which they saw as vital to their success. This reinforced the independent attitude of the Irish unions. Inevitably, as in Belfast in 1907, the lock-out had a deleterious effect on the men and their families, particularly the children, Soup kitchens were set up in Liberty Hall to mitigate the real threat of starvation. A crucial if understandable mistake was made when an offer from the British movement to find the children places with families of their members for the duration, was welcomed. However, this gave their opponents the opportunity to claim that the morals of the children would be in jeopardy if sent to Protes-

tant, or worse, 'atheistic' Socialist homes in England. An attack on the
evacuation of the children at the docks by militant Catholics, forced the
abandonment of the project. The damage was done in propaganda
terms, with Larkin and his colleagues now portrayed as bent on undermining both faith and fatherland.

The longer the lock-out went on the more bitter it became, with
strongarm police tactics against pickets leading to two deaths and many
injuries. The union set up a defence force armed mainly with hurleys.
Out of this would grow the Irish Citizen Army (ICA). The political
dimension of the strike came to the fore with Larkin and Connolly
telling sympathetic voters in Britain not to support Government candidates in three by-elections. Lloyd George's statement that the subsequent Government loss of the three was for several reasons, 'the most
prominent of which is Jim Larkin' points to the efficacy of the tactic.
However these successes were followed by failure in the Irish local
government arena in January 1914. This election was the touchstone of
which side had the support of the people of Dublin and the result
showed clearly that Labour was the loser in this respect.[7] Indeed so
obvious was the judgement of the people that Larkin and the other
leaders called off the action within a few days.

The post mortem was bitter, although not as despairing as some
commentators would have it . Dr Austen Morgan, for instance, portrays
Connolly the disillusioned Socialist retreating in an atavistic direction,
'. . . following the defeat of the Dublin workers, national chauvinist
recriminations intruded in the early months of 1914, when it was difficult to sustain a belief in proletarian action'.[8] Although the union had
been beaten on this particular occasion, they had lost a battle not the
whole war. The ITGWU did not break up as Murphy had meant it to.
Indeed after a short time membership was soaring again. The experience had been melancholy for the men and their families but in the long
term it became the stuff of legend, even for the participants a badge of
honour to show the grandchildren. For the Irish trade union movement
in general it was the baptism of independence. The leaders of 1913 had
gained the mastery of the ITUC which they would now push into a
political and industrial role going far beyond the parameters of the
talking- shop it had been thus far. The support of advanced Nationalists
in Sinn Féin and the IRB, while not sanctioned officially by their
organisations, reflected a significant strand of social radicalism devel-
oping in both. This coincided with a growing move towards separatist
Nationalism within the trade union movement. In this Larkin and
Connolly were prime movers. The latter through the ICA was already
taking the steps that would lead him to an accommodation with the IRB
and ultimately to Easter Week 1916.

Connolly and Home Rule

Although Connolly and Larkin and their supporters were aiming for a completely separate Socialist Ireland, they were certainly not maximalists to the extent that they would not welcome the passing of the Home Rule Bill in 1912, with a two year postponement under the new Parliament Act. However Connolly in Belfast couldn't fail to realise the determination of the Loyalist population to resist Home Rule to the point of civil war. Indeed the Protestant workers who were the mass of union members were militant in their resistance. The thousands of Catholics who were expelled from their workplaces in the summer of 1912 bore witness to that. Many Protestants also were expelled from the shipyards and engineering works for being regarded as politically unsound, the criteria for this being membership of a Socialist group or even holding union office. Even Walkerites came in for abuse in a situation where pluralism was being driven to the wall. If Connolly was to make headway in winning over the workers of Belfast to his vision, this was not the time. Nevertheless he stuck to his guns, though more and more he was being drawn into the Catholic politics of Belfast in the debate on Home Rule.

In his speeches he made no allowance for the susceptibilities of the Loyalist workers whom he portrayed as misguided dupes of the Orange bourgeoisie. For their own good they could not be allowed to stand in the way of Socialism and national independence. His activities were becoming more controversial attracting the kind of hostile attention that his movement colleagues in Belfast desperately wished to avoid. On his return from arrest in Dublin during the 1913 lockout, he was greeted at the railway station by a loyalist mob singing party songs and discharging firearms. He was only with difficulty rescued from this unwelcome welcoming party. A similar scene attended the return of his trade union day excursion in August 1913. He was increasingly only able to hold meetings in Catholic areas and even there he was several times attacked by Nationalist youths for voicing criticism of Joe Devlin and Redmond over their apparent willingness to water down the Home Rule measure.

The Exclusion of Ulster

The Exclusion of Ulster arose over the compromise put forward by the Government to allow counties in Ulster where Unionists were in the majority, to opt out of Home Rule for a limited period of six years. Connolly vehemently opposed the imposition of the exclusion amendment and in a famous phrase forecast that 'Partition would usher in a carnival of reaction north and south'.[9] Connolly and his supporters held a mass meeting to protest against exclusion, significantly in the Catholic St. Mary's Hall. Loyalist workers, partly as a riposte to Connolly's activities held a meeting in favour of partition, which they claimed with justification represented the views of the majority of workers of Belfast. Thus the workers were being further polarised and the Labour movement in the city marginalised almost out of existence in the Home Rule struggle. The debate within the movement was carried on vitriolically at the ITUC in Dublin in June 1914. This saw a majority of mainly southern delegates opposing exclusion, while most Belfast delegates took the opposing view, with exceptions like D.R.Campbell. In the end an anti-exclusion motion was carried by acclamation. In Belfast the Labour movement was further damaged in the light of its national body's opposition to partition. Partition was now an option towards which most northern Unionists significantly were moving.

War

The situation in the summer of 1914 was one of approaching civil war, with the UVF well armed and buoyed by the recent support expressed by the officers at the Curragh. The Irish Volunteers were equally prepared to defend the Home Rule measure when it became law. Within the Irish Volunteers, was an IRB minority which sought to exploit the situation to gain nothing less than complete independence. The political parties were failing to come up with a compromise that would avoid conflagration. Within the Labour movement attitudes were hardening, shaped to an extent by its experiences the previous year during the Dublin lock-out. This insoluble situation was postponed by the outbreak of war in Europe leading to the postponment of the introduction of Home Rule for the duration. The attitude of the Labour and trade union movement to the war was very varied given the political heterogeneity of its members. The Socialist International, prior to the war, had voted not to cooperate in the event of hostilities. They saw it as an imperialist war to bolster the ruling class for which the working class would provide cannon-fodder.The outbreak of war in the event saw most Labour movements, not least the British and German, fall into line behind their respective governments. The ITUC official attitude was expressed in a manifesto which called on the Irish working class to avoid a war in which, '. . . it is your fathers, husbands and brothers whose corpses will pave the way to glory for an Empire that despises you . . .'.[10]

The difficulty was reconciling this with the views of the vast bulk of Unionist workers in the north who saw support for the war as their patriotic duty. This was not to mention the bulk of Nationalist trade unionists who followed the Redmondite line in supporting the British war effort. Even members of Irish unions, whose leadership opposed the war, joined up in great numbers. In May 1915, William Partridge of the ITGWU rather shame-facedly admitted that no less than 2,700 former union members were in the trenches, over half the union's membership on the eve of the Easter Rising. P.T.Daly another leader of the Transport union, reported, in 1917, that 5,000 union members had joined up, of whom 2,000 had since died.[11]

Nevertheless the old separatist adage 'England's difficulty is Ireland's opportunity' found an echo in the attitude of Connolly and his supporters. He added to it the refinement of turning the war into a revolution against the rulers of Europe:

> Should the working class of Europe, rather than slaughter each other for the benefit of kings and financiers, proceed to erect barricades all over Europe . . . that war might be abolished, we should be perfectly justified in following such a glorious example, than contributing our aid to the vulture classes that rule and rob the world.[12]

His promotion of such views in his paper *The Irish Worker* and at open air meetings in Belfast created notoriety which his colleagues in the ILP(I) in the city found intolerable. Connolly took the opportunity of Larkin's departure for the United States to move to head the union in Dublin. He left in his wake a movement in Belfast sorely divided and marginalised by the polarisation caused by the issues of Home Rule, partition and the war. Given his failure to win over the Labour movement in Belfast, let alone the Protestant workers, it is little wonder that Connolly should have felt more at home in Dublin.There at least a substantial minority shared his views which were now coalescing with those of the IRB in the need for a rising during the war.

Easter 1916

Connolly headed the strongest industrial force in Ireland, the ITGWU, with its own militia, the Irish Citizens' Army. Though the ICA was never much more than 300 in active strength and was more symbolic than real as a military force, certainly in comparison to the UVF and Irish Volunteers, it nevertheless gave Connolly the right to assume the status of commandant when the revolutionaries admitted him to their counsels in January 1916. Connolly's participation in the Rising arose out of his revolutionary Socialist Republicanism and had the official blessing of neither his union nor the ITUC. The initial popular hostility to the Rising gave way to revulsion at the British for the executions of the leaders. In this Connolly merited a special place, being the last of the executees. Also the fact that he was wounded in the leg, necessitating his being strapped to a chair to face the firing squad, vested the occasion with a particular poignancy. The dignified manner in which he faced death, as reported by his confessor, was seen in marked contrast to the vengeful way in which William Martin Murphy's *Independent* had called for his execution. He was accorded instant entry to the Nationalist pantheon of martyrs and purchased for Labour the right to participate in the leadership of the emerging nation. The fact that many of its members particularly in the north were averse to this was illustration that Connolly would continue to be a source of division in death as in life.

The ITUC&LP Congress of 1916, held a few months after the Rising, illustrated the tightrope that the leadership now walked in trying to keep the disparate sections from splitting. The problem was how to acknowledge Connolly's sacrifice without offending northern susceptibilities. This fell to Tom Johnson who was now President. Indeed, he and D.R. Campbell had taken over the running of the movement from Belfast due to the virtual emasculation of the organisation in Dublin by the military authorities in the immediate wake of the Rising. Johnson, while alluding to the sacrifice of Connolly and other Congress members who had perished in the Rising, at the same time spoke of their comrades who had laid down their lives in the war. Thus for the moment a potentially serious crisis was headed off, though Connolly's legacy would remain to both be fought over by his adherents and eschewed by his opponents in the Labour movement, a situation that continues to this day.

The Irish Convention 1917

In the wake of the Rising in 1916, Lloyd George made an attempt to bring the political parties together, but to no avail. A more serious effort was made the following year spurred on by the need to demonstrate some progress to American public opinion, particularly to Irish-Americans, in order to draw them into the Allied war effort. The much respected Sir Horace Plunkett was made chairman of the Irish Convention with the brief of bringing the conflicting parties in Ireland to the conference table to try once more to achieve a settlement. The Unionists by now were determined not to move from the position of permanent exclusion for the six north-eastern counties of Ulster. The IPP, under the ailing John Redmond, was frightened that any further concessions would lead to a further erosion of support to the more extreme

Nationalists. Sinn Féin refused to attend, seriously weakening the Convention's credibility at the outset. The Congress Party although offered seven of the ninety-five Convention seats, also refused to attend, signalling how far it was now within the Nationalist camp. In fact the Congress only refused to send delegates on the casting vote of its chairman William O'Brien, Connolly's successor at the ITGWU, and this despite the support of Tom Johnson for attendance. However, Belfast Trades Council voted unanimously to send its President H.T.Whitley. He along with other delegates from Belfast trade unions took up the Labour quota in the Convention, thus reflecting a growing dichotomy between north and south within the movement.

In fact the northerners who attended were as representative of rank and file views as the Congress leadership. The experience of the Convention was one which allayed the fears of the essentially Unionist Whitley who enthused, 'If Ulster working-men could hear the debates ... they would see that the danger to their interests, from an Irish Parliament was wholly imaginary'.[13] The Labour delegates supported a measure of self-government within the Empire, as put forward in the Convention majority report, with some adjustments in the working-class interest. They were out of step with the Congress official view, but more importantly with the vast majority of Protestant workers in the north, now inalienably wedded to partition. Their attempt to produce the elements of an independent strategy for Labour was supported by Belfast Trades Council and the Belfast Labour Party set up in 1917. The Convention report itself though was a dead letter due to Unionist and Sinn Féin non-compliance. The impetus towards final rupture was gaining momentum.

The Conscription Crisis 1918

One of the most divisive issues for the movement, in the latter stages of the war, was the threat to introduce conscription in Ireland in April 1918. This provoked violent conflict, both rhetorical and physical that made the fissures between the north and south into chasm. The official Congress position was one of utter opposition to the measure. Tom Johnson was appointed to the national committee, set up at the behest of the Lord Mayor of Dublin to incorporate all shades of Nationalist opinion in resistance to conscription. Johnson became secretary of the committee and was thus raised to national stature as a result. The Unionist workers of the north naturally supported conscription which brought Ireland into line with the rest of the United Kingdom. They saw Labour's participation in a joint campaign with Sinn Féin against the Government's prosecution of the war as further evidence that it was

just another wing of the overall Nationalist separatist thrust. This split
was reflected in the Congress of that year in less than parliamentary
language but in an even more violent fashion on the streets of Belfast.
This was occasioned by anti-conscription meetings in Belfast addressed
by Johnson. On Tuesday 16th April a meeting in front of the City Hall
was attacked by a hostile mob and Johnson sustained a split head from
a missile, while, according to the Nationalist *Irish News,* prominent
Unionists looked on with satisfaction. The result was rioting between
rival mobs for the rest of the day.

   A meeting of the anti-conscription campaign convention on the 20th
of April had declared that, 'The passing of the Conscription Bill by the
British House of Commons must be regarded as a declaration of war on
the Irish Nation'. The Labour movement's principal action in the campaign was the organisation of a one day general strike. The strike was
solid all over Ireland except in the north-eastern counties where the
Protestant workers were hostile. The resistance continued with local
committees throughout the country manned by trade unionists and
Sinn Féin supporters, who worked together well in making preparations for an attempt to impose conscription by force. In effect this was
reinforcing on the ground the growing rapprochement between the
national leaderships of the two movements. This represented a high
tide for Labour which would recede soon enough when it allowed Sinn
Féin a free run in the 1918 election. In relation to the movement in the
north, however, it seemed to confirm what many loyalist workers saw as
a Nationalist trend beginning in 1912, with support for Home Rule,
continuing with opposition to the war and now compounded by anti-
conscription activities, particularly by Tom Johnson. Thus the Labour
movement was being identified largely with the Nationalist side in the
growing drift towards national conflict. In the event, the crisis on the
Western Front, which had precipitated the attempt to introduce conscription, ended with the defeat of the final great German spring offensive and the measure was dropped.

The 1918 General Election

However, the extent to which the whole conscription affair had allowed
Sinn Féin to assume the mantle of Nationalist leadership would become
clear in the general election soon after. Labour had become a major
force thanks to the legacy of Connolly, the growth of the ITGWU in
the last years of the war, and its role in resisting conscription. The
question now facing Labour was whether it should capitalise on this and
emerge as an independent force thus risking Nationalist unity in a
nation-making election, or step down and give Sinn Féin a free run.

Considerable heart searching ensued. By the autumn the defeat of the Germans now seemed imminent and Sinn Féin was calling for Nationalist unity to elect an assembly that would represent Ireland, at the ensuing peace conference, to demand self determination. Labour candidates would dilute national solidarity. The Congress also had to deal with the problem of the susceptibilities of its northern members, most of whom were opposed to independence for Ireland. The Congress executive members were in a genuine dilemma as the election date drew closer.

Sinn Féin were worried that Labour candidates could split the vote in some constituencies to the advantage of the Parliamentary Party. As a result they offered Labour a free run in some Dublin constituencies if they stood down in the rest. This would also be consequent on Labour candidates signing a pledge that they would abstain from Parliament if elected and would work for an independent Irish Republic, accepting nothing less than complete separation from England. For a time this was under serious consideration by the Labour Executive but was eventually rejected. First, it was felt that such an alliance would finally cause the northern membership to secede. As well, the question of whether to stand at all was the subject of a special delegate conference in early November. At this the delegates were presented with a motion from the Executive put by Tom Johnson in which he urged the temporary suspension of Labour's electoral ambitions:

> A call comes from all parts of Ireland for a demonstration of unity on this question (of self-determination) such as was witnessed on the conscription issue. Your Executive believes that the workers of Ireland join earnestly in that desire, that they would willingly sacrifice for a brief period their aspirations towards political power if thereby the fortunes of the nation can be enhanced.[14]

Furthermore, both the delegates and the Executive were aware that in Nationalist areas there was a groundswell among trade union members in favour of Sinn Féin, which they would oppose at their peril. Consequently, the motion to give Sinn Féin a clear run was passed by ninety-six votes to twenty-three. This was greeted by Sinn Féin with gratitude and by the Parliamentary party as the final nail in the coffin of a campaign that had run out of steam.

In the north the new Belfast Labour Party (BLP) made no such pact with Sinn Féin as they were opposed not only to it but also to the Congress Party's support for self-determination. At a meeting of Belfast Trades Council soon after, D.R. Campbell, reported on the election conference in Dublin:

He thought it was undesirable that Labour should withdraw (hear hear) . . . he believed that the working class as a whole should have been afforded an opportunity of voting for the representatives of the workers, apart from any political parties existing in Ireland. A delegate said he thought it was a terrible thing that Sinn Féin should have been allowed to capture Labour in Ireland . . . He could scarcely believe that any organisation of Labour in Ireland would lie down to Sinn Féin to the extent it did.[15]

Belfast Labour put up four candidates in constituencies with large concentrations of Protestant workers. They faced competition from the newly established Ulster Unionist Labour Association (UULA) which had been set up by the Unionist leadership to provide working-class Unionist candidates and to keep workers within the fold. This was an organisation affiliated to the party, the absence of which, as Dawson Bates wrote to Carson, '. . . frequently leads the younger members of the working-class to Socialist, i.e. extreme organisations, run by the ILP where they are educated in views very different to those held by our body'.[16]

Furthermore the Congress Party pact with Sinn Féin, although not endorsed by Labour in the north, provided Unionists with the opportunity to castigate them as 'Bolshevik/ Republicans'. The red /green tag was effective in alienating the majority of electors in Belfast from Labour's message, in itself little different from that being heard in Britain. The BLP came second in all four constituencies but polled a very small vote in each. In the face of a concerted Unionist campaign, itself a mirror image of Sinn Féin's in imposing consensus among loyalists, Labour was being squeezed out by the major players in the national struggle. If it had stood nationally it might not have achieved more than a few seats. Nevertheless in the 1918 election, two out of three were first-time electors who were not given a chance to vote Labour. Labour was thus absent from a political bonding process which in many cases would last a lifetime.

The 1919 Belfast Engineering Strike

The following year Belfast became the scene of a major industrial dispute in which the British orientation of the workers in that city was clearly demonstrated and in which neither the Trades Council nor the ITUC had any role. Instead it was the British Federation of Shipbuilding and Engineering Trades (FEST), a body set up in 1890 to combat the employers' combine, which was the organising centre for the craft unions in the industry that was involved. Thus, unlike Belfast in 1907 and Dublin in 1913, it was mainly an action by skilled unions. It was furthermore initially a national dispute involving all the great industrial centres in a demand for a forty-four hour week. In Belfast the vast majority of the workers involved were Protestant and to that extent there was no possibility of sectarianism being brought in to divide them. At the outset the FEST nationally settled with the employers for a reduction of hours from the existing 53/54 to a 47 hour week. A national ballot approved this by 337,029 to 159,887. There was opposition in Glasgow where the militant shopstewards' movement led an unsuccessful strike in January and February 1919 in a demand for a forty hour week. The Clydesiders were thus continuing with their militancy which had caused considerable dislocation of wartime production.

The Belfast members of FEST had seen the achievement of maximum productivity during the war as a patriotic duty and had accordingly suspended the normal restrictive practices associated with such skilled unions. This had been recognised by Sir Edward Carson, then First Lord of the Admiralty, addressing shipyard workers in December 1918 at a launch, 'Not only did you do your duty but nothing pleased me more than when I heard that the men of Belfast beat the records all round . . . But for the efforts you made we should never have won and now that we have we ought to be grateful'.[17] This kind of rhetoric was commonplace from Unionist leaders speaking on behalf of UULA candidates during the 1918 election and surely heightened expectations of a better deal in the industry post-war.

In Belfast the opposition to the FEST Executive was equally strong, and the local union officials, such as Charles McKay of the U.K.Patternmakers and Robert Waugh of the Carpenters' and Joiners' unions, put forward a demand for a 44 hour week. There was little connection between Belfast and the Clyde on these demands. McKay, who was Belfast chairman of the FEST proposed, after the national ballot, that Belfast should ballot on whether to accept 47 or go it alone for 44. The results of this were 13,508 to 1,184 against the national acceptance, and 20,225 to 558 in favour of drastic action for 44 hours. This showed the strength of feeling in Belfast, especially as the dispute being unofficial, strike pay in most cases was not forthcoming.[18]

The strike ran from 25th January to 15th February. It involved directly the members of the Amalgamated Society of Engineers (ASE), the Amalgamated Society of Carpenters and Joiners (ASC.&J), Plumbers, Sheet Metal Workers, Boilermakers, Iron and Steel Shipbuilders' Society, Patternmakers, and the NAUL and Workers' Unions. Outside the engineering trades, 3,500 employees of the Ropeworks were thrown out due to the action of 20 firemen. For the city of 400,000 inhabitants, there was no gas, electricity or trams for 21 days. Many thousands were on the dole for lack of power. The strike completely disorganised the municipal, social and domestic, as well as the industrial life of the city. It was a model of disciplined behaviour, given its length and significance, in marked contrast to Belfast 1907 and Dublin 1913. This can be partly attributed to the largely loyalist nature of the participants. Partly also it was due to the quashing by the strike committee, of outside extremist Socialist agitators, such as John Hedley (England), Charles O'Meagher (Dublin) and Simon Greenspon (Dublin, of Polish Jewish origin). Also, by arrangement with the police, 300 strikers were enrolled as special constables, and these helped keep order.

The strike ended when the leaders decided that, due to the collapse of Cross Channel opposition to the FEST, particularly on the Clyde, they could not go it alone. The *Whig* quoted this reason from *The Workers' Bulletin,* organ of the Strike Committee.[19] While the strike was a massive show of discontent and solidarity by the workers, it was not evidence that they were becoming politically conscious in a Labour or Socialist sense. Those who criticised the Strike Committee for not proceeding in a more radical fashion, given the power at their elbow, failed to understand the mood of the strikers. They were in conflict with their employers, but still committed Unionists, in most cases. Nevertheless the May Day parade that year was attended by over 100,000, and speakers cited the strike as evidence of the need for more solidarity among workers in the municipal elections, the following year, when Labour won thirteen seats, their best ever result.

The Democratic Programme of the Dáil

In the south all the running after the election of 1918 was being made by the first Dáil set up by Sinn Féin to undermine and replace the British writ in Ireland. Labour was not directly represented, but its electoral sacrifice was acknowledged when Tom Johnson was asked to draw up the Democratic Programme of Dáil Éireann. There was also a backward glance in this gesture at the legacy of Connolly. The programme borrowed from Connolly certainly, but also from Pearse, as expressed in the Proclamation of 1916. Nonetheless many of the members of the Dáil regarded it as 'Communistic' in its original form drafted by Johnson, and it was given to Sean T.O'Kelly to excise the more Socialist elements of the economic and social sections. Despite this the final version was as close to Labour's own programme as they had the right to expect given the socially conservative nature of most of the Sinn Féin deputies, Arthur Griffith being not least in this respect. In the end the programme was never implemented given the hostility to it of the Free State leadership especially Collins, Cosgrave and O' Higgins.

Ireland at Berne

The Congress Party and the SPI were jointly represented at the meeting of the Socialist International at Berne in 1919 by Johnson and Cathal O'Shannon. The latter was a northerner and acolyte of Connolly now based in Dublin, who was coming to the fore in the movement. The meeting at Stockholm, the previous year, had been declared off limits for British subjects by the Government on the grounds that it was wartime, but also because they suspected the motives of the organisers. The Berne conference was now under the auspices of more moderate elements and the Government this time placed no hindrances in the way of the British and Irish delegations. The importance of Ireland being represented as a separate delegation was that it was tantamount to a recognition of its independent statehood. This gave the Labour movement tremendous cachet vis a vis Sinn Féin, who received no such recognition of their delegation to the Paris Peace conference.

The Irish proposed that the Berne conference in effect should recognise the right of Ireland to complete sovereignty. Ramsay MacDonald for the British delegation countered with a proposal calling for Home Rule within the Empire, though the British were eventually persuaded to go along with resolutions passed by the conference calling for self-determination for Ireland and for the Paris peace conference to grant this. The gratitude of Sinn Féin was expressed by DeValera, speaking as Dáil president in April 1919, 'When we wanted the help of Labour in Berne, Labour gave it to us and got Ireland recognised as a distinct nation'.[20]

Labour and the Anglo-Irish War

The Berne experience was indicative of how closely identified Labour was with the national struggle at least in the south. The movement in the north could only look on at a process with which they could not identify and which exposed them to their Unionist enemies. By now, if not in name then to all intents and purposes certainly, there were two Labour movements anticipating what would soon become the partition of Ireland. In the south at leadership level the relationship was good between Labour and the political and military wings of the Republican movement. This permeated all levels of the two movements with many union members being IRA men and union halls the venues for Republican meetings. While the Congress Party functioned as a legal movement, the Government was well aware of its sympathies and consequently, in times of tension, its members were subject to arrest, its offices to raids and its property to confiscation.

Although Labour was unhappy at the social attitude of Dail deputies, after it made sweeping gains in the 1920 local government elections, its councillors gave de facto recognition to the Local Government Board of the Dail. Nevertheless it was prepared to use on a pragmatic basis the facilities of departments of both competing administrations, where the interests of the workers and of the movement were best served. They drew back from ultimate recognition of the Dail as the legitimate Government of Ireland. The main consideration in this was the need to preserve the unity of the movement nationally and not alienate the membership in the north to the extent of secession.

A much higher degree of involvement in the national struggle was pursued by the industrial side of the movement in the use of the strike weapon to frustrate the prosecution of British security measures. The first of these was in Limerick in April 1919 when the Trades Council called a general strike in the city, in response to its designation as a 'special military area' with permits required for access. With the support of the IRA, the strike committee took over total control of the city inevitably attracting the media attribution of Limerick *Soviet*. The strikers received some national support but it was largely through their own local efforts that they succeeded in forcing the authorities to withdraw the permits. The following April, the Labour movement held a nationwide general strike in sympathy with the hundred Republican prisoners on hunger strike in Mountjoy jail. The strike was solid everywhere except the north. Within two days the authorities acceded to the demands of the prisoners.

A month later began a strike of more direct military significance when the Irish members of the National Union of Railwaymen (NUR) began to refuse to carry munitions. Despite military intimidation and dismissal the action continued till the end of 1920. They gained support for their action both from the other Irish unions and the British movement, including the holding of a representative union conference in England which produced a demand for the end of British military occupation of Ireland. The effectiveness of the strike, in strategic terms, was according to General Macready, the British commander-in-chief, '. . . a serious set-back to military actions during the best season of the year'.[21] In the north such activities were interpreted as the result of a Labour-Republican alliance. There was a backlash when the NUR members in the south refused to allow the carriage home by train of the body of Colonel Smyth, a Banbridge man and commander of the RIC in Munster, murdered in Cork on 17th July 1920. On the day of his funeral, workplace expulsions of 10,000 Catholics in the Belfast area began. Along with them many Socialists and trade unionists known to their opponents as 'rotten Prods' were expelled. These would not be the only repercussions in the north of the nexus between the Labour and Republican movements.

Northern Nemesis

In the face of these developments D.R.Campbell, now leader of the Labour Opposition in the Belfast Corporation, decided to take action as he had in the previous expulsions in 1912. He decided to get the matter raised in the Corporation with a motion of support for the expelled workers. However, his motion, which called for reinstatement and asked the Corporation to set up peace patrols from all sections of the community, was jointly proposed with Sinn Féin councillors and this gave the Unionists the opportunity to link the two. It followed an earlier fracas in the Corporation when Labour had opposed a Unionist motion condemning the murder in Dublin of an Ulsterman, Assistant Police Commissioner Redmond. The *Newsletter* reported that this proved they were 'tinged with Sinn Feinism'.[22]

Now the situation in Belfast had become so tense that Campbell and his Labour colleagues thought better of turning up on the day of the motion. Their Sinn Féin co-proposers, however, did attend and were heckled and spat upon by a crowd of loyalist workers in the public gallery, some of whom brandished revolvers. On the defeat of the motion, both Unionist councillors and spectators broke into a rendition of 'God Save the King' which according to the sneering report in the *Northern Whig,* 'must have gratified little the Sinn Féiners who stuck to their guns and will please still less the Labour Socialists who ran away.'[23] The meeting of the Corporation on expulsions had shown that the shipyard workers were prepared to come out of the Queen's Island to smite their opponents. The work of Campbell and his Labour colleagues was in tatters. Labour was now just as unacceptable to loyalists as Sinn Fein.

Elections North and South

An indicator of just how low the Labour stock had sunk, came with the first Northern Ireland general election in 1921. The Labour candidates were James Baird, Harry Midgley, John Hanna and Congregationalist Minister Bruce Wallace, a veteran of Labour politics in the city in the eighties and nineties. Wallace ran an independent campaign opposing the anti-partitionist attitude of the other three. The three booked the Ulster Hall for an election meeting. However, at the hour of the meeting on the evening of 17th May, the hall was filled by 4,000 shipyard workers who had marched there after work, led by leading 'pogromists'.

Baird, Midgley and Hanna hid in a dressing room, while a triumphant loyalist meeting was held in place of that scheduled for Labour. This physical rout became an electoral one with only 1,877 combined votes for the three Labour anti-partitionist candidates, while Wallace fared no better. Labour was being squeezed out in the trauma attending the birth of the northern state.

In the south, where Sinn Féin treated the 1921 elections as being for the second Dail, a repeat of the 1918 policy of standing down was the only possibility for Labour. This was even more the case since the previous election, as the Republicans could now claim that they had purchased the right to stand for Ireland's independence unopposed, with the blood of their fallen comrades. Labour claimed that they were refusing to stand on the principle that the electoral act was partitionist. In reality they would have been swept aside in any contest as the vast majority of their own members were now committed to vote for Sinn Fein.They would again have been allowed some seats if they stood, by agreement, on the Sinn Féin programme of complete independence but this would have alienated the northern members to the point of splitting the movement. Their advice to workers was to vote, 'only for those candidates who stand for the ownership and government of Ireland by the people of Ireland'.[24] The result of the election in the south was again a complete whitewash for Sinn Féin, a mirror image of Unionist victory in the north. The Labour movement was being consigned to the margins in both areas. There they were essentially to remain.

Partition and after

The Anglo-Irish Treaty, in which Labour had taken no part, established the hegemony of essentially socially conservative elements in both parts of the island. Labour was now being marginalised in the emergent partitionist settlement that would indeed usher in Connolly's prophesy of a 'carnival of reaction north and south'. In both states the new governments were hostile to Labour as a possible rival as they set about establishing secure foundations for survival against internal and external threats. When these had subsided, after a few years, there was still no room for Labour in the eyes of the statesmen of the new dispensation. DeValera's edict at the time of the election in 1918, that 'Labour must wait'· was matched if not outdone by Craig's statement, made when announcing the removal of PR, which was aimed more at Labour than the Nationalists, 'What I want to get in this House and what I believe we will get very much better in this House under the old fashioned plain and simple system, are men who are for the Union on the one hand, or who are against it and want to go into a Dublin

Parliament on the other'.[25] This statement outlined loyalist non-acceptance of Labour as a third force between conflicting nationalisms.

Epilogue

The bitterness of sectarianism in the north continued to dog Labour's attempts to provide a viable alternative to the Unionist-Nationalist dichotomy. In the south, fratricidal strife ensued in the movement, over the influence to be accorded to Larkin on his return from America in April 1923. The party returned seventeen out of eighteen candidates in the 1922 general election. However, the fractious nature of Larkin's relations with O'Brien and the other Congress leaders split and weakened both the industrial and political sides of the movement. This culminated in the 1923 general elections in which Larkin entered five candidates and in which, in tandem with Sinn Féin, he castigated the Congress party as having sold out to Saorstat Eireann. The result was a drop in Labour deputies to fourteen. The demoralisation of the movement was completed in its industrial sector, in November of that same year, when the Larkin inspired Dublin docks strike ended in ignominious defeat. Nevertheless, the Labour movement in the south had come of age. Although it would not supplant either of the parties of the civil war it would a remain an integral part of the southern political set-up, including junior partnership in a number of coalition governments.

The movement was now de facto partitioned in the political sense, although unions in the north continued in membership of ITUC and its successors. In the north following the comprehensive defeat in the 1921 general election, the political section regrouped under the charismatic leadership of Harry Midgley. In the 1922 municipal elections only two Labour candidates were returned in Belfast, underlining Labour's fall from favour in that area. However, the gloom was soon unexpectedly dispelled in the following year, as a result of the general election contest in West Belfast. Midgley, in the absence of Joe Devlin, who was boycotting the election, stood against the Unionist incumbent, Sir Robert Lynn. This was a mixed constituency and Midgley adroitly played to the disparate susceptibilities of those on the Shankill and Falls roads. As a result, with 22,255, he fell short of Lynn by just 2,720 votes an impressive tally which his biographer estimates was split equally between Protestant and Catholic voters.[26]

This was a great boost both for Midgley personally and for the movement as a whole. It established a precedent in the north in which Labour would appeal jointly to the more radical Protestant workers and, in the absence of a Nationalist candidate to the Catholic protest vote This was a pattern which became all but systematised in later northern parliamentary elections. In the ensuing period of euphoria, a meeting was held on March 8 1924 of shipbuilding and engineering unions and political groups which set up the Northern Ireland Labour Party (NILP). Effectively Labour was recognising the reality of partition. The new party would indeed be a 'broad church' in terms of the National Question, with membership ranging from Walkerite Labour Unionists to followers of James Connolly. In the early days of the party, Midgley could be found in the latter camp. The party survived in the sectarian political fray of the north by avoiding 'non-essential' issues like partition and by stressing social issues in a programme akin to that of the British Labour Party. It avoided adopting a position on the National Question until the late forties, and then at the expense of a debilitating split. Organically, it was not linked to either the British or southern Labour parties which in turn were unable to offer more than moral support. There would be peaks of support, in the late fifties and early sixties, when the NILP formed the Official Opposition at Stormont, though this inevitably faded just as soon as the almost episodic community conflict broke out again. Thus far the dismal history of Labour on this island has been blighted by the national conflict and until that is settled, one way or another, politics in a Labour sense must wait.

Michael Collins (in centre) on Sinn Féin platform in Armagh, Sept. 1921, shortly after his election for Co. Armagh to the Northern Ireland parliament (photograph, Allison Collection, Public Record Office of Northern Ireland)

CHAPTER NINE

Michael Collins
by
Tim Pat Coogan

What sort of man was Michael Collins? Curiously, if he had taken his brother Pat's advice his life might have been very different. Indeed, the Republic of Ireland might not exist today. Watching the storm clouds of World War One gather over Europe, Pat had written to Michael from Chicago urging his younger brother to leave his job in a London financial institution and come to join him in America. Had they teamed up one is tempted to speculate that one of the all time great Pat and Mike success stories might have resulted. As it was Pat became a Captain of police in Chicago and Michael went on to destroy the Irish police force, the armed Royal Irish Constabulary (RIC). In so doing he laid the foundations for today's unarmed Irish police, the Gardai Siochána or Civic Guard. What we do know is that in the early stages of World War One, the then twenty-six year old Collins agonised over Pat's letters inviting him to America. He took long lonely walks through London's dockland, seeing the ships leave for the New World, wondering should he go himself. War meant conscription would come soon, bringing with it an unthinkable choice: Option one was to become a conscientious objector. This was a course he did not believe in. His party piece was called *The Fighting Race* by J.C.Clarke, about the numbers of Irishmen who have died fighting abroad. For some that would be doggerel. For Michael Collins it was dogma. Option one was ruled out. So was Option two: to don a British uniform and fight for the Crown.

Collins solved the problem in his own inimitable way. He put on an Irish uniform and went to fight for Ireland, in the 1916 Easter Rebellion in Dublin. He was captured and sent to a Frongoch Internment Camp in Wales, the Republican University as it was known, It was here, in prison, that he began to think out a new philosophy of warfare and to re-organise the Irish Republican Brotherhood, the IRB, which later spear-headed the fight for Irish independence and led to the creation of modern Ireland. He was also the founder of modern urban guerilla warfare, the first freedom fighter, or urban terrorist. Mao Tse Tung studied his methods. And Yitzak Shamir, the former Prime Minister of Israel, was so impressed with Collins that not alone did he study him, he took the codename 'Micail' for his Irgun unit during the Israeli war of independence against the British.

But before going on with his career, let us briefly diverge to look at his origins and examine what led him, a man like that, to a London counting house in the first place. He was born, the youngest of eight children, on a ninety acre farm, a good holding for Catholics of the time, near Clonakilty in West Cork in 1890 to a remarkable set of parents. His father was nearly thirty years older than his mother, Marianne, and was in his seventy-sixth year when Michael arrived. Neither parent had much formal education but they both knew French, Latin, Greek, Irish and English. And, apart from being an expert farmer and veterinarian, Michael senior was also noted for his knowledge of astronomy, mathematics and for his skill as a builder. The Collins, or the O'Coileains as they were known in Irish, were once a very considerable Munster clan. And the family, both in Michael Collins's day and in our own, are recognised as being unusually intelligent and well-doing.

However, Michael senior died when young Michael was six, leaving Marianne to run the farm and look after the eight children. One by one the children were forced to emigrate until only Johnnie, who ran the farm after Marianne contracted cancer, and Michael, who was then fourteen, were left at home. There was at the time a tradition of recruiting for the British postal service in the Clonakilty area. When a baby boy was born, the neighbours' first comment on looking into the pram was 'musha tis the fine sorter he'll make'. Collins attended a class in Clonakilty which prepared pupils for the post office exams and, at the age of sixteen, crossed over to London to live with his sister Hannie and take up work as a boy clerk in the Kensington Post Office Savings Bank. He became very active in the Irish-Ireland life of the city, joining the Gaelic League to learn Irish and the Gaelic Athletic Association to play Gaelic Football and hurling, one of the most skilful and dangerous stick games in the world. He was a natural athlete, a particularly fine hurler, with a cloud-burst temperament that meant he either initiated or was drawn to any fights that broke out on the field. He found time to continue his studies and to become a regular theatre goer, becoming a particular fan of George Bernard Shaw. He was an omniverous reader, mopping up anything he could find in the way of Irish Nationalist literature and a variety of other authors including Conrad, Arnold Bennet, Chesterton, Hardy, Meredith, Swinburne as well as Irish literary figures such as Wilde, Yeats, Padraig Colum and James Stephens.

And now we come to the point where Collins's shadow begins to fall across contemporary Ireland. In or around 1914 he was sworn into the oath bound secret society, the Irish Republican Brotherhood, by a fellow Corkman, Sam Maguire. The then political situation was that Ireland in 1914 seemed to be in a fair way to getting her own parliament. At Westminister the Irish Parliamentary party, the constitutionalist wing of Irish national self-assertion, had brought Home Rule to the Statue Book under the leadership of John Redmond. But there was opposition. The Protestants of north-eastern Ulster clung to their Scottish ancestry and British links. They wanted to remain in union with Westminster, just exactly as do the Unionists of the present. More importantly, they were backed to the point, and some would say beyond the point of treason, in this attitude by the British Conservative Party. The Tories dealt a death blow to Home Rule, which had been passed by a democratically elected majority in the House of Commons by two major acts of defiance of Parliament. One was their sponsorship of the illegal gun running at Larne which put teeth into the Protestants' resolution to resist. The second was their even more efficacious sponsorship of a move within the British Army to refuse to proceed against their rebellious co-religionists, known as the Curragh mutiny. The Conservatives were not acting just out of affection for the Ulster Protestants. They also used the Orangemen, as a weapon in domestic British politics, to undermine the Liberal Government led by Prime Minister Asquith which had been driven to sponsor Home Rule through dependence on Irish Party support for its majority. The tactic, known as playing the 'Orange Card', was invented by Randolph Churchill, Winston's father. He coined the phrase: 'Ulster will fight and Ulster will be right'. As his grandson, also called Randolph, wrote sixty years later, 'that pithy phrase explains why Ulster is part of the United Kingdom today.'

The IRB, or Fenian movement, distrusted British politics and politicians as a matter of dogma. The Fenians did not accept that the Britain would ever confer Home Rule, or any form of independence on Ireland unless she were forced to, not by parliamentary methods, but by physical force. However, to revert to Michael Collins, in his everyday working life he sought to broaden his range of experience by moving from the Post Office to a firm of stockbrokers, Horne and Co., and from there to a clerkship in the Board of Trade and finally, perhaps because of brother Pat's urgings, moved to gain a flavour of American business life, to the Guaranty Trust Company of New York's London Office where war found him.

He found his own war in Dublin in Easter 1916. It was a rebellion that should not have been allowed to happen. Had Home Rule for all Ireland not been aborted by the strength of the Unionist/Conservative alliance there would have been no subsequent Anglo-Irish war, no civil war, no partition and no IRA, or Northern Ireland problem today. But that searing week of flame and folly during Easter 1916 claimed the lives of some of the people Collins most admired: Tom Clarke, James Connolly, Sean Hurley, Sean MacDiarmada, Joseph Plunkett. To him their deaths were a debt owed, a charge against freedom, which England would repay. But he would not present his bill for retribution by means of conventional warfare. He still believed in fighting. In the parliamentary game as played at Westminister the rules were so arranged that the outnumbered Irish Nationalists always lost. But he now understood that static warfare, seizing a stronghold, be it a building such as Dublin's General Post Office in which he fought during the rebellion, or a mountain top, and then slugging it out with rifles and shot guns against an adversary who possessed heavy artillery would continue to provide the Irish with heroes and martyrs – and the British with victories.

Instead Collins evolved a new concept of guerrilla warfare based not on the capture of the enemy's bricks and mortar, but on his information. Traditionally Dublin Castle, the seat of British administration in Ireland, had used a network of spies and informers to infiltrate, and then snuff out, movements directed at securing Irish independence. Collins perfected a system of spying on the spies. Every important branch of the Castle system, be it banking, policing, the railways, shipping, the postal service, whatever was infiltrated by his agents. These were not highly trained, CIA-style operatives, but ordinary men and women, little people whom nobody had ever taken notice of before. Collins gave them a belief in themselves, a courage they did not know they possessed, and they in return gave him a complete picture of how their masters operated. That typist in Military Intelligence saw to it that Collins had a copy of the Colonel's orders to the Captain before the officer received the originals. This railway porter carried dispatches, the docker smuggled in revolvers, the detective told him who the informers were – and the Squad used revolvers to deal with them. The Squad was his particular brainchild. For the first time in her history the Irish had a team of assassins trained to eliminate informers. In the scale of modern warfare, the totals were tiny. Collins was careful about wasting human life. He struck selectively, to achieve the maximum political and psychological advantage. As he said himself: 'England could always replace a detective. But the man can not step into the dead man's shoes-and his knowledge'. He thus demoralised the hitherto invincible Royal Irish Constabulary, the armed police force which operated from fortified barracks and held Ireland for the Crown.

Generalised warfare broke out all over the country as the British introduced new men and new methods in a vain effort to counter the guerrilla tactics of Collins's active service units and the Flying Columns of volunteers which lived on the run, eating and sleeping where they could. Held back from making a full scale use of her army by the force of world opinion, largely Irish-American, the British tried to fight a 'police war' carried on by hastily formed forces of ex-servicemen and officers troubled by little discipline and less conscience. The Black and Tans and the Auxiliaries wrote new chapters of horror in the blood-stained story of the Anglo-Irish relationship. Reprisals for the activities of Collins and his colleagues included the burnings of homes and cream-eries, random murder and the widespread use of torture. Through it all Collins lived a 'life on the bicycle'. The most wanted man in Europe, he smiled his way through a hundred hold-ups never wearing a disguise, never missing an appointment, never certain where he would spend the night.

One of his central ideas was derived from G.K.Chesterton's *The Man Who Was Thursday*. He was given the book by Joseph Plunkett, his immediate superior in 1916. Plunkett, who was dying of tuberculosis, took part in the fighting and was married in his cell, ten minutes before facing a firing squad. Obviously any relic of such a figure would be prized by his lieutenant. And Collins prized in particular the advice of the Chief Anarchist, in the Chesterton book: 'if you don't seem to be hiding nobody hunts you out.' Accordingly Collins never seemed to be hiding. He always wore good suits, neatly pressed. And time after time, this young businessman was passed through police cordons unsearched, with his pockets stuffed with incriminating documents. It seems to be an iron law with policemen, both in Collins's time and ours, that terrorists are not expected to wear pin striped suits and clean collars and ties. He had a network of safe houses and secret rooms where he transacted business. In addition to his campaign of warfare he ran a national loan which was banned by the British so that either its advertisement or sale became illegal. Yet every subscriber got a receipt and the loan was fully subscribed. He was President of the omnipresent secret society, the Irish Republican Brotherhood which regarded him as the real President of the Irish Republic, and Minister for Finance in the Sinn Féin Cabinet. In addition he was Director of Intelligence of the Irish Republican Army (IRA). Any one of those jobs would have consumed the energy of an ordinary man, but Collins combined them all efficiently and effectively.

He combined a mind like a laser beam with a hawk-like eye for detail. Nothing escaped his attention. Everything attracted his interest. Shaw's latest play, the way the Swiss organised a Citizen Army, Benjamin Franklin's proposals for dealing with loyalists, or the latest edition of Popular Mechanics. An article in this journal in November of 1920 led to the first use in warfare of the Thomson gun. Collins saw the article on the recently invented weapon and had enquiries made about this 'splendid thing' which led to the Irish American leader Joseph McGarrity of Philadelphia buying five hundred of the weapons. Two Irish American ex-officers were sent to Ireland to train the IRA in the use of the weapons. Only a handful got through American customs, but these were duly used in a number of Dublin ambushes.

Collins was tough and abrasive with his male, and sometimes female colleagues. But he was gently and playfully with children and old people. Throughout the eighteen months that Eamon de Valera was in America, on a propaganda and fund raising mission, which lasted most of the Anglo-Irish war, Collins risked his life to call each week to his absent chief's family, bringing them money and companionship. Eventually the war effort Collins had spearheaded drove the British to a conference table and a settlement, that was unpalatable to many Irishmen and women, namely a partitioned Irish Free State that would owe allegiance to the Crown. It was a deal which had been foreshadowed to de Valera in four days of talks between himself and Lloyd George, the British Prime Minister, in London during July 1921. But de Valera did not want to be the man who faced up to the implications of that deal. Instead he repaid the kindness Collins had shown his family in Machiavellian fashion. He stayed away himself from the opprobrious negotiations, but manipulated Collins into going to London as part of the delegation which signed the Anglo-Irish Treaty of December 6th. 1921, the constitutional foundation document of modern Ireland. Collins took the leading part in the Treaty's negotiation. Facing one of the most powerful British delegations ever assembled. Winston Churchill only ranked fourth on the team which was led by Lloyd George and included the Lord Chancellor, Lord Birkenhead and the leader of the Conservative Party Austen Chamberlain. Subsequently Collins became Chairman of the Executive Council (in effect the Government) of the Irish Free State which emerged and later Commander-in-Chief of the Army.

The Treaty did not yield the Republic he had hoped for but provided what Collins prophetically termed a 'stepping stone' to today's Irish Republic. All the other stepping stones to the tragedy of today's Northern Ireland situation were part of that negotiation too. In a very real sense Collins's premature death was caused by the forces which still rage about the north-eastern corner of the land and people he fought for. The story of his life explains tomorrow's news from Belfast. He was forced into an impossible janus-faced policy. On one hand, as head of the infant Provisional Government of southern Ireland, he engaged in civil war to defend the Treaty against De Valera and his former comrades in the IRA. He argued fiercely for its potential for democracy and freedom. On the other, the plight of the Catholics in Northern Ireland, subject to pogrom and prejudice, drove him to secretly arm the IRA in the north. He did everything in his power to destabilise the northern state. He organised burnings, raids, kidnappings; and once, when some of his followers faced execution, sent two former members of the Squad over to England to shoot the British executioners who were detailed to hang them. At the last moment the IRA men were reprieved. So were the hangmen.

One of the great questions of Irish history is: If Collins had lived longer would he have brought fire or prosperity to his country? Or would he have died of drink or disillusionment at the effects of the civil war which broke out over the terms of the Treaty? Certainly he had more business acumen and vision than any of his contemporaries. He foresaw a role for Ireland in Europe long before the EEC was ever heard of. He preached that Ireland should study the lessons of German scientific advancement, Danish agriculture and bring them back home to develop a distinctive Irish economy and culture of its own. He loved the Irish language, but not merely as a medium of expression. He saw in the language a method of thinking and ultimately of acting, more suited to Ireland than the Anglo-Saxon inheritance. He believed in personal initiative, once writing:

> Millionaires can spend their surplus wealth bestowing libraries broad-cast upon the world. But who will say that the benefits accruing could be compared with those arising from a condition of things in which the people themselves were prosperous enough to buy their own books and to put together their own local libraries in which they could take a personal interest and acquire knowledge in proportion to that interest.

Tragically we will never know how Collins might have developed, for as Heine once remarked, the Irish always pull down a noble stag. A couple of months short of his thirty-second birthday, in a remote Cork valley, known in Irish as Béal na mBláth, the Mouth of Flowers, he died, not far from where he was born, in an ambush laid by a former comrade in arms. This man, ironically, had undergone sadistic tortures at the hands of British intelligence officers, rather than betray his boyhood friend, Michael Collins. Collins' career is a paradigm of the tragedy of modern Ireland. The suffering, the waste of talent, the hope, the bedevilling effect of history and nomenclature whereby one man's terrorist is another man's freedom fighter.

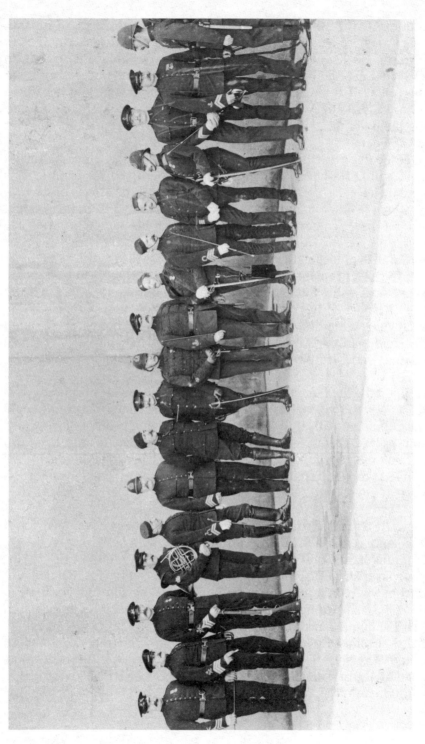

Photograph of members of the Royal Irish Constabulary, wearing all their different uniforms c. 1914 (Linen Hall Library)

CHAPTER TEN

British Security Policy in Ireland 1919–21
by
Keith Jeffery

During the period 1919–21 the British Government faced a protracted and violent challenge in Ireland which contained elements of colonial warfare, civil war and internal rebellion. The challenge, moreover, was both political and military, and in any discussion of British policy no hard and fast division can be made between security policy on the one hand and political developments and policy making on the other. It is very important to bear in mind that the problem which faced the British Government and the administration in Ireland was not just a security problem. It was both a violent challenge and a political problem as well. The two aspects are of course intimately connected, a fact perceived most clearly perhaps on the Irish Nationalist side.[1]

The strategy being pursued by Sinn Féin in this period was one which both pushed ahead as a violent challenge to the British administration in Ireland and as a political campaign to enlist the Irish people behind their demand for independence. The complex nature of the conflict is illustrated by the variety of names which can be applied to it. What, exactly, do you call the 1919–21 conflict? There are various options. The 'Irish War of Independence' is quite a popular title, though quite clearly all of Ireland was not independent at the end of hostilities in 1921. Indeed, even the twenty-six counties which comprised the Irish Free State were not fully independent. Do you call it the 'Anglo-Irish War', which is favoured a bit more by historians of the revisionist tendency? This title is, perhaps, a little less politically (and emotionally) loaded, but it is still highly problematic. It implies that it was a war between 'the English' and 'the Irish' which it certainly was not. There were English-men on the Irish side and Irishmen on the English side (not to mention Scots, Welsh and a few others), although I fully concede that there were more Irishmen on the 'English' side than there were Englishmen on the Irish side. But that's just the nature of the problems here. It is some-times called the 'Tan War', which emphasises only one element of the security situation, the Black and Tans. This description indicates perhaps the extent to which the conflict was not an 'real' war; it was not so much orthodox, regular warfare as an irregular, guerilla campaign. In that way, of course, what happens in Ireland sets the model for many subsequent wars of national liberation, particularly since the Second World War. Sometimes the period as a whole is simply called the 'Troubles' which is a pleasingly neutral term, but one which since 1969 has run the risk of being confused with the more recent conflict in Northern Ireland. Each of these different designations has its own validity, but the point to bear in mind is that each also implies a different interpretation of the conflict. I will call it 1919–21 and evade the issue altogether.

There are three main points which should be made concerning British policy making towards Ireland during this period before we examine the security aspects in greater detail.[2] First, there was a fatal (sometimes literally so) muddle between a civilian security strategy and a military one. Neither the Cabinet in London nor the administration in Dublin were quite sure how exactly to respond to the challenge. As it emerged in 1919 and 1920 the challenge was certainly explicitly military (as had been the case in 1916) but there were quite sound political reasons for the policy makers not to meet it with military measures. If London formally accepted that the struggle in Ireland were a 'war' and that they were fighting a real 'army', then this would bestow legitimacy upon the IRA and the Nationalist cause and concede part of the political battle.[3] What Sinn Féin wanted to establish was that they were fighting a legitimate war for national liberation; that one army was fighting another army. By contrast, the line initially taken by the authorities was that they were effectively dealing with a criminal conspiracy for which the use of the police, rather than the military, was more appropriate. Events on the ground in Ireland progressively undermined this view.

The second consideration is that at this time (as frequently since) Ireland was very low down on the British political agenda. Because the violence of 1919–21 so obsessed people and politicians (and the security forces) in Ireland, it is sometimes assumed that the policy makers in London were similarly affected. In fact, they were not. It was not really until about the spring of 1920, more than a year after the campaign had started, that the British Cabinet seriously began to look at the security problem. There were other, bigger problems to be solved. In the aftermath of the First World War the British Prime Minister, David Lloyd George and his colleagues were mostly concerned with the Paris peace conference and the re-establishment of peaceful relations in the postwar world. Notwithstanding the presence of Sinn Féin representatives at Paris, Ireland was very small beer indeed and was very much a side issue.[4] The intensity of violence, moreover, was only building up rather slowly in 1919. The crucial time regarding policy making (both in the political and security side) was really from the spring of 1920 through to the summer of 1921 – a relatively short period of just sixteen months. And in security terms, the authorities only began to adopt a coherent policy during the first half of 1921.

The third consideration is that Ireland has to be seen within the broader context. I have already mentioned this in regard to the postwar peacemaking, but within the British imperial system Ireland only represents one of a number of nationalist challenges which emerged after the First World War and which contributed towards a 'crisis of empire'[5] during the postwar years. In March 1919 there were quite serious Nationalist disturbances in Egypt. The same month there was unrest in India and the Amritsar Massacre when a political meeting in the Punjab was fired on by British Indian soldiers and over 300 people were killed; a military response to a political challenge if you like. Other manifestations of nationalism occur elsewhere in the Empire at the same time[6] and from the London perspective what was happening in Ireland was just one of a series of challenges. This undoubtedly made British policy makers cautious when dealing with Ireland. They were anxious not to concede anything in political terms which might simply encourage Nationalists all over the Empire. It made them equally careful, for example, in dealing with India where policy also involved granting a species of 'Home Rule'. You find senior British ministers saying at this time that they did not want 'another Ireland' in India, since that would signal a critical loss of control within the Empire. The series of imperial challenges also stretched the available British resources of manpower, and, indeed, of intellectual effort. It seems clear that the pressures under which the British Government were operating during the immediate postwar years adversely affected the quality of decision-making.[7] Irish security policy was certainly characterised by a tendency to cut corners and discover a 'quick fix' of some sort or other. In addition to the imperial problem there was a generalised fear of revolution after the First World War, which had precipitated the collapse of four empires: Russia, Germany, Austria-Hungary and the Ottoman (Turkish) empire. The Bolsheviks were seated in power in Moscow and apparently threatening revolution across the world. This prompted fears that there might be revolution within Great Britain itself,[8] not just in Ireland, which added a further complication for the policy makers in London.

We can date the beginning of the war (if that is what it was) – the conflict – to 21 January 1919 at Soloheadbeg in County Tipperary when a group of Irish volunteers captured a cart load of quarry explosives and killed two policemen escorting it. Throughout 1919 there was sporadic violence and gradually a well organised terror campaign developed. In June, District Inspector Hunt of the Royal Irish Constabulary was assassinated in the centre of Thurles, County Tipperary, in broad daylight by men who wore no disguise. Those who witnessed the killing gave no assistance to the police afterwards which illustrates a crucial advantage enjoyed by the volunteers (who quickly became known as the Irish Republican Army). They had a very substantial measure of popular support, however produced, by sympathy or by intimidation. This popular support increasingly gave them a considerable freedom of action over a large part of the country. The initial targets were the police and a series of raids were launched on police barracks, although by the autumn the IRA were beginning to attack military units as well The first soldier killed was in September 1919, when a party of soldiers on their way to church in Fermoy, County Cork, was attacked for their rifles.

In the early days, however, the brunt of the IRA campaign was borne by the police. The Royal Irish Constabulary (RIC) was a semi-military force. They were armed policemen; they lived in barracks; and they were organised on a military basis. On the other hand they were all Irish and very much still drawn from the community they served, except that a police recruit was always stationed away from his home area. (This still applies in the Garda Siochána, which has inherited many of the characteristics of the RIC.) In that sense they were not local policemen who had families in the neighbourhood. At the beginning of 1919 there were about 9,000 policemen, all living in the community and presenting soft – and obvious – targets for the IRA. The Republican attacks, however, had an odd affect on police recruitment. In the first half of 1919 the RIC was markedly under strength and intimidation of families led to numbers of resignations, but towards the end of 1919, as the terror campaign intensified, local enlistment picked up sharply.[9] What does this mean? There are a number of explanations, including the improvement of police pay and conditions, but clearly not all Irish people (north or south) supported Sinn Féin's methods. Some were still prepared to support law and order, even that of the increasingly unpopular British régime based in Dublin Castle. The Government, as already noted, was certainly anxious to avoid an overtly military solution to the Irish disorder and they began to expand the size of the police force. So, the first response by the Government was to recruit more policemen but by the end of 1919 local recruitment could not keep up with demand and at the end of the year the RIC, for the very first time, began to enlist non-Irishmen, many of whom were ex-servicemen. Owing to a shortage of police uniforms many of the early British recruits were kitted out in a mixture of the very dark bottle green RIC uniform and khaki army service dress, which is where the term 'Black and Tans' comes from – a term taken from a similar nickname applied to a pack of foxhounds in County Limerick. The nickname was also generally applied to a further reinforcement of the police called the Auxiliary Division which was raised from mid 1920 onwards and eventually reached a maximum strength of 1,500 in mid-1921, at which time there were also 14,000 regular policemen.[10]

The emergence of the Auxiliaries in the middle of the 1920s was the result of a British Cabinet review of policy in the spring of that year. A new army Commander–in–Chief was appointed: Sir Nevil Macready, who very reluctantly took up the post in March 1920. Macready had considerable expertise in the field of police-military co-operation.[11] He had been in command of the troops at Tonypandy in South Wales in 1911, at the time of a violent strike in the coalfield there. He was named as Military Governor of Belfast in 1914. Had the threat of a violent challenge from the Ulster Volunteer Force come to pass, and if the Government had introduced martial law in the North he would officially have been in charge. During the war he worked in the War Office as Adjutant General, (responsible for liaison with the civil power) until 1918 when there was a police strike in England and he was transferred to be Commissioner of the Metropolitan Police in London. He was perhaps the best qualified British general to take command in Ireland. He also had a very sharp political sense. He was a personal friend of Lloyd George, and was a Home Ruler with Liberal political sympathies. However, he was not at all keen to go to Ireland. In 1919 he had written to Ian Macpherson, who had just been appointed Chief Secretary for Ireland, that 'I loathe the country you are going to and its people with a depth deeper than the sea and more violent than that which I feel against the Boche [Germans]'.[12] It is not clear whether this attitude was regarded as an advantage or disadvantage for the Dublin job. In the end he was apparently persuaded to take the post by his old army chief Field Marshal Lord French, who was then the Lord Lieutenant in Ireland, and his move from London was sweetened by a £5000 disturbance allowance.

When Macready arrived in Dublin his first impression was that the Irish administration was completely flat on its back. The civil service had more or less given up in the face of the Sinn Féin challenge. Republican courts were operating in parts of the West where the writ of the British Government did not seem to be running any more. The police were demoralised and had not yet begun to train people properly to meet the new situation. He believed that they needed to develop expertise, and they were not really equipped to meet the challenge. The army, moreover, had been held back by the Government for the political reasons already outlined. Macready refused to take charge of all the security forces, civil as well as military, in Ireland – from his point of view a wise political move, but not one that made any sense in security policy terms. An early proposal, therefore, was for a new chief of police to help sort things out. It was easier said than done to get someone to accept this particular poisoned chalice. Macready's preferred candidate for the job was Lieutenant-General Sir Edward Bulfin, a Dublin Catholic who had done well in command of troops during the recent nationalist unrest in Egypt. But Bulfin refused the offer on the grounds that 'it would be most distasteful to him to do any work . . . which was not of a purely military character'.[13] In the end the post was given to Major-General Hugh Tudor, an artillery officer acquaintance of Winston Churchill (then in the Cabinet as Secretary for War). Tudor was credited with having invented the creeping smokescreen,[14] a First World War artillery technique, and one which might well have stood him in good stead as head of the Black and Tans, as it turned out.

Tudor adopted rather a 'gung ho' attitude to his job and enthusiastically supported the raising of the Auxiliary Division, which was a markedly more 'military' formation than the ordinary police. In effect he hoped that by taking a tough line the Black and Tans would frighten Sinn Féin out of existence. What in fact developed was that these recruits, who were predominantly ex-servicemen, were frequently sent out on duty having received only the most cursory of training.[15] The 'Tans' gained a fierce reputation for unflinching severity as they sped about the country in armoured cars of one sort or another and their activities represented the development, by the end of 1920, of a policy of counter-terror masterminded (if that is the right word) by Tudor backed up by Lloyd George. The Prime Minister was as anxious as anyone for a quick fix in Ireland and it appears that this was precisely what Tudor offered to provide. Rather like Henry II and Thomas à Beckett, Lloyd George asked 'who will rid me of these turbulent Sinn Féiners?' To which Tudor replied: 'I will'. Lloyd George (and here the parallel with Henry II breaks down) seems to have told him to get on with it and assured him that the Government would turn a blind eye to whatever happened in Ireland. Although there is no direct written evidence for this, it is confirmed by contemporary anecdotal reports.[16] Tudor's policy of reprisals – attacking people and property with alleged Sinn Féin connections, burning creameries in Republican areas, and so on[17] – flowed directly from the permissive and thoughtless approach to Irish security policy adopted in London. The policy did not work – in fact it made matters much worse – but it reflected the anxiety of Lloyd George and his colleagues to try to sort Ireland out without too much fuss, as it were, and without actually putting much intellectual effort into it.

By the turn of the year 1920–21, however, Lloyd George had begun to appreciate that the police policy was not working. Writing in February 1921 to the Chief Secretary for Ireland (Sir Hamar Greenwood) the Prime Minister summed up the problem with the Tans as it had begun to emerge:

> I am not at all satisfied of the state of discipline in the Royal Irish Constabulary and its auxiliary force. Accounts reach me from too many and too authoritative quarters to leave any doubt in my mind that the charges of drunkenness, looting and other acts of indiscipline are in too many cases substantially true ... [This is] causing grave uneasiness in the public mind ... It is vital that the violence and indiscipline which undoubtedly characterises certain units in the Royal Irish Constabulary should be terminated in the most prompt and drastic manner. It is weakening seriously the hands of the executive.

While this was the Prime Minister's private opinion, he was less inclined to be quite so critical in public. Indeed, his hard line in private contrasted strongly with assurances of support for the police in Parliament and elsewhere. In his letter to the Chief Secretary he also linked the indiscipline in Ireland with public opinion. If the ill behaviour continued, Lloyd George believed that 'public opinion, which is already unhappy, will swing round and withdraw its support from the policy which is now being pursued by the Government in Ireland'. The excesses of the Black and Tans had a clear political impact. 'There is no doubt', he wrote, 'that indiscipline, looting and drunkenness in the Royal Irish Constabulary is alienating great numbers of well disposed people in Ireland and throwing them into the arms of Sinn Féin'.[18]

A few days later Greenwood replied to Lloyd George in terms which illustrate some of the problems of command in Ireland: 'I have told Tudor that discipline [in the police] must be maintained or he and certain subordinates must go. He's a gallant man and it's hard to be blunt with him but he appreciates the position'.[19] Concern about the police reached the highest in the land. In March 1921 King George V told Field Marshal Sir Henry Wilson, the professional head of the British army and an Irishman born in County Longford, that he wanted 'to abolish *all* Black & Tans' and that he was concerned about Tudor. Wilson replied that in his opinion 'Tudor was a gallant fellow on service [i.e. during the war], but a man of no balance, knowledge or judgement & therefore a deplorable selection for his present post'.[20]

The 'police policy' in Ireland was exemplified by Lloyd George's clear affirmation to the Cabinet that 'you do not declare war against rebels'.[21] The intensity of the conflict at first lent some weight to the notion that the Republican campaign was not a full-scale military operation. The balance of advantage, however, lay clearly with the Republicans. From the beginning of 1919 to the end of 1920, 177 police and 54 soldiers were killed, as against only 42 IRA and civilian fatalities together.[22] As the struggle continued the number of IRA and civilian casualties over the whole period from January 1919 until the truce in July 1921, rose disproportionately, but still represented just about a third of the security force casualties: 751 people in all were killed and some 1,200 wounded. Of the dead 405 (54%) were police and 150 (20%) military, while 196 (26%) were civilian and IRA.[23] It is natural to try and draw parallels between then and now. The peak year (so far) for violence in the Northern Ireland conflict since 1969 was 1972, during which the proportions of casualties were almost exactly the opposite: about two-thirds civilian deaths to one-third security force. One of the reasons for this is the differing nature of the challenge between 1919–21 and since 1969. There was, for example, almost no urban rioting during the earlier period, which was much more in the nature of a guerrilla war with the specific targets being the security forces.

Another important point to bear in mind is that although the tempo of violence increased during 1920 and 1921, it did not affect all parts of the island equally. We might also hazard that (as in the twenty years or so since 1969, if looked at as a whole) most people most of the time were not physically affected by the struggle. Some parts of Ireland were more peaceful than might be expected. One example comes from a report submitted by a British army colonel in command at Strabane, County Tyrone, whose men were deployed across south County Donegal.

> We have left practically all the original area which is now perfectly quiet and I *hope* will remain so. The danger is the irresponsible youths . . . This place is very quiet and quite free from outrages. The harriers hunt, there is good shooting [presumably animals rather than people], and in the spring, excellent fishing. There is a cinema for the men which they much appreciate and I am getting a football ground.
>
> The men have worked wonderfully well and their behaviour has been so exemplary that the inhabitants of Killybegs were most sorry to lose them, even Sinn Féiners coming to say goodbye and good luck, and I have been overwhelmed with the compliments from all sorts of people on the men's behaviour. The R.C. priest even made a public speech in his Church on the subject.[24]

However this letter might be interpreted, it suggests that the situation in Ireland in 1920 was by no means absolutely straightforward. The position in Strabane and Donegal suggests that it was not simply a case of 'them and us' or 'English versus Irish'; it was something much more complex.

During 1920 matters hotted up. One of the targets identified by Michael Collins, a key strategist on the Republican side, was the British intelligence network. Those detectives working on political crime in the Royal Irish Constabulary and the Dublin Metropolitan Police had been virtually eliminated by the spring of 1920. Collins himself was a good example of how intelligence on the British side was defective. Collins had been interned after the 1916 Rising along with several hundreds of his colleagues in a camp at Frongoch in North Wales, but no one had troubled to question him systematically or take his photograph. He had actually been held by the British for several months but when he emerged during the Anglo-Irish War as a hugely important figure in the IRA the British knew very little about him, let alone what he looked like. What this sorry state of affairs (from the British perspective) confirms is not just the ineptness of the British intelligence effort,[25] but also the low level of perceived threat from Irish Republicans. Faced with the outbreak of violence in 1919–20 the British did not take it very seriously. This was understandable since the history of Irish risings had hitherto been a history of failure. But when the IRA emerged as sophisticated, able and ruthless, it caught the administration in Ireland on the hop. By contrast Collins's own intelligence was very good. He had agents in the police and Dublin Castle who kept him very well informed about security force plans.[26]

One of Collins's most notable successes was the simultaneous shooting of a dozen or so British intelligence officers on the morning of Sunday 21 November 1920. No bout of Irish 'troubles' passes without at least one 'Bloody Sunday' and this was a dramatic and horrifying operation. Some of the men were roused from their beds and shot in front of their families. That afternoon there were more deaths when a squad of auxiliary police opened fire at Croke Park Stadium in Dublin where 12 people were killed and 11 seriously injured. A week later another dramatic IRA operation marked the intensification of the rural conflict. It was led by the legendary Tom Barry who was in command of the 3rd West Cork Brigade. He was an ex-British soldier (as indeed were many of his colleagues). Barry had a formidable reputation as one of the most ruthless Republican commanders and at the end of November at a place called Kilmichael near Macroom in County Cork, Barry's force of 36 riflemen ambushed two lorries carrying auxiliary police and killed 15 of the 17, leaving the others for dead. This particular incident coming a week after Bloody Sunday seems to have persuaded Lloyd George that civil methods were no longer sufficient alone and he now told the Cabinet that he believed a species of war now existed in

Ireland. That meant stepping-up the security effort to a different level. Martial law – which in effect put the army in overall charge of security – was introduced for eight counties in the south and west of Ireland and there was an intense debate as to whether martial law should be imposed over the whole of Ireland or not. Representing the army, Sir Henry Wilson and Sir Nevil Macready argued that martial law should cover the whole country. They said it was absurd that someone could step over a county boundary and escape the full rigour of martial law, which could include detention without trial and very swift retributive justice or action against people caught, say, carrying arms.

At the end of 1920 there was a shift from civil to military methods. This stemmed partly from a reform of the security effort. The Castle administration gradually began to get control of the police and the allegations of reprisals fell off in the spring of 1921 because discipline was more fully enforced. But the shift away from the police, and from civilian methods, also indicated the extent to which general community support was slipping away from the Dublin Castle régime. Put simply, police forces really only work by consent. Armies on the other hand rely more on coercion. Once even the minimal level of consent which might still have existed in Nationalist Ireland – from people who had no great interest in politics but just wanted 'law and order' – was lost then there was no option but to move on to a military 'solution'. Militarising the security effort was an indication of the degree to which the Castle administration was losing the political war.

Martial law gave the British army very wide powers by the beginning of 1921 over a large swathe of the south and west (but not including Dublin, which was an important centre for Republicans).[27] These powers did enable the soldiers to restrict the activities of IRA flying columns. It is also true that in 1921 the British finally began to develop a well organised and co-ordinated security policy. With martial law the army took the leading role and the police came directly under their command in the designated area (that was the theory at any rate). Macready or his subordinates in Cork, therefore, effectively had command of all security operations in Munster, which was a martial law area, and parts of Leinster. They began to develop joint police-military operations. The whole intelligence structure was revamped at the end of 1920 and a lot of resources went into this but it would be some time (if ever) before the increased investment might bear fruit. The politicians, however, were, as always, anxious for immediate results.

During 1921 the army began to plan a major summer offensive. In May 1921 Sir Henry Wilson outlined the position in a letter to Sir Henry Rawlinson, an old friend who was the army Commander–in–Chief in India.

In Ireland [he wrote] we have had one of the worst week-ends since the beginning of the rebellion, and it is perfectly clear to me that unless the 'Frocks' [Wilson's nickname for politicians from the frock-coats they wore] shout out at the top of their voices and get England on their side, and then really set to work to stamp out this vermin we shall lose Ireland, and with the loss of Ireland we have lost the Empire. I want permission from the 'Frocks', the moment England gets temporarily quiet again,[28] to send over between 20 and 30 battalions, from here, some more cavalry, guns, aeroplanes, wireless, tanks, armoured cars etc. to place the whole of Ireland under Martial Law and to hand it all over to Macready. But even with this reinforcement no promise can be made that we can really knock out the murder gang in Ireland, all that I can say that he is more likely to be able to do so after being reinforced than he is today before he is reinforced. But to go on as we are now, which is neither trying to knock out the murderers nor handing the country over to them as a present, is sheer madness and when the weather breaks in September-October I am afraid we shall find that the troops whoever they are, who have been separated from their wives and families for a couple of years will be getting tired of the job and will say so, and then we shall be properly in the soup.[29]

Macready was also worried about the pressure of service in Ireland on the troops and he told the Government that the strain was 'incomparably greater that . . . in time of actual war'. He was sure that the 'present state of affairs in Ireland . . . must be brought to a conclusion by October, or steps must be taken to relieve practically the whole of the troops together with the great majority of the commands and their staffs'.[30]

In fact things were not quite so bad as that in the spring and early summer of 1921 when the security forces now began to achieve some success. The statistics of internment of IRA volunteers reflects this. In the four months from January to April 1921 about 1500 IRA suspects were interned but from May to July 1921 – two and a half months up to the truce on 11 July 1921 – another 1450 were interned. Collins certainly felt this intensification. The intelligence reforms at the end of 1920 began to pay dividends and Macready was also assisted by the reinforcements which started to arrive in the early summer, after the strike threat faded away in Great Britain. Ironically the peak number of troops in Ireland throughout the whole period (60,000) occurred in August 1921, after the truce had been agreed.

The rising tempo of security force activity, and the possibility of a major 'push' during the summer of 1921 played a part in bringing both sides to the conference table. As the soldiers pressed for reinforcements

Lloyd George became increasingly anxious about what would happen if a draconian or Cromwellian policy of repression was imposed in Ireland and he was alarmed about the way things might go. He was worried that British public opinion might not stand for it. Sir Henry Wilson, too, knew that nothing was possible without the support of the British public and that the 'Frocks' had to 'get England on their side'. In the end the Prime Minister decided that enough was enough, as did the Irish Republicans. It was to both sides' advantage that they paused as they did with the truce in July 1921 when the British security campaign by and large finished.

In conclusion, I want briefly to examine the extent to which British security policy failed in Ireland over this period. In the short-term it was a clear disaster which was felt most strongly by die-hard Conservatives and Unionists, such as Sir Henry Wilson. When he read the Treaty in December 1921 he thought it 'a shameful and cowardly surrender to the pistol'.[31] But Wilson's was an extreme view and for the British there were distinct advantages to the truce and the subsequent treaty. The truce let the British Government off the hook of a rigorous security policy. They were almost committed to running intensified operations in Ireland in the summer of 1921 which would have been on a scale much greater than anything that had happened before. The outcome would have been quite unpredictable. The trouble about going to war – any war – is its unpredictability, as demonstrated during the First World War, which was not 'over' by Christmas 1914. No one knew what they were letting themselves in for in Ireland, and even the army high command were reluctant to guarantee any sort of victory from the summer push. In that case Lloyd George and his colleagues were probably wise to halt 'the devil they knew' – a sort of medium level insurgency campaign – rather than opt for major military operations which might produce a huge military commitment in Ireland for decades.

So the truce let the British off the hook, as it did the IRA who were beginning to run short of arms and ammunition in the summer of 1921. After the truce, moreover, the IRA could not go back to active operations as before. Michael Collins, for example, 'went public'. He was openly identified and had his photograph taken. The reformed British military intelligence organisation took care to gather information about IRA leaders in order to prevent a revival of the sort of challenge that the Republicans had been able to pose before the truce. By the autumn of 1921 the British knew enough to make it very difficult indeed for an effective renewal of the Republican military campaign. And in the long term there were also advantages to be gained for the British. In the December 1921 treaty they secured all the strategic requirements needed in Ireland, with the 'Treaty Ports', and the promise of security co-operation in the event of a major war. In political terms Home Rule had already been conceded and what the debate was about from 1914 onwards was simply the extent of that Home Rule and how exactly it was going to be applied in Ireland. Thus, conceding 'dominion status' to the Irish Nationalists was no more than might well have been foreseen as a logical development of Home Rule in 1914.

The only bit of the 'Irish Question' remaining was Northern Ireland and London very deftly sub-contracted the management (and security) of the six counties to the new local administration in Belfast, and did so very satisfactorily from their point of view since Ireland was simply removed from the British political agenda. Whether that was satisfactory from an Irish or from a Northern Irish point of view is another question but from the British perspective it was fine. As A.J.P.Taylor remarked memorably in his *English History 1914–1945*, Lloyd George 'conjured' the Irish problem out of existence.[32] What Lloyd George could not so easily do was 'conjure out of existence' the damage done to Anglo-Irish relations by the conduct of the British security policy during the years 1919–21, especially the deplorable actions of the Black and Tans. Indeed, the very existence of the Black and Tans, who epitomised the poverty and incoherence of the Government's Irish policy, adds weight to the argument that for much of the 1919–21 period no real security 'policy' existed at all.

EXILED.

[Many ex-members of the Royal Irish Constabulary are paying for their loyalty by exile from their homes under threat of death at the hands of fellow-Irishmen. The British Government are undertaking the removal-expenses of married men and their families to any place in Great Britain or Ulster, and providing them with assistance in finding suitable accommodation until such time as they can safely return to their homes or settle elsewhere.]

Punch cartoon. Forced exile of R.I.C. ex member and family, post 1921
Punch, 10 May, 1922

CHAPTER ELEVEN

Partitioning Ireland, India and Palestine
by
Tom Fraser

The partition of Ireland in the Government of Ireland Act of 1920 set an important precedent for the peoples of the British Empire. Simply put, it was a constitutional device which the British had not tried before but which they were then to follow in two other important parts of the Empire, India and Palestine. Like most other imperial systems, the British Empire grew up taking little, if any, regard for ethnic or national differences. A close parallel is the Habsburg Empire which formed out of a series of finely-calculated marriages by the ruling family, then found a purpose in reconquering much of central and eastern Europe from the Ottoman Turks. By 1914, the Habsburg domains embraced Germans, Hungarians, Czechs, Poles, Slovaks, Slovenes, Croats, Bosnians, Serbs, Rumanians, Ruthenes, Italians and Jews, in a structure which made economic and strategic sense. Its existence was a standing affront to the age of nationalism and it was, of course, the national passions of one its peoples, the Serbs, which triggered the war of 1914 and set in train the events which were to shake the Empire into its various parts.

The British Empire was essentially little different. Spread across a quarter of the world, it could only continue as long as British sea power remained unchallenged and its peoples were immune from the heady doctrines of nationalism. By 1918, neither was any longer the case. The Royal Navy might have seen off the challenge of the Kaiser's High Seas Fleet, but the naval power of the United States and Japan, her allies in the war, pointed to new realities in the future. A country whose economy and manpower had been devastated by the war could no longer look with confidence to the maintenance of world naval supremacy. And nationalism was now a stark reality. The pre-war Irish demand for Home Rule had been transformed by the Easter Rising and Sinn Féin's success in the elections of November 1918 into a struggle for an independent Republic. In India, the modest growth of the Indian National Congress changed beyond recognition after the Amritsar Massacre of

1919. Led by one of the great leaders of the century, Mahatma Gandhi, it embarked on a mass campaign of non-violence to end British imperial control. By 1920, then, despite Britain's triumph in the war, dark shadows were gathering around the future of the Empire, at least in Ireland and India. Curiously, 1920 also saw the British adding to their Empire, this time in the Middle East, for the San Remo Conference awarded her the League of Nations Mandates for extensive territories in the region, including Palestine. It was hardly to prove an asset.

With benefit of hindsight we can see that the British Empire, at the moment of its greatest victory, had very similar problems to the less fortunate empire of the Habsburgs, which had just disappeared. The peoples of the latter empire were now embarking on a new future based upon the fashionable concept of 'self determination'. Proclaimed by President Woodrow Wilson in his famous Fourteen Points, the right of peoples to 'self determination' became part of the Allies' war aims and were central to their discussions at the subsequent Paris Peace Conference, a matter of no small consequence for the political shape of Ireland. As the victorious leaders soon discovered, to reconstruct central and eastern Europe on the basis of 'self determination' was easier said than done, for the ethnic map was one of frustrating complexity. The new Republic of Czechoslovakia contained the economically advanced area of Bohemia, long linked with Vienna, and the more backward Slovakia, whose connexions were with Budapest. More ominously, its population included three million Germans who bitterly resented their separation from Austria or Germany. Yugoslavia was little better or possibly worse. The Polish Corridor was to be the scene of a new war twenty years later. 'Self determination', which seemed so strikingly obvious at the time, proved to be a seriously flawed basis for the reconstitution of Europe.

For the British Empire, these issues of self determination were also present. They were not entirely new, for British politicians had earlier had to deal with the problems of the French in Canada and the Afrikaners in South Africa. In each case, the solution had been a full measure of self government linked with a federal constitution. In 1918, both Dominions seemed to be working, and federalism had long been mooted as a possible way forward for Ireland.[1] But before examining possible solutions, it is as well, briefly, to rehearse the problems of conflicting allegiance which Ireland shared with India and Palestine and which in each case was to result in partition. In the case of Ireland, the rise of Nationalism had been mirrored by the emergence of a specifically Ulster, as opposed to Irish, Unionism. It is unnecessary to chronicle the origins of the Ulster Protestant community in the plantations of the seventeenth century, but it is useful to be reminded that by the early part of the twentieth century Ulster Unionism had taken on many of the features usually associated with nationalist movements elsewhere. It had its own myths and traditions, stretching from the Siege of Derry and the Battle of the Boyne through the rituals and symbolism of its unique contribution to political and religious development, the Orange Order. Like continental national movements, it could claim to represent all social groups from the Belfast shipyard, engineering and linen workers, through the professional middle classes, to the farmers and landed aristocracy. It had its own economic agenda: unrestricted access to the markets of Britain and the Empire. In short, although their political thrust was adamantly opposed to the aspirations of Irish Nationalism, Ulster Protestants were bringing forward into the twentieth century characteristics not dissimilar to those emerging in other parts of Europe. 'Ulster has got her own ideas, her own thoughts, which are not common with those of the rest of Ireland', David Lloyd George was to claim in 1920.[2]

India was virtually a continent in its own right. Separated from the rest of the Asian land mass by the mountain barrier of the Himalayas, it had evolved in Hinduism its own distinctive religious and social system based upon a belief in reincarnation and the rigidly hierarchical caste system. From the Middle Ages, however, the political dominance of Hinduism had challenged by aggressive Muslim conquerors from Central Asia and the Middle East. The beliefs of Islam could not have stood in greater contrast to those of Hinduism, based as they were on a stern monotheism and the brotherhood of all believers. Until the British conquest of the mid eighteenth century, Muslim rulers dominated the political life of north India and in the process a quarter of the population converted to the new faith. When Indian politics sprang to life with the formation of the Indian National Congress in 1885, the lead was taken by Hindus and the Muslims were rather left behind. Like Irish Nationalists, Congress came to stand for independence from Britain, the unity of the country, and the assertion of distinctive national values and culture. But when leadership was assumed in 1920 by Mahatma Gandhi, a Hindu holy man, many Muslims came to question the direction the national movement was taking. By 1940, these fears had taken such concrete form that, inspired by Mohamed Ali Jinnah, they were prepared to demand the creation of the separate Muslim state of Pakistan. Jinnah, in turn, had taken this concept from the 'Two Nation' theory of Indian development developed by the Muslim philosopher and theologian, Sir Muhammad Iqbal in the 1930s. 'Why should not the Muslims of north-west India and Bengal be considered as nations entitled to national self-determination just as other nations in India and outside India are?', Iqbal had asked Jinnah in 1937.[3]

When Britain acquired the Palestine Mandate in 1920, the country was overwhelmingly Arab, some 500,000 according to the best estimates, most of them Muslim but with a thriving Christian minority. Glad to be free of the Turks who had ruled them since the sixteenth century, they looked forward to independence as part of the Arab Middle East, something which they believed the British had promised them in 1915. But there was another claimant, smaller in numbers but destined to grow in size and confidence, the Jews whose ancestors had been forced into exile by the Romans. The modern movement for Jewish statehood was largely the creation of the Austrian journalist Theodor Herzl who founded the Zionist movement in 1897. In 1917, in an attempt to win Jewish sympathy for the war effort in Russia and the United States, the British Government issued the Balfour Declaration which committed them to work for the creation of a Jewish National Home in Palestine. Jewish settlement was not dramatic until the rise of Hitler in 1933 unleashed a wave of persecution throughout Europe. Frightened Jews flocked to Palestine in such numbers that from being 180,793 in 1932, by 1936 they accounted for 370,483, compared with an Arab population which had grown to 1,336,518. They brought with them the way of life of middle class central Europe, confirmed when the great Italian conductor Arturo Toscanini came to conduct the Palestine Symphony 0rchestra. Faced with such a challenge to their established way of life, in 1936 the Arabs of Palestine rebelled. The British countered with military repression and the despatch of a Royal Commission under Lord Peel. Its most forceful member was Professor Reginald Coupland of Oxford University who quickly came to the view that the only possible solution was partition based upon his analysis that Palestine was inhabited by an 'Arab community predominantly Asiatic in character' and a 'Jewish community predominantly European'; in short, by Two Nations.[4]

So far, it has been argued that underpinning the partition of all three countries was the emergence of a 'Two Nation' theory. Two other things stand out. Firstly, the validity of the 'Two Nation' theory was vigorously denied by the opponents of partition. Thus, Nationalist MP for North East Tyrone, Thomas Harbinson, pleaded before the British House of Commons in 1920 that 'Ireland is a nation, one and indivisible, and this House has no moral right or power to divide Ireland'.[5] For Mahatma Gandhi, religion was not relevant to the concept of nationality. The fact that a person's ancestor had converted from Hinduism to Islam could not, for him, change his or her innate identity as an Indian. Palestinians argued rather differently. They could not concede the claim of a recently-arrived minority to carve a state out of Arab land. The second element all three cases had in common was the British.

Each was a part of the British Imperial system and decisions about their future would have to be reached in London. Did the British, as many suspected, have a partitionist agenda? Such a belief was all too plausible, for British leaders, well versed in the classics, knew the ancient Roman principle of divide et impera. The Imperial government was known to use such tactics as part of control. Hence, in India certain groups such as the Punjabi Jats were rewarded with special favours in return for their military reliability. To many in the Empire the partition of Ireland simply confirmed this belief and in the 1930s the British were accused of attempting to create 'Ulsters', not, it must be said, in a complimentary sense. Certain questions, then, inevitably arise. Were the British set on partition as a device of imperial control? If they were, then partition becomes easier to understand, but if they were not, then the problems multiply. Why did the opponents of partition who were, after all, a decisive majority in each case, fail to prevent it?

Close inspection of the key decisions made over Ireland, India and Palestine hardly sustain the view that partition was a device which British leaders found instinctively attractive. Although some form of Ulster exclusion from Home Rule had been widely debated between 1912 and 1914, and revived by Lloyd George in his negotiations with John Redmond and Sir Edward Carson after the Easter Rising, the immediate origins of the partition of Ireland are to be found in the deliberations of the Cabinet Committee on the Irish Question which met under the chairmanship of Walter Long in the early winter of 1919. The constraints acting upon this Committee tell us much about the nature of the partition which followed. The strength of electoral support for Sinn Féin in the 1918 election, the determined nature of the IRA campaign against the Crown forces, and the perceived need to persuade American opinion of Britain's good intentions, all demanded that Irish aspirations be satisfied. But what of Unionist Ulster? The events of 1912–1914 had demonstrated that Ulster could, if circumstances demanded, put together a formidable military force. Unionists were still an integral element in British Conservatism. It is true that the party was less enthusiastic about Ulster than it had been before the war but Andrew Bonar Law was still its leader and his commitment to the province of his father was undimmed. And Lloyd George needed his support. Lloyd George might be one of the three most important men in the world in 1919, along with Woodrow Wilson and France's Georges Clemenceau, but that dizzy eminence rested upon a flawed foundation. In December 1916 he had become Prime Minister only at the price of splitting the Liberal Party, much of which remained faithful to H.H.Asquith. Thus, in the election of November 1919 he found himself leading a Coalition of Conservatives and 'Coalition Liberals', a combination in which the former was easily predominant with 339 MPs to 136 for Lloyd George's Liberals. Naturally, Bonar Law had extracted a price and as far as Ireland was concerned this closed two possibilities, 'the one leading to a complete severance of Ireland from the British Empire, and the other to the forcible submission of the six counties of Ulster to a Home Rule Parliament against their will'.[6]

The significance of this pledge cannot be overestimated but the other factor which played upon influential figures was that of 'self determination', for it was precisely the principle over which they had been wrestling at the recent Paris Peace Conference. In particular, it affected the Foreign Secretary Arthur Balfour, who had not been notably warm to Ulster before the war. 'No one can think', he wrote, 'that Ulster ought to join the south and west who thinks that the Jugo Slavs should be separated from Austria. No one can think that Ulster should be divorced from Britain who believes in self determination'.[7] The idea of Ulster's right to 'self determination' proved to be a powerful new element in the political equation. Nor should it be forgotten that partition as a solution for the problems of divided communities was very much in the air in 1919–1920. Many of the elements in the partition of Ireland can be found in what was happening in the mixed German-Polish areas of Allenstein and Marienwerder in East Prussia and also in Silesia. Students of Irish history have tended to ignore these events, but Ireland was not in some kind of political vacuum isolated from the rest of the world and they need to be taken into account.

When Long's Committee reported to the Cabinet on 4 November 1918, these were the considerations behind their three recommendations. By the first, Ulster would have the right to vote itself out of the jurisdiction of a Dublin Parliament, retaining its existing status as part of the United Kingdom. Such a proposal would, so the Committee believed, have two drawbacks; it ran counter to the principle of Irish unity and to the right to self determination of the Nationalists of Ulster. The second possibility was also deemed unacceptable. This was to include Ulster under the jurisdiction of a Dublin Parliament but with the right to veto any legislation affecting the province. Such a mechanism would simply cripple the working of the Parliament. The third proposal contained the major elements of the subsequent Government of Ireland Act and hence the future political shape of the country. Arguing that Britain 'cannot compel Ireland to unite', the Committee tried to chart a way forward which would leave open the possibility of the future unity of the island. Ulster was to have its own Parliament, for all nine counties on the grounds that such an arrangement 'minimises the division of Ireland on purely religious lines'.[8] A Dublin Parliament would assume responsibility for the other three provinces. To ensure

that unity would consistently be on the agenda, the Committee pro-
posed a Council of Ireland, consisting of twenty members from each
Parliament. The hope was that it would work towards becoming an all-
Ireland Parliament.

Such, then, was the strategy behind what became the Government of
Ireland Act. Central to its purpose was the fostering of Irish unity, or at
the very least of ensuring that mechanisms were in place to facilitate
this. Over the next two years, admittedly with many twists and turns,
Lloyd George tried to hold to that strategy. During the negotiations in
1921 which eventually led to the settlement with Arthur Griffith and
Michael Collins, he put intense pressure on what had become the
Government of Northern Ireland to come under a Dublin jurisdiction.
But the Government of Ireland Act did not lead to Irish unity. Why
not? In the first place, the provisions of the Act were no longer acceptable to the bulk of Irish opinion. When elections for the Dublin Parliament were held, 124 Sinn Féiners were returned unopposed. The
Parliament, necessary if the Council of Ireland were to function, met
but once, attended only by the four representatives of Trinity College.
As important in wrecking the strategy of Irish unity was the political
skill, and notable lack of sentiment, of the Ulster Unionists. Led by Sir
James Craig, they quickly grasped the point that a Belfast Parliament
could be used to copper bottom their position, if only they could reduce
its jurisdiction to six counties. This view found strong support in the
Cabinet on the grounds of self determination, not least from Balfour
who argued that 'if the Peace Conference had been delimiting the new
frontier, in accordance with the general procedure adopted at Paris, we
should not have included in the Protestant area so large and homogene-
ous a Roman Catholic district as that (say) of the greatest part of
Donegal'.[9] If Craig showed his political skill in persuading the Cabinet
of this, he unsentimentally persuaded his followers to abandon the
Unionist communities of Cavan, Monaghan and Donegal, to whom
they were supposedly bound by the 1912 Covenant. 'We cannot hold
the nine counties', his brother Charles confessed.[10] But the six counties
which the Government of Ireland Act gave to the Belfast Parliament
ensured the Unionist position for many years to come, and hence the
partition of the island.

The Unionists' success owed much to the unswerving support of
Balfour and Bonar Law. Craig candidly acknowledged 'the open, frank,
courageous and splendid attitude of Mr Bonar Law'.[11] Lloyd George's
part is more mysterious, as he was never much of a correspondent. It is
fair to say, however, that he was forced to acknowledge partition as the
inevitable consequence of his electoral pledge to the Conservative
leadership but throughout the events of 1919–1922 he tried to manage

events in such a way as keep open the path to Irish unity, should circumstances permit. The British attitude towards partition may be seen as at best ambivalent, seeing it as an expedient way of resolving conflicting pressures. This problematic attitude was also to be reflected in their response to events in India in Palestine.

The initial British attitude to the Muslim League's 'Pakistan Demand' in 1940 was hardly to take it seriously. The prevailing attitude was to regard it as a shrewd bargaining position which would enable Muslims to bid for an effective position inside an independent India. In this they proved no wiser than Gandhi and the Nationalist leadership. Their belief was confounded by the dramatic growth of Muslim League support in the course of the war. In elections held at the end of 1945, Jinnah could claim the endorsement of the bulk of the Muslim population, not least of the large states of Bengal and Punjab. Faced with the Muslim demand for partition, in the spring of 1946 the British Government sent out the Cabinet Mission led by Sir Stafford Cripps. The ministers went armed with a devastating critique of the idea. Partition would carve out a Muslim state in the north-west and north-east of the sub-continent separated by over 1,000 miles and two to three weeks' sailing time. How could such a state have any sense of unity, be militarily defensible, or 'possess any reality from the economic point of view?'[12] Moreover, Jinnah's demand for the provinces of Bengal and Punjab as part of Pakistan on the grounds of Muslim self determination ignored certain uncomfortable facts: Bengal had 27,497,624 Muslims but 21,570,407 Hindus, while Punjab had 6,328,588 Hindus and 3,064,144 Sikhs to set against 13,332,460 Muslims.[13] When confronted with the argument that he could not deny the right to self determination of these Hindu and Sikh communities, which hated the idea of a Muslim state, and that Pakistan implied the partition of Bengal and Punjab, Jinnah was prepared to concede the British compromise position of federation. The federal scheme which was briefly accepted by both the Indian National Congress and the Muslim League would have allowed the Muslim areas the maximum amount of internal self government while retaining Indian unity for defence, foreign affairs and communications. It was the preferred British solution but it failed to stand up in the face of the Hindu-Muslim passions which had been unleashed. In the winter of 1946–1947 communal slaughter reached such proportions that when the last Viceroy, Lord Mountbatten, arrived he could see no alternative to partition. Neither could Gandhi or Jinnah.

British resistance to partition in India is closely paralleled by their attitudes in Palestine. In June 1937, the Peel Commission Report, drafted by Reginald Coupland, powerfully argued the case for partition into an Arab and a Jewish state based upon the 'Two Nation' theory.

Such was the power of Coupland's prose that it was initially accepted by the Government. But the Jewish response was lukewarm – they did not believe that the proposed Jewish state allowed enough scope for development – and the Arabs were passionately opposed to any dismemberment of their country. Arab hostility had to be given full weight, for in 1937 Mussolini began powerful reinforcement of his military positions in the eastern Mediterranean, and in the following year Hitler's moves over Austria and the Sudetenland brought the prospect of war into sharp focus. War could not be fought with the Arab world hostile to Britain. In 1938, Sir John Woodhead's so-called Palestine Partition Commission recommended that partition was unworkable and in the following summer the British committed themselves to the creation of a united Palestine with a guaranteed Arab majority. The Holocaust of the Second World War, with the death of some five million Jews in Hitler's death camps, fired Jewish determination to achieve statehood in Palestine. Their revolt against British rule was conducted with skill and ruthlessness and no less effective was their campaign to secure the support of the American President, Harry S.Truman. Their triumph came on 29 November 1947 when the General Assembly of the United Nations voted by the necessary two-thirds majority that Palestine should be partitioned into Arab and Jewish states with a special regime for the city of Jerusalem. Throughout all this process British hostility to partition remained undimmed. The Arabs continued to oppose it and Britain needed access to their oil resources to help rebuild after the war. For British leaders partition was 'so manifestly unjust to the Arabs' that they could not support it.[14] Not only that, they made it clear that they would actively impede any attempts by the United Nations to implement it. During the period between the passing of the Partition Resolution and the formal end of the Mandate on 14 May 1948, Britain refused to allow United Nations officials to enter the country, with the inevitable result that the scheme was not put into force. When the British did leave, the Jews proclaimed the existence of the State of Israel in the areas they controlled and the following day the first Arab-Israeli war began.

These summaries of what happened in India and Palestine show that if the partition of Ireland was a precedent then it was not one which the British particularly cared to follow. British politicians and officials were well aware of the pitfalls. Population mixture was the most obvious. One of the most persuasive arguments against the partition of Palestine in 1947 was that the projected Jewish state contained almost as many Arabs as Jews; in fact, by doing a hasty count of the semi-nomadic Bedouin population the Foreign Office was able to demonstrate that it might even have an Arab majority.[15] Here, of course, was the origin of the Palestinian refugee problem as Arabs fled, and were driven, from their homes in 1947–1948. The central Punjab was just as inflammable. In the central districts the Muslim proportion was as follows: Lahore, 61%; Gurdaspur, 51%; Amritsar, 47%; Jullundur, 46%; Ferozepore, 45%.[16] As the partition line cut its way through these districts hundreds of thousands found themselves on the 'wrong' side. At least 200,000 people died as a result and two million migrated. These problems had also been well known during the partition of Ireland. The fate of Fermanagh and Tyrone was never far from the centre of discussion during the years 1912–1922, and when partition came it left the Unionist minorities of Cavan, Monaghan and Donegal in the Free State and the Nationalist communities of West Belfast, Derry City, south Down and south Armagh in Northern Ireland. Perhaps it was inevitable that some would be left unsatisfied. 'Self determination' in 1919–1920 had proved an imperfect instrument, leaving Hungarians in Czechoslovakia, Rumania and Yugoslavia, Germans in Czechoslovakia, Italy and Poland, Poles in Germany, etc. Partition reflected divided societies and could never be a perfect solution. By satisfying some, it left others bitter and alienated. If the British adopted it, it was without enthusiasm but because no viable alternative seemed in sight. One eminent British official in the Punjab aptly described it as the policy of 'Divide and Quit'.[17] This was possible in India and Palestine. In Ireland it was not.

Notes and References

Chapter one: The 1885–6 General Elections – Brian Walker

1. For a more detailed study of these elections see B.M. Walker, *Ulster Politics: the Formative Years 1868–86* (Belfast, 1989) (hereafter cited as Walker, *Ulster Politics*); C.C. O'Brien, *Parnell and his Party 1880–90* (Oxford, 1957) (hereafter cited as O'Brien, *Parnell*); and James Loughlin, *Gladstone, Home Rule and the Ulster Question, 1882–93* (Dublin, 1986).
2. All information on election results has come from B.M. Walker, *Parliamentary Election Results in Ireland, 1801–1922* (Dublin, 1978).
3. See B.M.Walker, 'The Irish Electorate, 1868–1915,' in *I.H.S.*, xviii, no. 71 (Mar. 1973), pp 359–406.
4. Walker, *Ulster Politics*, p. 154.
5. O'Brien, *Parnell*, p.150.
7. Emmet Larkin, 'Church, State and Nation in Modern Ireland' in *American Historical Review*, lxxx, no. 4 (Oct. 1975), pp 1265–7.
8. Walker, *Ulster Politics*, p. 204; Michael Davitt, *The Fall of Feudalism in Ireland* (London, 1904), pp 466–9.
9. A.C. Murray, 'Nationality and Local Politics in Late Nineteenth-Century Ireland: the Case of County Westmeath' in *I.H.S.*, xxv, no. 98, (Nov. 1986) p.146.
10. Walker, *Ulster Politics*, p.213.
11. P.J. Buckland, *Irish Unionism, 1885–1923* (Belfast, 1973), pp.95–9.
12. B.M. Walker, 'Party Organisation in Ulster, 1865–92: Registration Agents and Their Activities' in Peter Roebuck (ed.) *Plantation to Partition: Essays in Ulster History in Honour of J.L. McCracken* (Belfast, 1981), pp 201–3.
13. E.G., D.C. Savage, 'The Origins of the Ulster Unionist Party, 1885–6' in *I.H.S*, xii, no. 47, (Mar. 1961), p.186.
14. Walker, *Ulster Politics*, pp 177–92.
17. Ibid, pp 207–8.
19. T.M. Healy, *Letters and Leaders of My Day* (2 vols, London, 1928), i, pp 231–3.
20. Walker, *Ulster Politics*, pp 190, 209–11.
21. Ibid, pp 215–9.
22. P.J.O. McCann, 'The Protestant Home Rule Movement, 1886–95' (M.A. thesis, N.U.I., U.C.D., 1972): see also James Loughlin, 'The Irish Protestant Home Rule Association' in *I.H.S.*, xxiv, no. 95 (May 1985), pp 341–60.
23. For further valuable information on the issues involved see James Anderson, 'Ideological Variations in Ulster During Ireland's First Home Rule Crisis: an

Analysis of Local Newspapers' in C.H. Williams and E. Kofman (eds) *Community Conflict, Partition and Nationalism* (London, 1989), pp 133–66.

24. Mary Daly, *Industrial Development and Irish National Identity 1922–39*, (Dublin, 1992), p.3.
25. B.M. Walker, 'The Irish Electorate, 1868–1915,' in I.H.S., xvii, no. 71 (Mar. 1973), pp 359–406.
26. *Belfast Morning News*, 10 Nov. 1885.
27. See W.E. Vaughan and A.J. Fitzpatrick (eds), *Irish Historical Statistics: Population 1821–1971* (Dublin, 1978)
28. See B.M. Walker, M. O'Dowd and C. Brady (eds), *Ulster: an Illustrated History*, (London, 1989), p. 164.
29. W.E. Vaughan, *Landlords and Tenants in Ireland, 1848–1904* (Dublin, 1984).
30. W.E. Vaughan and A.J. Fitzpatrick (eds) *Irish Historical Statistics: Population 1821–1971* (Dublin, 1978), pp 57–9.
31. See Walker, *Ulster Politics*, pp 15–38; David Hempton and Myrtle Hill, *Evangelical Protestantism in Ulster Society, 1740–1890* (London, 1992); Emmet Larkin, 'The Devotional Revolution in Ireland, 1850–75' in American Historical Review, lxxvii, no. 3 (June 1972), pp 625–52.
32. *Weekly Examiner*, 13 Mar. 1886.
33. Walker, *Ulster Politics*, p.26.
34. Emmet Larkin, 'Church, State and Nation in Modern Ireland' in *American Historical Review*, lxxx, no. 4 (Oct. 1975), p.1267.
35. For valuable discussions of these movements see D.G. Boyce, *Nationalism in Ireland* (London, 1982; new edition, 1991) and Alvin Jackson, *The Ulster Party: Irish Unionists in the House of Commons, 1884–1911*) (Oxford, 1989).
36. See A.T.Q. Stewart, *The Narrow Ground: the Roots of Conflict in Ulster* (London, 1977; new edition 1989), p. 163; John Coakley 'The Foundations of Statehood' in John Coakely and Michael Gallagher (eds) *Politics in the Republic of Ireland*, (Galway 1992), p. 8; and Tom Garvin 'Democratic Politics in Independent Ireland' in ibid, p. 222.
37. See S.M. Lipset and Stein Rokkan, 'Cleavage Structures, Party Systems and Vote Alignment: an Introduction' in S.M. Lipset and Stein Rokkan, *Party Systems and Vote Alignment* (New York, 1967), pp 50–6; Gordon Smith, *Politics in Western Europe* (London, 1972; 4th edition, London, 1983), pp 12–14, 44–6; A.R. Ball, *Modern Politics and Government* (London, 1988), pp 82–4.
38. See Gordon Smith, *Politics in Western Europe* (London, 1972; 4th edition, London, 1983), pp 18–26; Jan Erik Lane and S.O. Erson, *Politics and Society in Western Europe* (London, 1987), pp 56–64, 97–9; J.H. Whyte, *Catholics in Western Democracies* (Dublin, 1981), pp 47–75.
39. See Alf Kaartvedt, 'The Economic Basis of Norwegian Nationalism in the Nineteenth Century in Rosalind Mitchison (ed.), *The Roots of Nationalism: Studies in Northern Europe* (Edinburgh, 1980), pp 11–19; Gordon Smith, *Politics in Western Europe* (London, 1972; 4th edition, 1983), pp 297–302, 308–10.
40. For a valuable discussion of some of the ideological conflicts to emerge over questions of nationality and sovereignty see Thomas Hennessey 'Ulster Unionist Territorial and National Identities 1886–93: province, island, kingdom and empire' in *Irish Political Studies*, vol. 8, 1993, pp21–36.

Chapter two: The Legacy of Arthur Balfour to Twentieth Century Ireland – Catherine B. Shannon

1. Quoted in C.B. Shannon, *Arthur J. Balfour and Ireland 1874–1922.* (Washington, 1988) p.19.
2. Ibid., p.53.
3. Ibid., pp.52–3.
4. Ibid,. p.186.
5. Ibid., p.206.
6. Ibid., p.280.
7. Ibid.
8. Ibid., p. 287.

Chapter three: Irish Unionism 1905–21 – Alvin Jackson

1. The best general studies of Irish Unionism between 1885 and 1922 remain Patrick Buckland, *Irish Unionism I: The Anglo-Irish and the new Ireland, 1885–1923* (Dublin 1972) and *Irish Unionism II: Ulster Unionism and the Origins of Northern Ireland, 1886–1922* (Dublin 1973). See also Michael Laffan, *The Partition of Ireland, 1911–25* Dublin, 1983); and Alvin Jackson, *The Ulster Party: Irish Unionists in the House of Commons, 1884–1911* (Oxford, 1989). For an excellent documentary source see: Patrick Buckland, *Irish Unionism 1885–1923: A Documentary History* (Belfast, 1973).
2. For this alternative approach see Ian D'Alton, 'Southern Irish Unionism: A Study of Cork Unionists, 1884–1914' in *Transactions of the Royal Historical Society, xxiii (January 1973)*, pp 71–88; and also Alvin Jackson, 'Unionist Politics and Protestant Society in Edwardian Ireland' in *Historical Journal, xxxiii,* 4 (June 1990), pp 839–66.
3. For more information on Colonel Saunderson see: Reginald Lucas, *Colonel Saunderson MP: A Memoir* (London, 1908) and Public Record Office of Northern Ireland (hereafter PRONI), *Edward Saunderson Papers: T.2996.* For Walter Long see: *Walter Long, Memories* (London, 1923); Charles Petrie, *Walter Long and his Times* (London, 1936); Richard Murphy, 'Walter Long and the Conservative Party, 1905–21' (Bristol Ph.D., 1984). For Edward Carson see: Edward Marjoribanks and Ian Colvin, *The Life of Lord Carson, three volumes* (London, 1932–4); H. Montgomery Hyde, *Carson: The Life of Lord Carson of Duncairn* (London, 1953); A.T.Q. Stewart, *Edward Carson* (Dublin, 1981). Carson's papers are largely in PRONI. For James Craig, see St. John Ervine, *Craigavon: Ulsterman* (London, 1949) and Patrick Buckland, *James Craig* (Dublin, 1980). Craigavon's papers are also in PRONI.
4. Alvin Jackson, 'The Rivals of C.S. Parnell' in Donal McCartney (ed), *Parnell: The Politics of Power* (Dublin, 1991), p.79.
5. Jackson, *The Ulster Party,* pp 322–6.
6. British Library (hereafter BL), Walter Long Papers, Add.Ms.62413: Long to Acland-Hood, 14 April 1908 (copy).
7. BL, Long Papers, Add.Ms.62411: Cadogan to Long, 4 Jan. 1907.
8. The devolution crisis has received considerable attention from historians. See F.S.L. Lyons, 'The Irish Unionist Party and the Devolution Crisis of 1905–6' in *Irish*

Historical Studies, vi, 21 (March 1948), pp 1–22; J.R. Fanning, 'The Unionist Party and Ireland, 1906–10' in *Irish Historical Studies, xv, 58 (September 25 1966)*, pp 147–71. See also Andrew Gailey, *Ireland and the Death of Kindness: The Experience of Constructive Unionism, 1890–1905* (Cork, 1987), pp 235–91; Jackson, *The Ulster Party*, pp 243–83.

9. Some recent work has offered a more subtle and complex picture of the Conservative stand on Ireland in 1912–14. See, for example: W.S. Rodner, 'Leaguers, Covenanters, Moderates: British Support for Ulster, 1913–14' in *Eire-Ireland, xvii, 3 (1982)*, pp 68–85.

10. J.C. Beckett, 'Carson – Unionist and Rebel' in Beckett, *Confrontations: Studies in Irish History* (London, 1972), pp 160–70.

11. Laffan, *Partition of Ireland*, pp 61–2.

12. Hyde, *Carson,* pp 413, 438.

13. Alvin Jackson, 'Unionist Myths 1912–85' in *Past & Present,* no.136 (August 1992), p.181.

14. Charles Townshend, *Political Violence in Ireland: Government and Resistance since 1848* (Oxford, 1983), pp 250–1.

15. See David W. Miller, *Queen's Rebels: Ulster Loyalism in Historical Perspective* (Dublin, 1978), pp 87–108; Marianne Elliott, *Watchmen in Sion: The Protestant Idea of Liberty* (Derry, 1984).

16. For some comments on the Unionist sense of the past see Terence Brown, *Ireland's Literature: Selected Essays* (Mullingar, 1988), pp 223–42; and Jackson, 'Unionist Myths'.

17. See chapter three.

18. Nicholas Mansergh, *The Unresolved Question: The Anglo-Irish Settlement and its Undoing, 1912–72,* (Yale, 1991), p.130; Laffan, *Partition of Ireland,* pp 65–66.

19. Buckland, *Irish Unionism I*, pp 1–2, 16–17.

20. Jackson, *Ulster Party*, pp 235–40.

21. John Harbinson, *The Ulster Unionist Party, 1882–1973* (Belfast, 1973), pp 35–60.

22. Jackson, *The Ulster Party*, pp 311–12.

23. For the role of women in Unionism see Nancy Kinghan, *United We Stood: The Official History of the Ulster Women's Unionist Council, 1911–74* (Belfast, 1975).

24. A.T.Q. Stewart, *The Ulster Crisis* (London, 1967), p.70.

25. Stewart, *Ulster Crisis,* pp 94–5.

26. Townshend, *Political Violence in Ireland*, p.253.

27. The complex national identity of Ulster Unionists has been the subject of considerable scholarly debate. See John Whyte, *Interpreting Northern Ireland* (Oxford, 1990), pp 127–9.

28. There is a copy of this intriguing and rare pamphlet in the Linenhall Library, Belfast. See the analysis by Miller, *Queen's Rebels*, pp 110–111.

29. See J. Magee, 'The Monaghan Election of 1883 and the Invasion of Ulster' in *The Clogher Record, viii, 2 (1974)*, pp 147–66.

30. Laffan, *The Partition of Ireland*, p.33; Mansergh, *The Unresolved Question*, pp 52–3.

Chapter four: Nationalist Ireland 1912–22: Aspects of Continuity and Change – Gearóid Ó Tuathaigh

1. For a lively collection of essays, including suggestions for further reading, see D.G. Boyce (ed), *The Revolution in Ireland 1879–1923*. (1988). On Irish nationalism in

general, see D.G.Boyce, *Irish Nationalism* (1980), Robert Kee, *The Green Flag: A History of Irish Nationalism* (1972), and Seán Cronin, *Irish Nationalism* (1980).

2. For Pearse, see Ruth Dudley Edwards, *Patrick Pearse: The Triumph of Failure* (1977), and, more recently, Brian P.Murphy, *Patrick Pearse and the Lost IRB Idea* (1991).
3. On the franchise, see N.Blewett, 'The Franchise in the United Kingdom,1885–1918', in *Past & Present*, xxxii, (1965), pp 27–56.
4. Michael Laffan, *The Partition of Ireland 1911–1925.* (1983), p.24.
5. F.S.L.Lyons, *The Irish Parliamentary Party 1890–1910* (1951); *John Dillon* (1968) ; 'Dillon, Redmond and the Irish Home Rulers', in F.X.Martin (ed), *Leaders and Men of the Easter Rising:Dublin 1916* (1967); Joseph V.O'Brien, *William O'Brien and the Course of Irish Politics 1881–1918* (1976); J.Anthony Gaughan, *A Political Odyssey: Thomas O'Donnell, M.P. for West Kerry 1900–1918* (1983); D.Gwynn, *The Life of John Redmond* (1932).
6. J.M.Curran, *The Birth of the Irish Free State 1921–23* (1980).
7. See J.Hutchinson, *The Dynamics of Cultural Nationalism: The Gaelic Revival and the Creation of the Irish Nation State* (1987), and, also, Seán O Tuama (ed), *The Gaelic League Idea* (1972).
8. For a recent sympathetic study of Home Rule idealists, see Brian P.Murphy, *op. cit.* n.2 above.
9. For election results, see B.M.Walker (ed), *Parliamentary Election Results in Ireland, 1801–1922* (1978).
10. A.T.Q.Stewart, *The Ulster Crisis* (1967); Alvin Jackson, *The Ulster Party: Irish Unionists in the House of Commons 1884–1911* (1988); Nicholas Mansergh, *The Irish Question 1840–1921* (1975 edn) ch.vi, pp 204–239.
11. Patrick Buckland, *Irish Unionism. II. Ulster Unionism and the Origins of Northern Ireland* (1973), and, *Irish Unionism 1885–1923: A Documentary History* (1973). also, A.T.Q.Stewart, *op.cit.* above.
12. For Redmond, see Gwynn, *op.cit.* A critical assessment of the Nationalist position can be found in J.J.Lee, *Ireland 1912–1985* (1989), pp 1–55.
13. Gwynn's sympathetic study of Redmond, published in 1932, has not been superseded by any more recent study.
14. Laffan, *op.cit.* n.4 contains a lucid discussion of the options available.
15. Lee, *op.cit.*, p.23.
16. J.Fergusson, *The Curragh Incident* (1964).
17. John Bowman, *De Valera and the Ulster Question 1917–1973* (1982); also, Maurice Moynihan (ed), *Speeches and Statements by Eamon De Valera 1917–1973* (1980).
18. See Geoffrey J.Hand's Introduction in *Report of the Irish Boundary Commission 1925.* (1969).
19. See, for example, the three essays on the Treaty debate by F.S.L.Lyons in Brian Farrell (ed), *The Irish Parliamentary Tradition* (1973), pp 223–256.Also, F.Gallagher (T.P.O'Neill, ed .), *The Anglo-Irish Treaty* (1965).
20. For a perceptive contextualisation of MacNeill's intervention, see J.J.Lee, *op. cit.* pp 14–22.
21. On the IRB see Leon O Broin, *Revolutionary Underground: The Story of the Irish Republican Brotherhood 1858–1924.* (1976). See, also, Charles Townshend, *Political Violence in Ireland: Government and Resistance since 1848* (1983).
22. F.X.Martin, '1916 –Myth, Fact and Mystery', *Studia Hibernica,* no.7, pp 7–126 ; and Padraig O Snodaigh, *Comhghaillithe na Réabhlóide 1913–1916.* (1966).

23. O.D.Edwards, 'Press reaction to the Rising in general', in O.D.Edwards and F.Pyle (eds), *1916:The Easter Rising* (1968), and more recently Lee, *op.cit.* pp 28–36.

24. George Dangerfield, *The Strange Death of Liberal England* (1935).For perspectives on the Anglo-Irish dimension see, also, Dangerfield's *The Damnable Question* (1977), S.M.Lawlor, *Britain and Ireland 1914–23* (1983). and D.G.Boyce, *Englishmen and Irish Troubles: British Public Opinion and the Making of Irish Policy 1918–22.* (1972).

25. The most original local study is David Fitzpatrick, *Politics and Irish Life 1913–21.* (1977).

26. Tom Garvin's work is especially important: see his *Nationalist Revolutionaries in Ireland 1858–1928* (1987), and 'Great Hatred, Little Room: Social Background and Political Sentiment Among Revolutionary Activists in Ireland, 1890–1922', in D.G.Boyce (ed), *The Revolution in Ireland 1879–1923* (1988), pp 91–114.

27. See Brian P.Murphy, *op.cit.* n.2 above; also, e.g.Florence O'Donoghue, *No Other Law* (1986 edn), J.A.Gaughan, *Austin Stack, Portrait of a Separatist* (1977).

28. The releyant documents are printed in Arthur Mitchell and Pádraig O Snodaigh (eds), *Irish Political Documents 1916–1949* (1985).

29. Brian Farrell, *The Founding of Dáil Eireann: Parliament and Nation-Building* (1971).

30. See Fitzpatrick, *op.cit.* n.25 above; also, his 'The Geography of Irish Nationalism 1910–1921', *Past & Present,* no.78, pp 113–144.

31. M.Laffan, 'Labour Must Wait': Ireland's Conservative Revolution', in P.J.Corish (ed), *Radicals, Rebels and Establishments: Historical Studies XV* (1985), pp 203–222. Also, A.Mitchell, Labour in Irish Politics 1890–1930 (1974); Emmet O'Connor, Syndicalism in Ireland 1917–1923 (1988), and C.Desmond Greaves, Liam Mellows and the Irish Revolution (1971).

32. Garvin, 'Great Hatred, Little Room', *art.cit.* pp 112–114.

33. See Hutchinson, *op.cit.* n. 7; also Janet Egleson Dunleavy and Gareth W.Dunleavy, *Douglas Hyde* .(1991), M.Ní Mhuiríosa, *Réamhchonraitheoirí* (1968).

34. See, for example, K.Bowen, *Protestants in a Catholic State: Ireland's Privileged Minority* (1983), and Dennis Kennedy, *The Widening Gulf : Northern Attitudes to the Independent Irish State 1919–49.*(1988).

Chapter five: Carson, Craig and the Partition of Ireland – Patrick Buckland

1. St John Ervine, *Craigavon. Ulsterman,* (London, 1949) p.4. Carson and Craig have been included in the excellent 'Gill's Irish Lives Series: A.T.Q.Stewart, *Edward Carson,* (Dublin, 1981); and P. Buckland, *James Craig* (Dublin,1980). The Public Record Office of Northern Ireland has an extensive collection of documentary and other sources relating to Irish Unionism which would inform project work. A good range of the documentary material has been published by the Record Office: *Irish Unionism 1885–1923. A Documentary History,* ed. P. Buckland, (Belfast, 1973)

2. R. B. McDowell, 'Edward Carson', *The Shaping of Modern Ireland,* ed. C.C. O'Brien, (London,1960), p. 87

3. H. Montgomery Hyde, *Carson. The Life of Sir Edward Carson, Lord Carson of Duncairn,* (London,1953), p. 449.

4. Ervine, *Craigavon,* pp 47, 507–8

5. Lady Craig's Diary, 5 May 1921, Public Record Office of Northern Ireland, D 1415/ B/38.

6. I. Colvin, *The Life of Lord Carson, II,*(London, 1934), p.16.
7. Ibid., p.162
8. Lessons from Craigavon, (Belfast,1911), quoted in Ervine, *Craigavon*, p.193–4.
9. Ibid., p.195.
10. Hyde, *Carson*, p.308.
11. P. Buckland, *Irish Unionism 1885–1923. A Documentary History*, (Belfast, 1973) p.49.
12. Hyde, *Carson*, p. 286.
13. Ibid., p. 291.
14. Ibid., p. 341.
15. Colvin, *Carson*, p.282.
16. Ibid., p.283.
17. E. Holt, *Protest in Arms. The Irish Troubles 1916–1923* (London,1963), p.35.
18. Public Record Office of Northern Ireland, D 1415/E/21.
19. P. Buckland, *A History of Northern Ireland*, (Dublin 1981), p.152.
20. Hyde, *Carson*, p.359.
21. C. F. D'Arcy, *The Adventures of a Bishop. A Phase of Irish Life: A Personal and Historical Narrative,* (London,1934), p. 66.
22. Ervine, *Carson*, p. 227.
23. Northern Ireland Parliamentary Debates (House of Commons), I, cols 36–7.
24. Lady Craig's Diary,4 April 1922.
25. Ibid., 5,7, November 1921.
26. Ibid., 21 January 1922.
27. Buckland, *Craig*, p.77.
28 Colvin, *Carson*, p.104–5.
29. United Kingdom Parliamentary Debates (House of Commons), ser.5, CXXVII, col. 991
30. Ibid., cols 989–90.
31. Hyde, *Carson*, p.465.
32. Lady Craig's Diary, 8 February 1921.

Chapter six: British Politics and the Irish Question, 1912–1922 – George Boyce

1. D.G.Boyce, *The Irish Question and British Politics 1868–1986* (London, 1988), pp 38–41.
2. D.G.Boyce (ed.) *The Crisis of British Power: the Imperial and Naval papers of the Second Earl of Selborne, 1895–1910* (London 1990), p.252.
3. John Ramsden (ed.) *Real Old Tory Politics: The Political Diaries of Robert Sanders, Lord Bayford, 1910–1935* (London,1984) pp 46–7.
4. John Turner, *British Politics and the Great War: Coalition and Conflict, 1915–1918 (London, 1992)*, p.23.
5. See e.g. Alan Parkinson, 'The Presentation of the Anti-Home Rule Case in Great Britain 1912–1914', Polytechnic of Central London M.A. thesis, 1989.
6. Ramsden (ed.), *Real Old Tory Politics,* p.73 (Diary entry for 12 March 1914).
7. Ibid., p.74 (Diary entry for 19 March 1914)
8. Ibid., p.75 (Diary entry for 26 March 1914)
9. Lord Selborne to Sir Edward Grey, 3 April 1914, in D.G. Boyce (ed.), *The Crisis of British Unionism: The Domestic Papers of the Second Earl of Selborne, 1885–1922* (London, 1987), p.105.

10. Patricia Jalland and John O.Stubbs, 'The Irish Question After the Outbreak of War in 1914: Some Unfinished Party Business', in *English Historical Review,* Vol. xcvi, No. cclxxi (Oct. 1981), pp 178–807, at pp 778–9
11. Ramsden (ed.), Re*al Old Tory Politics*, pp 76–77 (Diary entry for 30 April 1914).
12. Ibid., p.79 (Diary entry for 21 July 1914).
13. Austen Chamberlain to Lord Selborne, 2 May 1914, in D.G. Boyce (ed.) *Crisis of British Unionism*, pp 109–10.
14. Jalland and Stubbs, 'Some Unfinished Party Business'. pp. 779–80.
15. Ibid., p. 783.
16. Selborne to Austen Chamberlain, 12 August 1914, in D.G. Boyce (ed.), *Crisis of British Unionism*, pp 114–5.
17. Jalland and Stubbs, 'Some Unfinished Party Business', p. 793.
18. Ibid., pp 799–804.
19. Lord Selborne to Walter Long, 26 April 1916, in D.G. Boyce (ed.), *Crisis of British Unionism,* pp 166–7.
20. D.G. Boyce, 'British Opinion, Ireland and the War, 1916–1918', in *Historical Journal,* Vol. 17, No. 3 (Sept. 1974), pp 575–93, at pp 580–83; John O. Stubbs, 'The Unionists and Ireland 1914–1918', in H*istorical Journal,* Vol. 33. No. 4 (1990), pp 867–93, at pp 876–7.
21. Stubbs, 'Unionists and Ireland', p. 877.
22. Lord Midleton to Lord Selborne, 10 June 1916, in D.G. Boyce (ed.), *Crisis of British Unionism,* pp 170–71.
23. Ibid., pp 173–77.
24. Stubbs, 'Unionists and Ireland', pp 879–80.
25. Ibid., p. 881.
26. Ibid., pp 882–3.
27. John Turner, Bri*tish Politics and the Great War,* pp 176–85.
28. Stubbs, 'Unionists and Ireland', pp 887–90.
29. Turner, B*ritish Politics and the Great War*, p.178.
30. Stubbs, 'Unionists and Ireland' p.890.
31. Turner, B*ritish Politics and the Great War*, p. 287.
32. Ibid., p. 290.
33. Ibid., p. 291.
34. Stubbs, 'Unionists and Ireland', p. 891.
35. F.S. Oliver to Lord Selborne, 23 Sept. 1918, in D.G. Boyce (ed.), *Crisis of British Unionism*, p. 222.
36. Stubbs, 'Unionists and Ireland', pp 892–3.
37. Turner, B*ritish Politics and the Great War,* pp 332–3.
38. D.G. Boyce, 'British Conservative Opinion, the Ulster Question, and the Partition of Ireland, 1912–21', in *Irish Historical Studies*, Vol. xvii, No. 65 (Mar.1970) pp 89–112, at p. 102; Richard Murphy, 'Walter Long and the Making of the Government of Ireland Act, 1920', in I.*H.S.* vol. xxv, No. 97 (May 1986) pp 82–96.
39. Charles Townshend, T*he British Campaign in Ireland, 1919–1921* (Oxford, 1975), p. 40. Ibid., p. 201.
41. Ramsden (ed) *Real Old Tory Politics,* p. 163 (Diary entry for 8 Nov. 1921).
42. Patrick Buckland, *The Factory of Grievances: Devolved Government in Northern Ireland, 1921–1939* (Dublin, 1979), pp 110–16.
43. Keith Middlemas (ed.), *Tom Jones: Whitehall Diary, Vol. III: Ireland 1918–1925* (London, 1971), p. 161 (Diary entry for 10 Nov. 1921).

44. Ramsden (ed.), *Real Old Tory Politics*, pp 163–4. (Diary entries for 27 Nov. and 8 Dec. 1921).
45. For Carsons's speech and Birkenhead's reaction see John Campbell, *F.E. Smith: First Earl of Birkenhead* (London, 1983), p. 579.
46. Buckland, *Factory of Grievances*, pp 197–99.
47. D.G. Boyce, *Englishmen and Irish Troubles: British Public Opinion and the making of Irish Policy, 1918–22* (London, 1972), p. 174–5.
48. Lloyd George to Winston Churchill, 8 June 1922, Lloyd George Papers, F10/3/3.
49. Buckland, F*actory of Grievances*, p. 200.

Chapter seven: Northern Nationalists, Ulster Unionists and the Development of Partition 1900–21 – Eamon Phoenix

1. Patrick Buckland, *Ulster Unionism* (Dublin, 1973) pp 1–19.
2. See J.R.B. McMinn, *Against the Tide: J.B. Armour, Irish Presbyterian Minister and Home Ruler* (PRONI, 1985)
3. Denis Gwynn, The Life of John Redmond (London, 1932) p.15.
4. Memo by K. O'Sheil (Irish Free State's legal adviser) January 1923 (SPO, S2027).
5. D.W.Miller, *Church State and Nation in Ireland, 1898–1921*(Dublin, 1973) pp 97–99.
6. J.W.Boyle, 'The Protestant Association and the Orange Order 1901–1910' in *Irish Historical Studies* v.13 (September, 1962) p.142.
7. F.S.L. Lyons, The Irish Parliamentary Party 1890–1910 (London, 1951) pp 104–5.
8. For a study of the AOH see M.Foy, 'The AOH: An Irish Political Pressure Group1884–1975' (M.A. thesis Q.U.B. 1976).
9. F.J.Whitford, 'Joseph Devlin' in *Threshold* v.1., no.2.(1957) p.27.
10. N.I. Parliamentary Debates (House of Commons) v.xvi cols. 279–80.
11. Fraser to Robinson, 12 October 1913 quoted in *Lovat Fraser's Tour of Ireland in 1913* (Belfast Historical and Educational Society, 1992) p.18.
12. R.F.G. Holmes, 'Ulster Will Fight and Ulster Will Be Right: the Protestant Churches and Ulster's Resistance to Home Rule, 1912–1914' in *Studies in Church History*, v. 20, pp.321–35.
13. *Irish News*, 25 September1913.
14. Gwynn, *op. cit.*, pp.258–9.
15. Michael Laffan, *The Partition of Ireland 1911–1925* (Dundalk, 1983), p.32.
16. RIC County Inspector's Report for March 1914 (PRO, CO 904/92).
17. Denis Gwynn, *The History of Partition, 1912–25* (Dublin, 1950), pp 130–2.
18. RIC 'Precis of Information' April 1915 (PRO, CO 904/120/2).
19. *The Workers' Republic*, 8 April 1916.
20. RIC Report for Belfast, 1916. (PRO, CO 904/120/3).
21. Devlin to Editor, *Irish Independent* 29 June 1916.
22. Logue to Bishop O'Donnell, 7 June 1916 (Armagh Archdiocesan Archives; Logue Papers).
23. Rev.P. O'Doherty ('Red Hand'), T*hrough Corruption to Dismemberment: A Story of Apostacy and Betrayal* (Derry, 1916) pp 3, 29.
24. F.S.L.Lyons, *John Dillon: A Biography* (London, 1968) p.424.
25 Devlin to Dillon, 28 November 1918 (T.C.D., Dillon Papers, 6730/201).
26. Devlin to Dillon, 15 May1919 (Dillon Papers 6730/224).
27. Ian Colvin, *Life of Carson*, v.3 (London, 1936) pp 365–6.
28. On 4 November 1919, the Cabinet Committee charged with drafting the Partition

Act (the Long Committee) recommended a 9 county Northern Ireland. A week later, however, James Craig, then a junior minister in the Coalition, informed the Committee of his preference for the six-county unit on the grounds that . . .'Protestant representation in the Ulster Parliament would be strengthened and . . . six counties would be...easier to govern than the whole province.' By February 1920, the Parliament had capitulated to this view. (PRO, CAB 27/68).

29. Laffan, op. cit. p.65.
30. Devlin to Bishop O'Donnell, 13 February 1920 (Armagh Diocesan Archives: O'Donnell Papers).
31. RIC Inspector- General's Report, July 1920 (PRO, CO 904/112); G.B.Kenna, *Facts and Figures of the Belfast Pogrom, 1920–22* (Dublin, 1922) pp.18–20. ('Kenna' was the pseudonymn of a Belfast priest, Rev.John Hasson).
32. RIC County Inspector's Report for Co. Antrim, August 1920 (PRO, CO904/112).
33. See for example *Daily Herald*, 31 August 1920.
34. Martin Gilbert, Winston S. Churchill, v.iv, 1916–22 (London, 1975), p.729. The fatality figures for the Belfast troubles of 1920–22 were: 267 Catholics, 185 Protestants and 3 unascertained. For a detailed discussion of the subject, see Eamonn Phoenix, 'Political Violence, Diplomacy and the Catholic Minority in Northern Ireland' in J.Darby, N. Dodge and A.C. Hepburn (eds.), *Political Violence: Ireland in a Comparative Perspective* (Belfast, 1990) pp 29–47.
35. S.G. Tallents to Sir J. Masterton-Smith 4 July 1922 (PRO CO 906/30).
36. *Irish Independent*, 8 April 1921.
37. *Irish Weekly*, 12 April 1919. The speaker, the Antrim Sinn Fein leader Louis J. Walsh urged the Sinn Fein Ard Fheis to treat the 'Ulster Question' more seriously.
38. See Collins' statement to the Newry Nationalist deputation on 1 February 1922, Frontier Sentinel, 4 February 1922.
39. For a full analysis of the impact of partition on the northern Nationalists, see Eamonn Phoenix, *Nationalist Politics, Partition and the Catholic Minority in Northern Ireland 1890–1940* (Ulster Historical Foundation, Belfast 1994).

Abbreviations
PRO   Public Record Office (Kew)
SPO   State Paper Office (Dublin).

Chapter eight: Irish Labour and Politics in the Late Nineteenth and Early Twentieth Centuries – Peter Collins

1. S. Cody 'The Dublin Trades Council and the Dublin Labour Movement 1893–1913' (M.A. thesis U.C.D.Dublin,1982) p.x.
2. *Belfast Labour Chronicle* 7/10/1905
3. Ibid., July 1905.
4. *Belfast Trades Council Annual Reports 1900* p. 19
5. J.W.Boyle, The Belfast Protestant Association and the Independent Orange Order 1901–1910', in *Irish Historical Studies* vol.13, 1962 pp 138–9.
6. A.Mitchell, *Labour in Irish Politics 1890–1930; The Irish Labour Movement in an Age of Revolution* (Dublin, 1974) p.33.
7. Ibid., p.51.
8. A.Morgan, *James Connolly, A Political Biography* (Manchester, 1988) p.122.
9. C.D.Greaves, *The Life and Times of James Connolly* (London, 1976) p.341.

11. Quoted in D.Fitzpatrick 'Strikes in Ireland 1914–21' in *Saothar 6, Journal of the Irish Labour History Society* 1980, p.27
12. *Irish Worker* 8/ 8/ 1914.
13. R.B.McDowell, *The Irish Convention 1917–18* (London, 1971) pp 176–7.
14. Mitchell op.cit.p.99.
15. *Irish News* 9/ 11 / 1918.
16. Quoted in H.Patterson, *Class Conflict and Sectarianism* (Belfast, 1980), p.99.
17. *Belfast Newsletter* 18/12/ 1918.
19. *Northern Whig* 20/ 2 / 1919.
20. Mitchell op.cit., p.112.
21. Ibid., p.121.
22. *Belfast Newsletter* 13/ 1/ 1920.
23. *Northern Whig* 2/8/20.
24. Mitchell op.cit., p.129.
25. *Hansard (Northern Ireland)* vol.8 coll.2276.
26. G.Walker,*The Politics of Frustration, Harry Midgley and the Failure of Labour in Northern Ireland.*(Manchester, 1985)

Chapter ten: British Security Policy in Ireland 1919–21 – Keith Jeffery

1. And in the works of Charles Townshend, especially *The British Campaign in Ireland 1919–1921: the Development of Political and Military Policies* (London, 1975), which is essential reading for an understanding of the period.
2. The following remarks are based on the argument in Keith Jeffery, *The British Army and the Crisis of Empire 1918–22* (Manchester, 1984), especially chapter 5.
3. This point is lucidly covered in W. K. Hancock, *Survey of British Commonwealth Affairs, vol. i, Problems of Nationality 1918–1936* (London,1937), pp 119–24.
4. Ireland does not even warrant an index entry in the definitive work on Britain and the peacemaking: Michael L. Dockrill & J. Douglas Gould, *Peace Without Promise: Britain and the Peace Conferences 1919–23* (London, 1981).
5. The concept is the late Jack Gallagher's. See his 'Nationalisms and the Crisis of Empire, 1919–1922', *Modern Asian Studies,* vol. xv, no 3 *(1981)*, pp 355–68. It also underlies my book cited above in n. 2.
6. For example Malta, which in 1919 'represented in miniature the nationalisms which were challenging and distracting a victorious and tranquillity-craving empire'. Hancock, *Survey, i,* p. 407. For an account of the Middle Eastern problems beset-ting British at this time, see John Darwin, *Britain, Egypt and the Middle East: Imperial Policy in the Aftermath of War* (London, 1981).
7. A point made with regard to Egyptian policy in Elie Kedourie, 'Sa'ad Zaghlul and the British', in A. Hourani (ed), *St Anthony's Papers No. 11* (London, 1961), p. 151.
8. For a discussion of the likelihood of revolution in Britain and an account of some of the preparations made to counter it see Keith Jeffery & Peter Hennessy, *States of Emergency: British Governments and Strikebreaking since 1919* (London, 1983).
9. Townshend, *British Campaign in Ireland,* pp 28, 42.
10. Townshend, *The British Campaign in Ireland,* appendix iii, pp 211–2, provides detailed figures for the police forces in Ireland during 1920–21.
11. Macready's career is fully, though not very critically, described in his memoirs: *Annals of an Active Life,* 2 vols, (London, 1924).

12. Quoted in Townshend, *The British Campaign in Ireland*, p. 20. It is perhaps also worth noting that Macready had Irish ancestry.
13. Quoted in Jeffery, *The British Army*, p. 82
14. In Sir Ormonde Winter, *Winter's tale: An Autobiography'* (London, 1955), p. 259; and 'A Woman of No Importance' [Charlotte Menzies], *As Others See Us*, (London, 1924), p. 89.
15. See, for example, the one day's training received by Douglas V Duff, which he recounts in his *Sword For Hire: the Saga of a Modern Free-companion* (London, 1934), a rare example of a Black and Tan's memoir.
16. See Jeffery, *The British Army*, pp 85–6.
17. Valuably narrated in Dorothy Macardle, *The Irish Republic* (London, 1937).
18. Lloyd George to Sir Hamar Greenwood, 25 Feb. 1921, Lloyd George Papers (House of Lords Record Office) *F/19/3/4.* The impact of public opinion on Briish policy is very well covered in D. G. Boyce, *Englishmen and Irish Troubles* (London, 1972).
19. Greenwood to Lloyd George, 3 Apr. 1921, *Lloyd George Papers F/19/3/7*
20. Diary of Sir Henry Wilson, 28 Mar. 1921 (Imperial War Museum).
21. 'Note of conversation', 30 Apr. 1920, Public Record Office, CAB 23/21/23(20)A.
22. Irish Office statistics, reproduced in Townshend, *The British Campaign in Ireland*, appendix v, p. 214.
23. According to the Irish Office figures, the comparison of wounded between security forces and IRA/civilians is even more striking. Of 1212 wounded, 682 (56%) were police, 345 (29%) army and only 185 (15% and fewer than the number killed) civilian/IRA.
24. Colonel W. Davies (commanding 2nd battalion, Rifle Brigade) to the Duke of Connaught (Colonel-in-Chief of the regiment), 30 Oct. 1920, copy in Wilson Papers (Imperial War Museum), HHW 2/54/6.
25. Covered by Eunan O'Halpin, 'British Intelligence in Ireland 1914–21', in Christopher Andrew & David Dilks (eds), *The Missing Dimension: Governments and Intelligence Communities in the Twentieth Century* (London, 1984), pp 54–77; and Keith Jeffery, 'British Military Intelligence Following World War I', in K. G. Robertson (ed), *British and American Approaches to Intelligence* (London, 1987), pp 55–84.
26. See Tim Pat Coogan, *Michael Collins* (London, 1990), chapters 4–6 for a good account.
27. Martial law eventually covered the following counties: Cork, Kerry, Tipperary, Limerick, Clare, Kilkenny, Waterford and Wexford.
28. A major industrial dispute in the British coal mines was worrying the Government by its apparent revolutionary potential.
29. Wilson to Rawlinson, 18 May 1921. Reprinted in Keith Jeffery (ed), *The Military Correspondence of Field Marshal Sir Henry Wilson, 1918–22* (London, 1985), pp 266–7.
30. 'Ireland and the General Military Situation', paper for the Cabinet, 24 May 1921, Public Record Office, CAB 24/123 C.P. 2965.
31. Diary of Sir Henry Wilson, 7 Dec. 1921 (Imperial War Musuem).
32. A J P Taylor, *English History 1914–1945* (Harmondsworth,1970) p. 213.

Chapter eleven: Partitioning Ireland, India and Palestine – Tom Fraser

 1. See John Kendle, *Ireland and the Federal Solution* (Kingston and Montreal, 1989);

Angus Macintyre, 'Home Rule for Ireland: A Failure of Federalism?', in Preston King and Andrea Bosco (eds.) *A Constitution For Europe* (Lothian Foundation Press, 1991), pp 247–252.

2. D. Lloyd George, *House of Commons Debates, 5th series, 1920, vol. 127, cols. 1322–36.*
3. Iqbal to Jinnah, 21 June 1937, *Letters of Iqbal to Jinnah* (Lahore 1943), pp 18–23.
4. *Palestine Royal Commission Report (Cmd. 5479. 1937)*, p.375.
5. Thomas Harbison, as 2 above, 1308–13.
6. Robert Blake, *The Unknown Prime Minister* (London, 1955), p. 386.
7. A.J. Balfour, 'The Irish Question', 25 Nov. 1919, PRO CAB 24/93.
8. First Report of the Cabinet Committee on the Irish Question, 4 Nov. 1919, PRO CAB 24/92.
9. Note by Balfour, 19 Feb. 1920, PRO CAB 24/98.
10. Charles Craig, as 2 above, cols. 984–93.
11. James Craig, *N. Ireland House of Commons Debates, 12 Dec. 1921, cols. 542–6.*
12. 'Viability of Pakistan', India Office, 13 Feb.1946, P.N.S. Mansergh (ed.).*The Transfer of Power in India (HMSO),* pp. 951–63.
13. These figures are taken from the 1931 Census of India, the last significant census before partition. The 1941 Census was, of necessity, a perfunctory affair.
14. Cabinet Meeting, 20 Sept. 1947, PRO CAB 76(47).
15. The rural Arab population of Palestine was broadly divided between the fellahin, settled cultivators, and bedouin, who were nomadic or semi-nomadic.
16. Memorandum by Sir Stafford Cripps, c. 9 April 1946, as (12) above, pp 174–80.
17. Penderel Moon, *Divide and Quit* (London, 1962).

Index